How to Do Everything with Windows Vista™ Media Center

About the Authors

Joli Ballew, 2007 Microsoft Windows–Shell/User MVP, is a technical author, a technology trainer, and Web site manager in the Dallas area. She holds several certifications, including MCSE, A+, and MCDST. She's written almost two dozen books, including *Degunking Windows* (awarded the IPPY award for best computer book of the year in 2005), *CNet's Do It Yourself 24 Mac Projects, PC Magazine's Office 2007 Solutions, Breakthrough Windows Vista* (Microsoft Press), and *Windows Home Networking* (Microsoft Press). In her free time, she enjoys golfing, yard work, exercising at the local gym, and teaching her cat, Pico, tricks.

Justin Harrison is an expert in digital media and a three time Microsoft Windows Media Center MVP. He has written for *TechNet Magazine* and has been quoted as a source in the *Hartford Business Journal*. In the past he has worked with the Casual Games team at Microsoft and has authored more than eight columns and webcasts for the Microsoft Windows XP Expert Zone. In his free time, he enjoys mountain biking and photography.

About the Technical Editor

Sally Slack has more than 17 years experience writing and editing technical works. She is also the author of eleven books, including *Do-It-Yourself Digital Home Office Projects* (McGraw Hill, 2007).

How to Do Everything with Windows Vista™ Media Center

Joli Ballew and Justin Harrison

New York Chicago San Francisco
Lisbon London Madrid Mexico City
Milan New Delhi San Juan
Seoul Singapore Sydney Toronto

The McGraw·Hill Companies

Cataloging-in-Publication Data is on file with the Library of Congress

How to Do Everything with Windows Vistaó Media Center

1 2 3 4 5 6 7 8 9 0   FGR FGR   0 1 9 8 7

ISBN: 978-0-07-149864-7
MHID: 0-07-149864-8

Sponsoring Editor	**Copy Editor**	**Illustration**
Roger Stewart	Lisa McCoy	International Typesetting
Editorial Supervisor	**Proofreader**	and Composition
Patty Mon	Carol Shields	**Art Director, Cover**
Project Manager	**Indexer**	Jeff Weeks
Sam RC (International	Valerie Perry	**Cover Designer**
Typesetting and	**Production Supervisor**	Pattie Lee
Composition)	Jean Bodeaux	
Acquisitions Coordinator	**Composition**	
Carly Stapleton	International Typesetting	
Technical Editor	and Composition	
Sally Slack		

For Pat Cosimo (1922-2006). May his music live on in our hearts forever.

—Joli

In remembrance of the thirty-two that perished on April 16, 2007.

—Justin

Contents at a Glance

Contents

Acknowledgments

As has always been the case, in my experience at least, a book is never written by any single person. It takes writers, editors, experts, publishers, managers, and various other people who I never come across during the process. There are a few people who I have worked directly with, however, including my acquisitions editor, Roger Stewart, who keeps selecting me to write books that challenge my intelligence and creativity; my coauthor, Justin Harrison, a media expert and engineering student at Virginia Tech; and a special contributor, Deanna Reynolds, who can always be counted on to step up and step in when she's needed. Of course, it wouldn't have come together properly without our technical editor, Sally Slack, and copy editor, Lisa McCoy, who spent their days scouring the words and steps to look for mistakes. What a job that would be!

There are a few people not directly involved with the book who need mentioning, too. My agent at Studio B, Neil Salkind, PhD, is always by my side, looking for projects that are perfect for me and always offering words of encouragement; my family, Jennifer, Cosmo, Mom, and Dad; and Pico, my cat, who enjoys watching me type and chases the "mouse" on the screen when I'm testing a product or set of instructions.

—Joli Ballew

Finally having the opportunity to work with Joli on this book has been a pleasure. Her experience and wisdom has been invaluable and without her guidance the last several years there are many opportunities that I would have missed. There are, of course, many other people who need mentioning as well; Roger, Sam, Sally, Lisa, and the entire team who have put countless hours in to making this publication possible; and my parents, grandfather, and friends, all who helped give me ideas and feedback about the content of this book.

—Justin Harrison

Introduction

The most unique part of Windows Vista, Windows Media Center is a key component of the Windows Vista Home Premium and Ultimate editions of Microsoft's newest operating system. You can use Media Center to watch live television; record TV shows and series; rewind, pause, stop, and fast-forward through TV shows; listen to music and radio; and much, much more.

Media Center builds on the previous versions of the application to deliver powerful functionality and many new features, along with an eye-catching and easy-to-use interface. If you're new to Media Center, you've got a lot to discover. If you're coming to Media Center as an experienced user of earlier versions, there's still plenty to experience, because the newest version included with Home Premium and Ultimate editions offers lots of new features and changes. Whatever the case may be for you, this book will get you up to speed quickly.

Who Is This Book For?

This book is designed to help beginning and intermediate users get the most out of Windows Vista Media Center in the shortest time possible. If you fall into either of those categories, you'll benefit from this book's comprehensive coverage, focused approach, and helpful advice. If you're an expert seeking super-advanced tips, tweaks, and hacks, you'll want to visit newsgroups and Media Center communities for that kind of information.

What Does This Book Cover?

Here's what this book covers:

- Chapter 1, "Meet Windows Vista Media Center," shows you how to launch Media Center; what Media Center is and how it can be used; and how you can employ Media Center to view, manage, and save media.

- Chapter 2, "Recognize and Distinguish Between Required and Optional Hardware," discusses the hardware you need to run Media Center and what components you can add. For instance, while you can view photos and listen to music using Media Center without a TV tuner, you'll have to have a tuner to watch live TV.

- Chapter 3, "Make the Physical Connection," starts by explaining how to connect to a wired network, connect to the Internet, connect to a TV signal, and then shows you how to connect an additional monitor and speakers.

- Chapter 4, "Complete the Required and Optional Setups," discusses how to join a wireless network, configure privacy settings, set up a TV signal, set up the display, set up the library, share media, and more.

- Chapter 5, "Take Advantage of Advanced Settings," shows you how to change the ways in which Windows starts and behaves by default, how to set up parental controls, how to fine tune Media Center when necessary, and how to configure closed captioning, among other things.

- Chapter 6, "Navigate Media Center," explains how to access Media Center's categories, including TV + Movies, Sports, Online Media, Tasks, Pictures + Video, Music, and Now Playing.

- Chapter 7, "Explore Live and Recorded Television, Movies, and the Guide," covers things like navigating the TV + Movies option; playing DVDs; navigating the Guide; watching, pausing, and rewinding live TV; forwarding through cached TV; searching for and watching sports programs and movies; and using the remote control.

- Chapter 8, "Record Live TV," starts by teaching you how to record a single live TV show. After that, you'll learn how to record a series of shows, work with recording settings, manage recorded TV, and even burn a DVD of a TV show you've recorded.

- Chapter 9, "Working with DVDs," shows you how to play a DVD you own, configure the DVD player for optimal playback, change DVD settings, and more.

- Chapter 10, "Download and Watch Online Media," discusses how to select and sign up for a media subscription service, install required components, and download a movie from the Internet and watch it using Media Center.

- Chapter 11, "Create a Personal Music Library," explains how to use Media Center to play songs and albums, rip a CD collection, move and copy media, edit songs in the library, and more.

- Chapter 12, "Buy or Rent Music Online," discusses how to select and sign up for a music subscription service. Once signed up, you'll learn how to install required components, download and play media, and listen to Internet radio stations.

- Chapter 13, "Manage Your Music," covers how to play music in auto-playlists, search the library, manage the music queue, and create additional playlists in Media Player 11.

- Chapter 14, "Enjoy Music on the Go and at Home," explains the range of features that Media Player and Media Center offer for burning CDs, synching mobile devices, streaming music, using visualizations, and configuring high-end speakers.

- Chapter 15, "Create a Personal Photo and Video Library," describes how to navigate the libraries, how to import media, how to view sample media, and how to edit what's in your library. You'll also learn how to configure options for your pictures and videos, and how to find, sort, and play the media you want to view.

- Chapter 16, "Share Your Photos and Videos," discusses how to transfer media so that others can view it. This chapter includes but is not limited to e-mailing media, burning media to a CD or DVD, creating a slideshow, and getting photos printed online.

- Chapter 17, "Access Your Media from an Xbox 360 or Other Windows Vista PCs," describes how to add a media extender, specifically an Xbox 360. You'll learn how to physically connect the extender, add the extender to the network, and stream media to the extender.

- Chapter 18, "Purchase and Install a DVD, HD DVD, or Blu-ray Disc Drive for Your Computer or Xbox 360," explains how to install a DVD burner if you don't have one. You'll learn about all of the DVD choices and options, as well as how to physically install the burner.

- Chapter 19, "Install and Configure a Second TV Tuner," explains how to choose, install, and configure a TV tuner if you need to add one.

- Chapter 20, "Install and Configure a Preferred Display," explains how to choose, install, and configure a second monitor for use with Media Center.

- Chapter 21, "Install and Configure a Cable Card," explains how to install and configure a cable card for use with Media Center.

- Chapter 22, "Install, Configure, and Back Up with an External Hard Drive," explains how to select, install, and use an external hard drive as a backup device. The Windows Backup And Restore Center is also introduced.

Conventions Used in This Book

To make its meaning concise and clear, this book uses a number of conventions, three of which are worth mentioning here:

- Note, Tip, and Caution paragraphs highlight information that you should pay extra attention to.

- Most check boxes have two states: *selected* (with a check mark in them) and *cleared* (without a check mark in them). This book tells you to *select* or *clear* a check box rather than "click to place a check mark in the box" or "click to remove the check mark from the box." (Often, you'll be verifying the state of the check box, so it may already have the required setting, in which case, you don't need to click anything at all.) Some check boxes have a third state as well in which they're selected but dimmed and unavailable. This state is usually used for options that apply to only part of the current situation.

Part I

Get Acquainted with Vista's Media Center Features

Chapter 1

Meet Windows Vista Media Center

How to...

■ Know what Media Center is

■ Know what Media Center is not

■ Use Media Center to change how you view and manage media

Windows Media Center is a feature (application, program, part) of Windows Vista Home Premium and Windows Vista Ultimate editions. Media Center, as it is referred to throughout this book, offers new and improved options for managing all types of media. Media includes, but is not limited to, pictures, videos, movies, home movies, music, online media, live television, recorded television, sports, media stored on DVDs and CDs, radio, podcasts, vodcasts (video podcasts), and media stored on portable media players.

Thus, the purpose of this book is to help you get the most from Media Center. While you may already know you can record a television series weekly and watch it later (skipping through the commercials), you may not know that you can change where the media is stored, configure the recording quality to save space or get a better recording, or even configure a show to record when it is shown on a channel other than the one you've selected. And this is just the beginning!

In this chapter you'll learn just what Media Center is and is not, gain an understanding of the purpose of Media Center, and learn how you can use it to forever change how you access, play, store, and manage your media.

> NOTE   *If you're new to Media Center, you may be confused as to just what Media Center is (and what it is not). In this first section, you'll learn what it is; in the second, what it is not.*

Understand What Media Center Is

Media Center offers a one-stop shop to access, play, and manage media. It includes the menus TV + Movies, Sports, Online Media, Tasks, Pictures + Videos, and Music. Each category offers subcategories, where you can access media libraries you create or libraries you access from third-party online retailers, as well as access to live television, sports, and online media. Figure 1-1 shows the Media Center interface after it's been set up.

You can obtain media from several sources if you have the proper equipment included with or attached to your Windows Vista PC:

■ A personal library of photos, music, videos, and home movies already on your PC

■ Data on an older PC

■ Media from backup devices, CDs and DVDs, and network drives

■ Your digital camera or camera phone

■ Portable media devices, such as MP3 players, handheld PCs, Pocket Phones, or smartphones

FIGURE 1-1   The Media Center interface

- ■ Older media players, including VCRs and reel-to-reels
- ■ Live television
- ■ Recorded television
- ■ Online media retailers, including URGE, Showtime, Movielink, Fox Sports, Nickelodeon, and more
- ■ Internet and local radio
- ■ XM Radio
- ■ On-demand programs from NPR News, the Discovery Channel, Comedy Central, and more

NOTE   *In this book, Media Center describes a feature of the Windows Vista operating system used for viewing and managing media. In contrast, the term media center is often used to describe a specific type of PC, one created with the media enthusiast in mind. Media center is also used to describe a type of shelving unit that holds and makes accessible a grouping of media hardware, such as a high-definition TV (HDTV), surround sound, and gaming system.*

Understand What Media Center Is Not

Media Center, in the context used in this book, is not a specific type of computer; rather, Media Center is an application included with Windows Vista Home Premium and Ultimate editions that you use for organizing your media on your PC and network. However, Media Center is not a standalone program either. It is part of Windows Vista and integrates fully with the operating system. As an example, any music you download using Windows Media Player is also accessible from inside Media Center. The same is true of any pictures you upload from your digital camera to Windows Photo Gallery or videos you add to the Videos folder.

To further define what Media Center is and is not, note that you won't generally use Media Center to obtain music online. Windows Media Player is better suited for that. You also won't generally use Media Center to upload and work with home movies. Movie Maker is better suited for that. Finally, you won't upload pictures from your digital camera directly to Media Center; Windows Photo Gallery is better suited for that.

So just where does that leave Media Center? As noted, Media Center is best used for accessing, playing, and managing your personal media. Note that *obtaining* is not included in that list, at least when talking about personal media you already own and music acquired online. However, Media Center is the only place you can obtain all other types of online media easily, such as downloadable movies, movie trailers, television shows, live sports programs, and special online media, including that from XM Radio, Internet radio, and even local radio broadcasts. There are also Internet-based television shows, including shows offered from the Discovery Channel, Comedy Central, Yahoo! Sports My Channel, MTV.com, and NPR News. That's where Media Center shines: It's where you can find, preview, obtain, and access all kinds of public media, while at the same time having access to all of your private, personal media! Figure 1-2 shows the online media options.

What Media Center Can Offer You

You may be thinking that all of this is just a little too much to deal with. Why not just open Windows Photo Gallery when you want to view pictures and Windows Media Player to listen to music? Why not just visit NPR's Web site and locate their on-demand programming when you miss it in real time? The answer is simple: With Windows Media Center, you need only open one program, and everything you want is right at your fingertips.

As you get to know Media Center, you'll also find that watching television on it is much better than watching "regular" TV. You can turn on *Judge Judy* at 4 p.m., for example, pause it

FIGURE 1-2   Online media you can obtain and access through Media Center

until 4:10, and then watch the program in 20 minutes instead of 30, all the while fast-forwarding through the commercials!

The same is true of radio. You'll no longer need to be in front of your radio to listen to your favorite radio programs. If you miss your favorite NPR program, just click the Online Media link, select NPR News, and select from All Things Considered, Day to Day, Talk of the Nation, and more. If you're interested in playing fantasy football, from the Online Media menu option, select Yahoo! Sports, and click the Fantasy Football link to get started. Don't miss out on Comedy Central's Internet editions of *Reno 911!* or *South Park* either.

Again, there are lots of ways you can use Media Center to change how you view, access, obtain, and manage media. And that's what we're all about here. Stay tuned!

Chapter 2

Recognize and Distinguish Between Required and Optional Hardware

How to...

■ Determine if your computer meets the minimum requirements

■ Decide what components you need

■ Decide what components you want

■ Locate and purchase missing components

There are many aspects of Media Center. You can view your personal photos, listen to music you've ripped from your own CD collection, and watch DVDs you've purchased from the local video store. You can do all of this without any hardware other than what you'd need to support a basic PC. As you know, you can also watch, record, and rewind live TV; listen to Internet radio stations; and download online media. For this though, you need more than a basic PC. You need additional hardware, like a TV tuner, cable connection, and Internet connection. And you may also *want* better speakers, headphones, or a nicer monitor!

So how do you know, first of all, what hardware you already have, what hardware is required, and what hardware is optional? Beyond that, where can you get the additional hardware you crave? That's what you'll learn in this chapter.

Minimum and Recommended Requirements

Microsoft has a list of minimum and recommended requirements for Windows Vista Home and Ultimate editions. These include things like how fast the central processing unit (CPU) must be, how much random access memory (RAM) has to be installed, and how much free hard drive space must be available to install an edition of Windows Vista that contains Media Center. What is considered "minimum" is ultimately in the eye of the beholder, however. Sure, you'll need to meet minimum requirements for CPU and RAM, but a person who wants to burn DVDs must have a DVD burner, while a person that does not, well, does not! In the same vein, if you aren't interested in watching TV, there's no reason to have a TV tuner. That being said, here is a list of truly *minimum* requirements, those that you absolutely must have to install Windows Vista and start Media Center:

■ An 800-megahertz (MHz) processor and 512 megabytes (MB) of system memory

■ A 20-gigabyte (GB) hard drive with at least 15 GB of available space

■ Support for Super Video Graphics Array (SVGA) graphics

■ DVD drive. You can't install Windows Vista without this.

Of course, if you want to do more than simply install Windows Vista Home Premium or Ultimate, you'll want to strive for the recommended requirements:

■ A 32-bit (x86) or 64-bit (x64) processor

■ At least 1 GB of system memory

■ A 40-GB hard drive with at least 15 GB of available space

- Support for DirectX 9 graphics with:
  - Windows Vista Display Driver Model (WDDM) driver
  - 128 MB of graphics memory (minimum)
  - Pixel Shader 2.0 i-
  - At least 32 bits per pixel
- DVD-ROM drive
- Audio output
- Internet access (fees may apply)
- TV tuner card required for TV functionality (compatible remote control optional)
- A system with a Trusted Platform Module (TPM) 1.2 chip if you want to use BitLocker Drive

Encryption (BitLocker Drive Encryption is available with Windows Vista Ultimate Edition only) Notice again that there are items missing from the minimum and recommended requirements that you may deem completely necessary. You will need more than 15 GB of hard drive space or a secondary hard disk to save the hours of TV programming you plan to record. You'll have to have a DVD burner to archive movies you create with your video camera. You may even feel you need a media extender so that you can watch the media you obtain in another room of the house without having to move your Windows Vista PC. If these seem like necessities to you, in reality, they are not. You can use Media Center to view and manage photos, music, and videos already on your hard drive without so much as an Internet connection. And Media Center will certainly run without a TV tuner installed, although you won't be able to watch TV without one!

Learn What Your PC Currently Includes

There are lots of ways to find out what your PC includes, and one of them is to take a physical inventory. You can likely look around and see if you have speakers, for instance, and you probably know if you have an always-on Internet connection or a remote control. However, it may be harder to tell if you have components like a rewriteable DVD burner, a TV tuner that supports both live television and local radio, or enough hard drive space to record a couple of season-long television series. So instead of relying on what you can see when you peek behind the PC and monitor, you'll want a more in-depth look at what's included with your PC by letting Vista do the work of finding out for you.

View Basic Information

To view basic information about your computer, such as how much RAM you have, what processor (CPU) is installed, and to see the rating Windows Vista has applied to your current hardware setup:

1. Click Start, and click Control Panel.
2. Select System And Maintenance. (If you're in Classic View, System Maintenance does not appear. Select System instead.)
3. Select System.

The Windows Experience Index, shown in Figure 2-1 as 3.2, is based on the scores Vista applies to your CPU, RAM, graphics, gaming graphics, and your primary hard disk. Better equipment means higher scores; higher scores mean better performance.

To see more information about the Windows Experience Index, click Windows Experience Index under System. You'll note in the results what exactly can be improved upon and learn how you can improve your computer's performance. As you can see in Figure 2-2, this computer is fairly well-endowed; the Windows Experience Index is based on the lowest component subscore. With the highest rating in any category being a 5.9, the Graphics subscore is perfect.

NOTE *You can also get basic information from the Welcome Center. The Welcome Center is almost always located in the left pane of the Start menu, but you can access it by choosing Start | All Programs and from the Accessories subfolder, too. After opening the Welcome Center, under Get Started With Windows, select View Computer Details. Not only will you see CPU information, RAM, and video card statistics, you'll also have access to what version of Windows Vista you are running.*

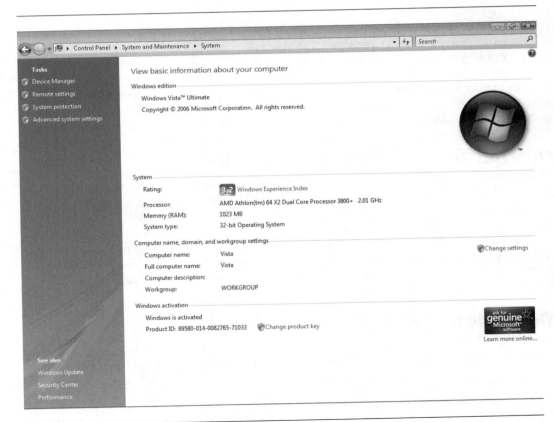

FIGURE 2-1 Windows Experience Index

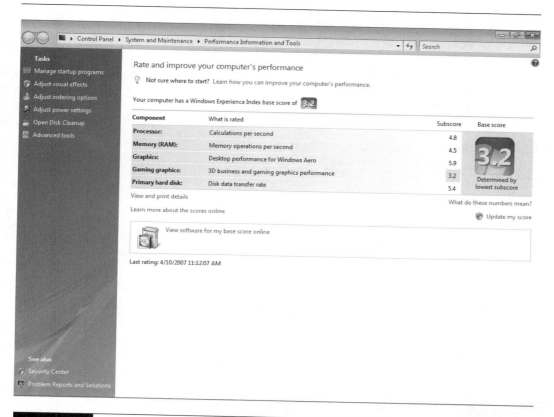

FIGURE 2-2   Windows Experience Index is based on the lowest subscore.

View Advanced Information

One of the best ways to view advanced information about the hardware installed on your PC is to use Device Manager. As you can see in Figure 2-1, Device Manager is available from the Tasks pane. To open Device Manager:

1. Click Start, and click Control Panel.

2. Select System And Maintenance. If you're in Classic View, select System.

3. Select System.

4. In the Tasks pane, select Device Manager.

5. In Device Manager, click View, and then click Devices By Type.

6. Expand any item in the list by clicking the plus sign (+) to see the installed components. Double-click any component to get more information about it. Figure 2-3 shows an example.

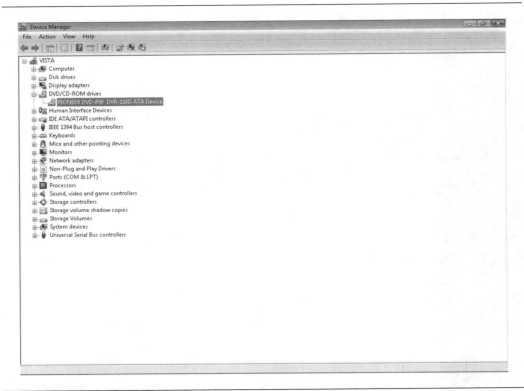

FIGURE 2-3   Device Manager and a DVD-RW DVR-110D ATA device

Note that from here you can upgrade your device driver, enable and disable the device, and more.

View Technical Information

There are lots of options for viewing advanced information. You may have noticed this in Figure 2-1 earlier. In the Tasks pane, for instance, you have options for Advanced Information and Device Manager. Both are good options to explore. However, there is another way to view what's on your PC: System Information.

To open System Information and browse through the data offered:

1. Click Start, and in the Start Search window type **System Information**.

2. In the results list under Programs, select System Information.

3. Expand Components, and select or expand subcomponents as desired. Figure 2-4 shows an example. Here you can see three drives: C:, D:, and E:. The size and available space are also available.

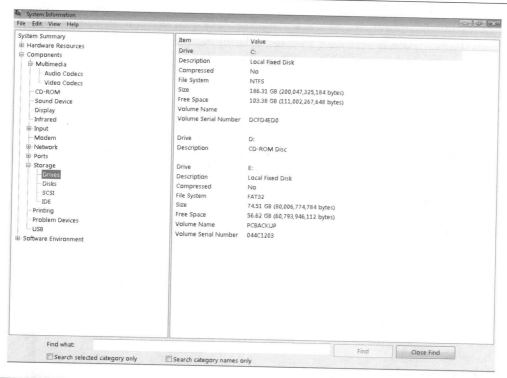

FIGURE 2-4   Advanced system information

You may need to access this information when troubleshooting hardware resources, components, or your software environment. Generally, the only time you'll be doing that is when/if you're ever on the phone with a company's technical support line.

Optional Components

We're sure your PC meets the minimum requirements; otherwise, you wouldn't have Windows Vista installed on it. However, your PC may not have all of the recommended requirements, and you may want to add some of the additional components to enhance your media experience. (For example, while the recommended requirements set free hard drive space at 15 GB, that is probably not enough if you plan to record several TV series at a time.)

In this section, we'll introduce optional components that you should consider installing. You'll likely want or need to obtain additional hardware to get the most from Media Center, like a TV tuner, DVD burner, speaker system, or a better monitor.

NOTE   *The following optional components are not listed in any particular order.*

TV Tuner and TV Signal

You'll need a TV tuner as well as access to a TV signal if you want to watch television on your Windows Vista PC. You may not have a TV tuner, as many PCs simply don't ship with one. However, if it turns out that you don't, you can purchase and install an internal or external tuner fairly easily. Later in this chapter you'll learn where to get a TV tuner; in Chapter 19, you'll learn how to install one.

Here's how a TV tuner works: The TV tuner accepts the incoming television signal, which can be anything from an antenna to cable to satellite. It then processes the signal and sends it on to Media Center, from where you watch television. When setting up the TV signal, you select what type of signal you use, whether or not you have a set-top box (such as a cable receiver), if you have one or two TV tuners, and if you want Media Center to automatically download information regarding the media you watch. You'll also input your ZIP code, and Media Center will offer television options in your area.

To see if you have a TV tuner installed:

1. Open Media Center.

2. Click TV + Movies.

3. Select Live TV. (Note that Live TV will not be an option if you have not connected your TV tuner to the television signal.)

If you see the screen in Figure 2-5 (or a similar warning), you do not have a TV tuner installed. If you are prompted to set up the TV signal or if live TV plays, you have a TV tuner.

Remote Control

A remote control is certainly an optional component. You can control Media Center with a basic mouse or keyboard, or a keyboard and mouse that are specifically designed for media applications. If you are using a keyboard and mouse, however, make sure you have a wireless set. You won't want to get up and walk over to the PC each time you want to fast-forward through a commercial or change playlists when listening to music. For the most part, TV tuners come with a remote control, which looks and acts similarly to any other remote control you've used in the past.

Media Center Extender

Another item you might want to consider is a Media Center Extender. An Xbox 360 is one example. A Media Center Extender is a hardware device that you connect to any TV in the house, which, after setup, allows you to access all of your media on that TV, even though your PC running Windows Vista is in another room, provided you have a home network. Initially, the Xbox was created for gaming, but it has since become a central place for accessing media in the home.

If you want to install and use a Media Center Extender, you'll need the following:

■ An Xbox 360 or a Media Center Extender device connected and configured to work with a television set

■ A wired or wireless connection to a home network (you might want to select a wireless A + G dual-band router if you're going wireless, but there will be much more on that later)

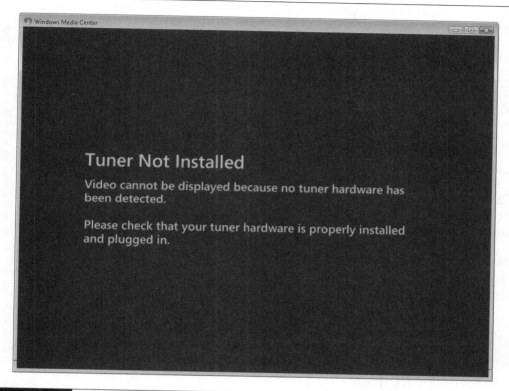

FIGURE 2-5 This message appears if a TV tuner is not installed.

■ A PC running Windows Vista Home Premium Edition or Windows Vista Ultimate Edition connected directly to the network router through an Ethernet cable.

NOTE *We'll cover installing a Media Center Extender in Chapter 17.*

Backup Hard Drive

A backup hard drive, preferably an external one, is considered an optional component, but if left up to us, we'd make it required. Having an external hard drive makes it easy to back up data and media as often as you like, and also offers an easy way to take the backups offsite if need be. With an external hard drive, you can back up your data once a week and leave the external drive at your parents' or friend's home, a safe deposit box, or other safe spot until you are ready to perform next week's backup. This way, if anything happens to your PC, like your hot water heater bursting and flooding your home, a fire occurring, or a similar disaster, you can count on your backups being safe. We'll cover installing and configuring a backup drive in Chapter 22.

Beyond having an external backup device, you can now pay for space on a Web server somewhere else. You might want to consider this option if you'd rather not hassle with a physical drive and instead save data to a third-party server in another city or state (or even country). This option also makes it easy to access data from anywhere in the world.

NOTE   *Of course, there's the option to burn data CDs and DVDs, and if this is what you've been using, that's fine, too. However, we find it's less work to use the Windows Backup And Restore Center to back up to an external hard drive versus a CD or DVD.*

CD and DVD Burner

Almost all computers come with CD burners these days, and many come with DVD burners as well. If you plan to burn a lot of CDs or DVDs of the movies or television you record, or if you have a lot of home movies to share or a lot of music to record, you'll want to make sure that you have the appropriate burner.

Some CD and DVD burners are writeable, which means you can write to the media only one time. Some are rewritable, meaning you can write to the disks again and again. You'll pay more for the latter, so decide what you need and want before investing.

Selecting, purchasing, and installing a DVD or CD burner is covered in Chapter 18. Note that you can install an external burner quickly, however, generally by connecting the burner to the PC via a USB port.

NOTE   *Windows Backup And Restore, a great program for backing up your data regularly, now writes to CDs and DVDs. The Backup program in Windows XP did not offer this option.*

High-End Monitor

There are many styles of monitors. There are plain old cathode ray tubes (CRTs) and there are newer flat screens. You can also connect your Vista PC to an existing television if you have the right options for connecting and a newer television. There are lots of sizes to choose from no matter what you decide on, and some options come with speakers included and some without. To choose a monitor that suits your needs:

- If you want a great performance, get a flat screen. CRTs are bulky and don't offer the features that flat screens do. Flat screens often offer a better picture and truer colors.

- If you're going to use the monitor to watch media on exclusively, get the largest one you can afford, but that also fits comfortably in the space you have for it and that is a good size for the distance you'll be sitting away from it.

- If you're going to use your own speaker system, there's no need for your monitor to include sound.

- Ask what resolutions are supported. The higher the resolution, the better the picture. Your video card will also have to support the resolution you choose, so take your PC's spec sheet with you.

- Make sure you know what your Windows Vista PC offers in the way of connections. If your new PC has a digital visual interface (DVI) connection, get a monitor that can connect to it—you'll get better performance. You can see what kinds of connections your PC offers by looking at the back of the PC's tower or the back of the laptop. Look for the monitor output.

■ If you are selecting a television, make sure the television and the PC can connect to each other. We prefer DVI or high-definition multimedia interface (HDMI) connections, but there are other options, like VGA, composite, S-Video, and others.

Even More Options

There are certainly more ways to spend your money, and once you get Media Center up and running, you'll quickly find out what other items you'd like to have. Some additional items you may want to consider include:

■ A speaker system, such as a surround-sound or high-definition speaker set.

■ Headphones for listening to music, movies, or other media without bothering others. (This is an excellent choice for laptops, especially when you're on a plane!)

■ A Webcam for visiting with contacts online.

■ A microphone for adding verbal notes to home movies.

■ An analog-to-digital recorder for transferring VHS tapes to digital format (and then burning them to DVD).

Purchasing Missing Components

Although you may know that you're missing some hardware, don't be hasty and order the first thing you see on the Internet and expect it to work flawlessly. It probably will, but that's not the point! The point is that it's ultimately better if you spend some time to look for and then purchase hardware that is known to work with Windows Vista.

Although you can visit your PC's manufacturer's Web site, browse store shelves at your local computer store, and ask friends and neighbors what they suggest, your best option for information is Microsoft. You want to make sure that whatever you purchase is compatible with Windows Vista, and Microsoft offers lots of options for comparing brands and models so there's no guessing involved.

There are a couple of places to get information about the hardware you need. One is Windows Marketplace; the other is www.microsoft.com/hardware.

For most hardware, we prefer Windows Marketplace. You can compare hardware options, view ratings for the devices you select, compare prices, and view hardware from many manufacturers. Keep in mind that you don't actually have to purchase your hardware here! You can, of course, but first and foremost, you want to gain information. Here's how to work through Windows Marketplace:

1. Visit www.windowsmarketplace.com. Select the Hardware link.

2. In the Search box, type what you'd like to view (speakers, headphones, etc.). Make sure you search All Hardware, not Game Downloads or something else that doesn't apply. Click Go.

3. Browse through the results. If you want, you can narrow the results by manufacturer, hardware category, delivery method, compatibility, and more.

4. Click any device to see the ratings and customer reviews, and to compare prices from various manufacturers. As shown in Figure 2-6, you can also see who offers free shipping.

Another option for locating hardware is at www.microsoft.com/hardware. What you'll find here is more Vista-related and is a great place to start. One place you might check is the Media Center Peripherals section. You can also enter your ZIP code and locate retailers near you.

No matter what you decide to buy, at least try to upgrade your Windows Vista PC to the following; you'll be glad you did:

- A processor with more chores
- At least 1 GB of system memory
- A 40-GB hard drive with at least 15 GB of available space
- Support for DirectX 9 graphics
- DVD-RW drive
- Media speakers
- Internet access (fees may apply)
- TV tuner card required for TV functionality (compatible remote control optional)

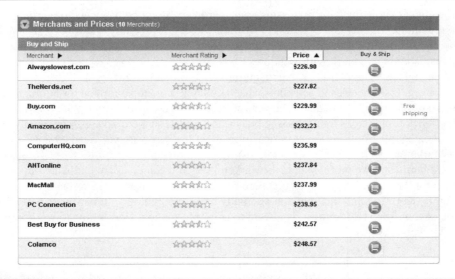

FIGURE 2-6 Compare prices at Windows Marketplace

Chapter 3

Make the Physical Connection

How to...

- Connect to a wired network
- Connect to the Internet
- Determine the appropriate connection type for a specific display type
- Set up a monitor or television set
- Set up speakers

Software can do a lot of things. Today, software is responsible for transferring electricity to your home, controlling the robotic arm that manufactured your car, running the controls that keep a plane in the air, operating the motors that drive elevators, and more. Millions of lines of software code bring us pictures all the way from the *Spirit* and *Opportunity* Mars exploration rovers, satellite imagery from high above the earth, and the ability to instantly communicate with loved ones no matter where they are in the world.

Still, despite the intergalactic, global, or even cross-continental potential and ability of software, the one common thing that any person has to do before they can interact with it is... connect a display! Computers are capable of doing incredible things, but you've got to have a way to interact with the computer to get started.

More About Media Center and Displays

Imagine you're on your way home from work. You stop at an intersection, and you're waiting for the traffic light to turn green. You're driving a typical, reliable, four-door sedan. It gets the job done of getting you to and from work. As you're waiting, a bright red convertible with the top down pulls up beside you. Loud music is blaring, you hear laughter, and the driver seems to be having quite a bit of fun. As the light turns green, the convertible speeds off into the distance.

If the typical, reliable, four-door sedan is your ordinary home computer—great for checking e-mail and browsing the occasional Web site—then the red convertible is a Media Center PC: perfect for having a little fun with and showing off to your friends and family.

Usually, you interact with a computer through input and output devices—typically a keyboard, mouse, and display. The ordinary computer has a keyboard, mouse, display, speakers, and a network connection.

However, Media Center PCs are different from ordinary computers. Ordinary computers play music, browse the Internet, and display e-mail. Media Center PCs are capable of doing much more, and as a result have many more input and output connections. Media Center PCs display movies on high-definition displays, play music in surround sound, and show large slideshows of photographs from vacations or adventures.

In this chapter, we'll take a look at how to physically set up your Media Center PC so that you can take advantage of the Media Center software. You'll learn how to connect to the Internet, bring television into your computer, connect displays, and configure speakers.

> NOTE
>
> *If you already have all of your hardware connected and don't want to purchase any new hardware, you may want to skip to the next chapter. In this chapter, we'll discuss the differences between different sound systems and displays, but not how to configure them with Media Center. That's in the next chapter.*

Connect to a TV Set or Monitor

As display technologies have changed, so have the quality of displays. Older displays offer standard-definition quality, while many newer displays offer high-definition quality. Standard-definition television sets have traditionally been used for analog television sources such as cable and antenna. With the rise of high-definition television sets, more digital television sources are becoming available. High-definition television quality is at least twice the resolution of standard-definition television quality. This allows for more details to be shown and, therefore, a better picture. High-definition television sets also support widescreen (sometimes referred to as 16:9) theater-style viewing, while on standard-definition sets, sometimes stretching or distortion may occur in order to view shows in this manner.

Know Your Connections

Display connections have evolved just like display technology in order to provide better ways for high-quality images to be transmitted across the wire. There are two main types of display connections: analog and digital. *Analog connections* are less precise than digital connections and provide lower-quality pictures, as they usually must be converted from the original digital signal in the computer to an analog signal when transmitted over the wire and then back to a digital signal at the display (if you're using an LCD display or similar digital display). *Digital connections* offer exact pixel-to-pixel image reproduction on digital displays. Some displays produce better images with digital connections, while others produce better images with analog connections. We'll discuss which connection is best for which display soon.

Digital video interface (DVI) is an up-to-24-pin digital video connection made for connecting to digital displays, and is suitable for high-definition video. DVI is one of the only connection standards that can carry analog as well as digital data. There are four types of DVI connections: DVI-DL (dual-link) DVI-A (analog), DVI-D (digital), DVI-I (analog and digital). DVI-DL is used for high-resolution monitors that need to process more information at once due to their large screen size and high resolution. DVI is usually used to connect a computer to a digital display. Table 3-1 offers a summary of connection types and a description of each.

High-Definition Multimedia Interface (HDMI) is a 19-pin digital video and digital audio connection similar to DVI, but with two exceptions. An HDMI connection carries both digital audio and digital video in an uncompressed high-quality format. HDMI is also compatible with the high-bandwidth digital content protection (HDCP) standard. HDCP prevents unauthorized copying of content that is protected under copyright. It is an up and rising connection type that can be found on newer video game consoles and high-definition televisions.

Separate Video (S-Video) is a 4- to 7-pin analog video connection that is popular on computer video cards. S-Video connections do not provide high-bandwidth connections and therefore are not used for high-definition video connections.

Connection Type	Description
Digital Video Interface (DVI)	Digital video; great for liquid crystal display (LCD), plasma, and projection displays
High-Definition Multimedia Interface (HDMI)	Digital video and digital audio; great for LCD, plasma, and projection displays
Separate Video (S-Video)	Analog video
Composite	Analog video
Component Video (Y-Yr-Pb)	Analog video
Video Graphics Array (VGA, RGB, D-Sub)	Analog video, used most often on cathode ray tube (CRT) displays
Coaxial (F Connector, RF)	Analog video and analog sound; used to connect cable boxes to televisions

TABLE 3-1 Connection Types

Composite connections use an RCA-type connector (sometimes referred to as a phono connector) and carries analog video. Often, it is paired with two other RCA-type connectors for the left and right channels of sound. The video connector is yellow, and the sound connectors are red and white. On consumer electronics where S-Video is offered, you will almost always find plugs for composite connections as well. Composite connections are usually used to connect consumer electronics (VCRs, game consoles, DVD players, etc.) to televisions, though composite connections are quickly being phased out for component video connections.

Component video is an analog video connection that consists of three RCA-type plugs: one colored red (Yr), another colored blue (Pb), and the last colored green (Y). It is similar to S-Video, but it offers better high quality because data is transmitted on three distinct wires, rather than all on one wire. Component video connections are suitable for high-definition video as a result. Component video connections can be found on new video game consoles, DVD players, and high-definition televisions.

Video graphics array (VGA) connections, sometimes referred to as RGB or D-Sub connections, are analog video, 15-pin connections. Each pin on a VGA connector carries different information, such as red, green, or blue color information. It is similar to component video and is usually used to connect computers to analog displays.

A *coaxial* connection carries analog audio and video. It is similar in quality to composite and S-Video and has traditionally been used to connect devices such as video game consoles and cable boxes to older televisions.

Know Your Displays

Before we begin figuring out how to connect an additional display to the Media Center PC, it may be helpful to learn about the different types of display technologies and the associated connections they utilize.

Traditionally, most displays have been *cathode ray tube* displays (sometimes referred to as CRT displays). These are large, heavy tube-based displays that have quite a bit of depth to them.

The contrast is crisp and colors are accurately reproduced—in fact, CRT monitors often produce the best picture quality of all display technologies. The only downside to CRT monitors is that they are large and usually heavy. Often you can also notice a screen flicker as the cathode ray scans the screen and updates it many times per second. For some people, this may bother their eyes. CRT monitors usually offer a VGA connection, although a few offer a digital connection.

Liquid crystal displays (LCDs) are the opposite of CRTs. LCD displays are usually flat—you can hang them on your wall quite easily, for example. They weigh very little, and there is no screen flicker when the screen updates. On the downside, light on the screen is provided by a fluorescent front or back light mounted inside of the LCD display case just by the LCD panel. As a result, the LCD display is very bright, but sometimes too bright to accurately reproduce sensitive colors such as black. The quality of the image is also dependent on the angle at which you view the screen. LCD displays are great for computer usage because they offer high resolution and display the clear, fine details often found on a computer very well. LCD displays usually offer VGA and DVI connections.

Plasma displays are similar to LCDs. They're flat like LCD displays and offer as good or sometimes better color reproduction. On the downside, they can be quite heavy and consume a lot of electricity. Plasma displays usually offer better viewing angles than LCD displays, which means you can see the picture better from the sides than you can on an LCD display. Plasma displays usually offer DVI and component connections.

Finally, there are *digital light processing* projectors, or DLP projectors. DLP projectors offer great image quality and color reproduction that is almost on par with CRT monitors. In fact, as of this writing, DLP projectors offer the best way to show a large picture without image degradation. The only downside is that some DLP projectors are rather loud because of the fans required to cool it. You also have to purchase new light bulbs and sometimes they can be rather expensive. Projectors usually offer RGB, DVI, and component connections. Table 3-2 offers display technologies and a description of each.

Display Technology	Description
Cathode ray tube (CRT)	Pros: Great image quality
	Cons: Takes up a lot of space; heavy; harder to read fine text; screen flicker
Liquid crystal display (LCD)	Pros: Great at displaying fine text; bright displays; high resolution
	Cons: Quality varies on viewing angle
Plasma	Pros: Great at displaying fine text; bright displays; wider viewing angles than LCDs
	Cons: Heavy; quality varies on viewing angle; high power consumption; shorter life span
Display light processing (DLP)	Pros: Great image quality (on par with CRTs); large screen size
	Cons: Projection only; noise

TABLE 3-2   Display Technologies

Configure Windows Vista for Displays

Knowing the different kinds of displays and connections was the hard part. Now that you're familiar with the different types of displays and connections, it's time to connect your Media Center PC to a TV set or monitor. Windows Vista makes this easy.

First, identify how many displays you are going to connect to your Media Center PC, what types of displays you own, and the types of connections that you are going to use. Second, determine which display will be your primary display and which will be your secondary display, if you plan to attach more than one display to your Media Center PC. Table 3-3 shows display types and recommended configurations.

If you own an LCD display, plasma display, or projector, you should use a digital connection (DVI) from your computer for the most accurate image and color reproduction. If you own a CRT display, then an analog VGA connection is appropriate. If your Media Center PC only has a DVI connection and you are trying to connect it to a CRT that only has a VGA connection, you can purchase a DVI-to-VGA adapter. If you're trying to connect your Media Center PC that only has a DVI connection to a projector that only has an HDMI connection, you can purchase a DVI-to-HDMI adapter.

If you plan to use your Media Center PC in an entertainment center configuration and do not plan to use it like an ordinary PC and you will only attach it to one display, then you will want this display to be your primary display.

If you plan to use your Media Center PC from a desk where you will be sitting close to it and working, you'll want your primary display to be the one at your desk and your entertainment display (should you own one) to be secondary. You'll see why this matters shortly.

Windows Vista will treat your primary display as the default monitor to show applications, the logon screen, and the taskbar. If you connect more than one display to Windows Vista, it'll ask if you want to clone your display output or extend your desktop to both displays. If you clone your display, you'll see the exact same thing on both displays. If you extend your displays, you'll be able to drag applications from one display to another.

If you only have one display attached to your Media Center PC, then you won't need to make a decision between cloning your displays and extending. If you attach two displays to your Media Center PC, however, you'll have to pick one. You can always change your decision later.

Once you've physically connected your Media Center PC to your displays, just turn the computer on. Make sure your displays are set to show the appropriate input. You may need to do additional configuration to make the picture look correct on the display. In the case of an LCD or plasma display, this may involve setting the output resolution from the computer to the display's native resolution.

Display Type	Recommended Configuration
LCD	DVI (from the computer) to DVI (on the LCD display)
CRT	VGA (from the computer) to VGA (on the CRT display)
DLP or other projector	DVI (from the computer) to DVI (on the projector); you may also be able to purchase an HDMI adapter to connect DVI (from the computer) to HDMI (on the projector)
Plasma	DVI (from the computer) to DVI (on the LCD display)

TABLE 3-3　Display Types

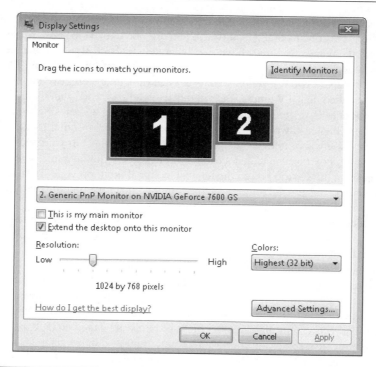

FIGURE 3-1   Configure Windows Vista displays

To access the display settings in Windows Vista, right-click the desktop and click Personalize, and then click Display Settings. You may recognize this diagram from previous versions of Windows—it looks almost exactly the same in Windows Vista. By default, your first monitor is the primary monitor (displayed with a 1 on it in the Settings dialog box), and your second monitor is the secondary monitor (displayed with a 2 on it in the Settings dialog box), as shown in Figure 3-1. To extend the desktop to the secondary monitor, click the secondary monitor, and then select Extend The Desktop Onto This Monitor.

Connect a TV Signal

Most Media Center PCs include a specialized component called a TV tuner (Not all Media Center PCs are required to include a TV tuner, so look carefully before you purchase if you plan to watch television on your computer!). TV tuners receive the television input signal from your set-top box (sometimes referred to as a cable box), satellite receiver, antenna, or directly from your cable line and then translate it to a form that the computer can understand. Then, using Media Center, you can set particular shows to record, rewind, or fast-forward television.

A television signal can only be used to view one channel at a time. For example, if you only have one television signal, it is not possible to watch two different shows at the same time over one connection. This means that if you want to record one television show while watching another on a different channel, you must have two separate television signal connections and, therefore, two TV tuners in your computer, one for each signal respectively. Some TV tuners include the ability to handle two television signals at once (and, therefore, two connections). These TV tuners are called dual TV tuners, and we'll discuss how to work with them in Chapter 19. In this chapter, we'll only cover the aspect of physically connecting a television signal to your Media Center PC. In Chapter 4, we'll discuss how to configure Media Center to use it.

There are several sources of television signals that you can connect to your Media Center PC. If you use a set-top box (as also called a cable box) to receive digital cable, you'll need to connect the output from the set-top box to the television signal input on your TV tuner. If you have satellite television, you'll need to do the same thing: connect the output from your satellite receiver to the television signal input on your TV tuner.

If you do not receive digital cable, you can connect your cable directly to the television signal input on your TV tuner and skip going through the set-top box. The same applies if you receive your signal from an antenna.

When you connect the output from a set-top box to the input of your TV tuner, Media Center can only display the output from the set-top box. In order to change the channel, Media Center needs to be able to communicate with the set-top box; the same applies if you have connected the output from a satellite receiver to your TV tuner input. Media Center communicates with your set-top box or satellite receiver through an extra piece of hardware called an IR blaster. The IR blaster connects to your IR receiver for your Media Center remote control via a 3.5-mm jack input on the rear of the IR receiver. Then the IR blaster is placed in front of the IR receiver for your set-top box or satellite receiver. When you change the channel in Media Center, it communicates with the set-top box or satellite receiver through infrared, just like a remote control, and asks the set-top box or satellite receiver to change the channel.

Connect to a Wired Network

Many people have more than one computer—for example, a laptop you bring to work and a desktop computer at home. If you want to be able to access the Internet on both computers, or if you want to share files between the two, they both must be connected to a computer network. A computer network is a common forum that computers share information through.

Computers can communicate with each other in many different ways. In this case, we'll be talking about how to connect your Media Center PC to a wired computer network. There are also wireless computer networks or Wi-Fi (wireless fidelity) networks.

Almost all computers include a network adapter that can connect the computer to other computers in the outside world. The most common type of network adapter is called an Ethernet adapter. Windows Vista can tell when it is connected to a wired network and can also tell when it is not connected to a wired network. As soon as you connect a Windows Vista PC to a wired network, Windows Vista begins speaking with other services and computers on the network in order to get more information about nearby computers and devices.

If you have more than one computer, or if you have a Media Center PC and another Ethernet-enabled device, such as an Xbox, Xbox 360, or the newer Xbox Elite (which offers high definition), you can set up a home network for all of your devices to communicate through. This is as easy as purchasing a router (such as a Linksys, Belkin, or Netgear router) and simply plugging in all of the devices to it. Media Center PCs and the Xbox 360 get along particularly well. Later, we'll discuss how to establish communication between an Xbox 360 and Media Center PC so that you can watch recorded television shows and listen to music stored on your Media Center PC through your Xbox 360.

Connecting a Media Center PC to an Ethernet network is as simple as plugging the Ethernet cord in to the Ethernet jack on the back of your PC. Ethernet uses an RJ-45 connector—it looks exactly like an oversized telephone cord. (Don't worry, they're two different sizes; an Ethernet cord will not fit into a telephone jack, and a telephone cord will be too small for an Ethernet jack.)

Every time you connect Windows Vista to a new wired network, it'll ask you what type of network it is: home, work, or public (See Figure 3-2 to see what this screen looks like). This sets the security on the Windows Firewall. If you select Home or Work, Windows Vista assumes that it is connected to a private network and enables computer-to-computer file sharing, media library

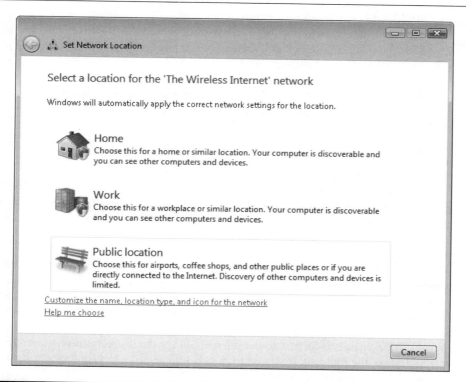

FIGURE 3-2   Every time you connect to a new network, Windows Vista asks what type of network it is so that it can secure your system against network threats.

sharing, and other features. If you select Public, then Windows Vista assumes it is connected to a public network and disables extra network-related features and increases security on Windows Firewall for that connection.

Connect to the Internet

These days, it's hard to do work and research on a computer that does not have an Internet connection. You also miss out on cool features in Windows Vista that use the Internet, such as the Online Media and Electronic Program Guide features of Media Center.

Fortunately, connecting your computer to the Internet is easier than ever with Windows Vista—the computer almost connects itself! If you use cable, digital subscriber line (DSL), or other broadband Internet access that uses an Ethernet connection and your Internet service provider does not provide a user name and password for you to log on to the Internet with, just connect your computer directly to your cable modem, DSL modem, or other network device Windows Vista detects the new connection and automatically connects to the network without the user name and password.

After Windows Vista has connected to the network, try opening a Web page. Open up Internet Explorer (You can just type **Internet Explorer** on the Start menu; or click Start, go to All Programs, and click Internet Explorer). Then type the address in the address bar. If the Web site loads, you're done! Congratulations—your computer is connected to the Internet. If the Web site fails to load, or if you are connecting to a home wireless network, you'll want to use the new Connect To The Internet feature in Windows Vista.

If you are starting Windows Vista for the first time, after you log on to Windows, the Welcome Center appears. If it doesn't, click Start, type **Welcome Center** into the Search text box, and press ENTER. You can also click Start, click All Programs, click the Accessories folder, and then click Welcome Center.

In the Welcome Center, under Get Started With Windows is Connect To The Internet. Double-click it to begin (see Figure 3-3).

In the first page, you're asked how you connect to the Internet: through a wireless connection, broadband (PPPoE), or dial-up. DSL typically uses Point-to-Point Protocol Over Ethernet (PPPoE). You most likely use PPPoE if your Internet service provider has provided you a user name and password to connect with and you're connecting to the Internet with a cable or DSL modem. If you're not sure whether your Internet service provider uses PPPoE, call and ask them before you continue.

Select the method that you're using to connect to the Internet. If you have your own wireless network or use a nearby wireless network, select Wireless. Windows Vista displays a list and walks you through the process of connecting to either a protected or unsecure wireless network. Otherwise, select Broadband or Dial-Up. Both options ask for the user name and password that was issued by your Internet service provider in order to continue.

If Windows Vista is unable to connect to the Internet, follow the instructions on-screen to diagnose or troubleshoot the problem. If all else fails, call your Internet service provider for assistance.

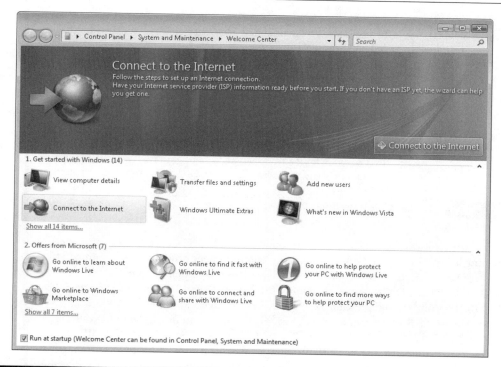

FIGURE 3-3   Accessing Windows Vista's Connect to the Internet wizard

Connect Speakers

Sound is the most important part of a Media Center PC—from listening to music to watching movies or television shows, without sound, you'll miss a big part of the experience. Fortunately, Media Center PCs are well equipped to deal with high-fidelity sound. Surround sound is an integral part of the Media Center experience.

Surround sound is a general term used to describe the technology of improving sound by adding speakers to reproduce more channels of sound. Surround sound first became popular in theaters, and as costs dropped, moved in to home theater systems and then high-definition television, DVDs, and computer games.

Sound system configurations are usually referred to by the number of speakers and subwoofers present. For example, a 4.0 speaker sound system has four speakers and zero subwoofers. A 4.1 speaker sound system has four speakers and one subwoofer. Typical speaker configurations include 4.0 (called quadraphonic, for four speakers), 4.1 (four speakers, or channels, and one subwoofer), 5.1 (five speakers and one subwoofer), 6.1, and 7.1. Table 3-4 shows configuration options and a description of each.

Configuration	Description
4.0 (quadraphonic)	Two speakers for the front (left and front right), two speakers for the rear (left and rear right)
4.1	Two speakers for the front (left and front right), two speakers for the rear (left and rear right), one subwoofer
5.1	Two speakers for the front (left and front right), two speakers for the rear (left and right), one center speaker, one subwoofer
6.1	Two speakers for the front (left and front right), two speakers for the sides (left and right), one center speaker, one rear speaker, one subwoofer
7.1	Two speakers for the front (left and front right), two speakers for the rear (left and right), two speakers for the sides (left and right), one center speaker, one subwoofer

TABLE 3-4   Sound Configurations

There are two ways to get high-fidelity sound from a Media Center PC to speakers. If you're connecting a Media Center PC to a pre-existing entertainment center, you may already own a digital receiver. A digital receiver takes sound encoded in a particular format (such as one of the many Dolby formats: Dolby Surround, Dolby Pro Logic, Dolby Digital, etc.) and decodes it, sending the appropriate audio channels to the correct speakers.

You can use the S/PDIF output on your Media Center PC to input sound to your digital receiver. S/PDIF stands for Sony/Phillips Digital Interconnect Format. The S/PDIF output connector is usually black and the S/PDIF input connector is pink. To use S/PDIF output for audio output on your Media Center PC, you must configure Windows Vista to use it as the default sound device. To do this, click Start, type **Sound** in the text box, and click the resulting Sound item in the Programs list. You can also click Start, click Control Panel, and then double-click Sound. Table 3-5 shows connection types and a description of each. (Note that throughout this book we're using Classic View. If you aren't using Classic View, the directions are Start | Control Panel | Hardware And Sound | Sound.)

The new Sound dialog box in Windows Vista Control Panel lists all of your Media Center PC's sound outputs on the Playback tab, microphones and other inputs on the Recording tab, and Windows system sounds on the Sounds tab. When you open the Sound dialog box, it should display the Playback tab by default. If your Media Center PC has an S/PDIF output, it may be labeled as Digital Output. Select Digital Output, and click Set Default.

Connection Type	Clock Speed (Range)
Jacks (phono plug)	Most common; 3.5-mm stereo jack
RCA	Red and white color connectors
S/PDIF	Sony/Phillips Digital Interconnect Format; black input; pink output
Jacks (phono plug)	Most common; 3.5-mm stereo jack

TABLE 3-5   Sound Connections

Next, you must configure the S/PDIF output. Select Digital Output and then click Properties. Click the Supported Formats tab. Select the formats and sample rates supported by your digital receiver, and then click OK when finished (see Figure 3-4). If you're not sure about what encoded formats your digital receiver supports, consult the instruction manual for the digital receiver.

If you are not connecting your Media Center PC to a pre-existing entertainment system, or if you do not own a digital receiver, you can connect speakers directly to your Media Center PC. Most Media Center PCs support 6.1 audio output through four separate 3.5-mm jack outputs on the rear of the PC. The speaker jack outputs are green. Windows Vista uses the speaker jack outputs by default. For more information about what speaker jack outputs correspond to which speakers, consult your Media Center PC manual.

To configure speakers that are directly connected to your Media Center PC, open the Sound dialog box in Control Panel. Then select Speakers, and click Configure. Windows Vista shows a list of speaker configurations that your sound card supports, such as Stereo (2.0 or 2.1), Quadraphonic, 5.1 Surround, and 7.1 Surround. Select your configuration, and then click Test to test your speaker connections (see Figure 3-5). You can also click individual speakers shown in the image to the right to play a test tone on them.

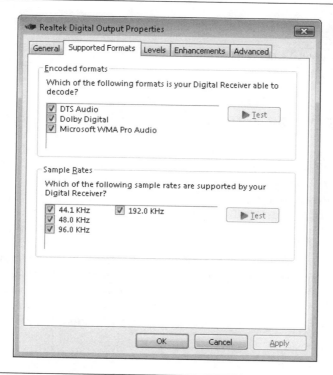

FIGURE 3-4   S/PDIF encoded format options

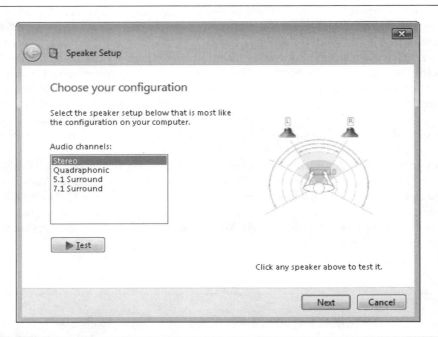

FIGURE 3-5 Windows Vista speaker configuration options

Audio in Windows Vista has leapt into the big league. Windows Vista contains a variety of advanced audio options built-in that are new or that were not available without third-party applications in Windows XP. To access them, click the Enhancements tab on the Properties dialog box for your sound output in the Sound dialog box in Control Panel. The manufacturer of your sound card may provide additional enhancements that are specialized for your sound card. Microsoft provides several built-in enhancements that come with Windows Vista, depending on the type of the sound device. S/PDIF only supports the bass management, virtual surround, loudness equalization, and room correction enhancements. The Headphones option only supports the bass boost, headphone virtualization, and loudness equalization enhancements. The 5.1 and 7.1 speaker configurations only support bass management, speaker phantoming, speaker fill, loudness equalization, and room correction. The 2.0 or 2.1 speaker configurations only support bass management, bass boost, virtual surround, loudness equalization, and room correction enhancements. Note that these enhancements may or may not appear, depending on your sound device and sound drivers. Table 3-6 lists enhancements and a description of each.

Enhancement	Description
Bass management	Enhances or redirects frequencies below a specific crossover point to reduce distortion of bass signals.
Bass boost	Adds gain in the mid-bass range; good for use on a laptop or computer with small speakers.
Speaker phantoming	Spreads sound intended for one speaker across two nearby speakers. Useful if you turn off a specific speaker or do not have one to begin with. (For example, it takes sound from the center speaker and spreads it between the left and right nearby speakers.)
Speaker fill	Extends sounds that would only play from two speakers to play on all speakers. (This is useful if you're listening to music that isn't encoded in surround sound on surround sound speakers, as you'll only get audio on the front two speakers otherwise.)
Virtual surround	Combines sound intended for multiple speakers into sound for two speakers, which can then be sent to a Pro Logic decoder and decoded back into sound for multiple speakers.
Headphone virtualization	Transforms sound so that you perceive it as being surround sound, even though you only have left and right sound from the headphones.
Loudness equalization	Reduces sudden jumps in sound volume.

TABLE 3-6   Sound Enhancements

As you can see, there are lots of display options to choose from. Hopefully, you can now decide exactly what kind of display you want and connect it with ease.

Part II

Configure Media Center for Optimal Performance

Chapter 4

Complete the Required and Optional Setups

How to...

- Join a wireless network
- Connect to the Internet
- Set up the display
- Set up a TV signal
- Set up the library

Windows Media Center is easy to set up, and once configured, your entire collection of digital music, movies, and photographs is available at your fingertips. The first time you open Media Center, you'll be able to select among Express Setup, Custom Setup, and Run Setup Later. This chapter walks you through the process of joining a wireless network, connecting to the Internet, setting up your display, setting up a TV signal, and setting up the Media Library, all of which you might not have gotten a chance to do with Express Setup or if you selected Run Setup Later.

Connect to the Internet

After you've taken your new Windows Vista PC out of the box and plugged it in, you'll probably want to start playing with Windows Media Center right away. Windows Media Center is easy to set up, and you can do it in no time with little hassle. First, you'll want to configure your Internet connection.

The most important part of setting up a new computer is getting it connected to the Internet. Without an Internet connection, you can't check your e-mail, read the news, or send instant messages to friends and family. An Internet connection is particularly vital for Media Center. Many features in Media Center depend on an Internet connection to download additional information.

If you have an "always-on" Internet connection, there is little that you need to do in the way of setup. This procedure that follows is mostly for those with dial-up Internet connections. Follow these instructions to connect Media Center to the Internet.

1. Open Media Center, scroll down to Tasks, and then scroll left to Settings.
2. Click General, and then click Windows Media Center Setup.
3. Click Set Up Internet Connection.
4. Click Next to begin configuring your Internet connection, as shown in Figure 4-1.
5. If you connect to the Internet using an "always-on" Internet connection, select Yes, and then click Next. Otherwise, click No, click Next, and skip to step 7.
6. Click Test to test the connection. Click Finish.

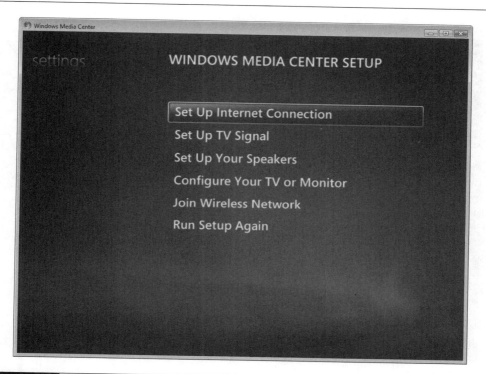

FIGURE 4-1   Set up your Internet connection.

7. If you do not have an "always-on" Internet connection, you'll need to select the connection that you use, an example of which is shown in Figure 4-2. (This connection should be made prior to continuing here. To create a new connection in Windows Vista, click Start, click Control Panel, and then click Set Up A Connection Or Network.) If you've already created a connection for the Internet, select it from the list that Media Center displays, and click Next.

8. Provide the user name and password that is associated with your Internet connection.

9. Click Test to test the connection (see Figure 4-3). Click Finish.

After you set up your Internet connection, the next step is to set up your TV signal. If you don't have a TV Tuner, skip ahead to "Set Up the Display" later in this chapter. You can't set up a TV signal if you don't have a TV tuner with which to watch TV.

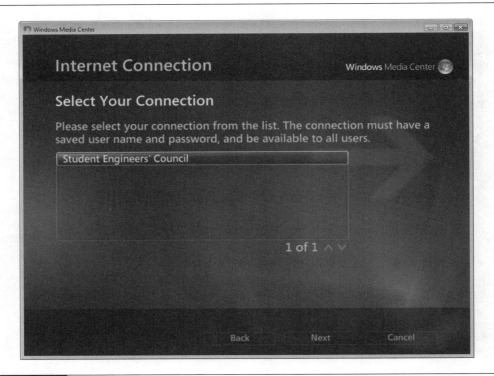

FIGURE 4-2 Internet connections.

Set Up a TV Signal

Although this section is optional, if your Windows Vista PC includes a television tuner card, this section is particularly important for you to understand. Before you can use a television card to receive a television signal on your Windows Vista PC, you need to set up your TV signal in Windows Media Center. Setting up a TV signal in Windows Vista is easy to do—just make sure that you do some background research first!

First, identify what kind of television signal you receive. Media Center supports three kinds of television signals:

- Cable (from a cable set-top box or directly)
- Satellite (from a satellite receiver box)
- Antenna (over-the-air television signal)

If you have cable television and use a set-top box, you'll want to connect the set-top box television output to your Windows Vista PC.

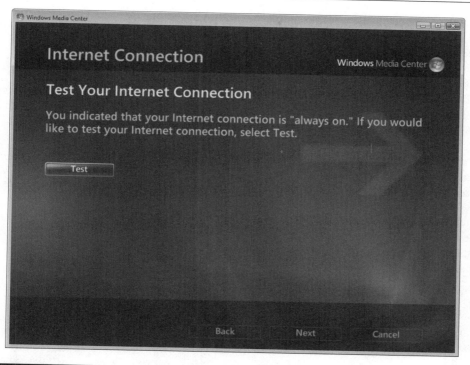

FIGURE 4-3   Test a new Internet connection.

Next, you'll want to consider the region that you are receiving your television signal from. For example, if you live on the border between two countries and can receive over-the-air television from either country, consider your selection carefully, as this may affect your television guide listings and your ability to receive a signal later on. For example, if you live in Canada but are close enough to the United States to watch television from that country, selecting Canada as your region will restrict your television guide to postal codes in Canada.

Once you have identified the type of television signal that you receive and the region your television signal originates from, you're ready to begin setting up your TV signal!

1. Open Media Center from the Start menu.
2. Scroll down to Tasks, and then scroll left to Settings.
3. Scroll down to General, and select it.
4. Select Windows Media Center Setup.
5. Scroll down and select Set Up TV Signal.

Media Center walks you through the process of setting up a television signal. If your Windows Vista PC includes more than one television tuner, don't worry! Setting up two television signals is just as painless as setting up one. For more information about how to add a second television tuner, see Chapter 19.

Setting up a television signal in Media Center by letting Media Center do most of the tasks automatically is a simple three-step process. First, Media Center confirms your television signal region. Then Media Center downloads TV Setup Options. Finally, Media Center automatically sets up your TV signal or lets you do it manually. After you've selected Set Up TV Signal, make sure that the region Media Center displays is correct, and then click Next, as shown in Figure 4-4. If it isn't correct, change the region now; otherwise, you'll have to set up your TV signal all over again later.

After Media Center downloads TV setup options, it can automatically configure your TV signal, or you can manually do it. In almost all cases, it is better to let Media Center automatically configure your television signal. Before you click Next, make sure that your computer hardware is all set up. This means that your television signal should be connected to your TV tuner card. If your television signal is not connected to your TV tuner card, Media Center won't be able to continue the TV signal setup process. After you select Configure My TV Signal Automatically, follow the steps on the screen (see Figure 4-5). Media Center walks you through the process of making sure that your computer is set up for a television signal.

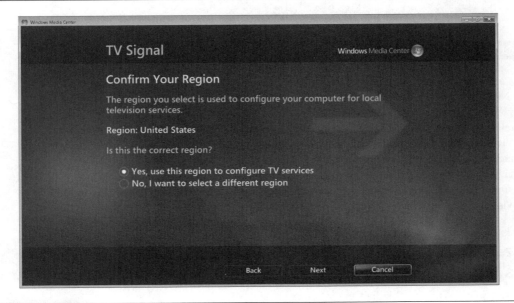

FIGURE 4-4   Media Center TV signal region

FIGURE 4-5   Configure the TV signal automatically.

If you decide to manually configure your television signal, follow these steps:

1. Select I Will Manually Configure My TV Signal, and then click Next.

2. There are three options: Cable, Satellite, or Antenna (see Figure 4-6).

    a. If you select Satellite, Media Center assumes that you receive your TV signal directly from a set-top box.

    b. If you select Cable, you can choose whether your TV signal is from the output of a set-top box or direct from a cable signal.

    c. If you select Antenna, Media Center assumes that you are using an antenna that is connected directly to the TV tuner.

3. Select the correct choice, and then click Next.

4. Exit setup or set up the Guide by selecting Set Up The Guide.

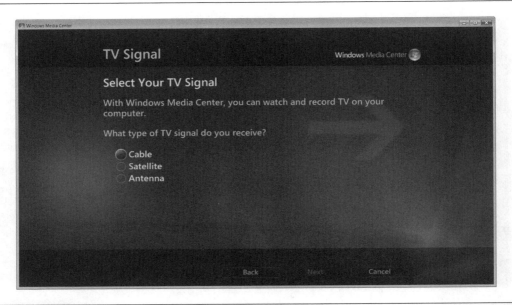

FIGURE 4-6   Configure the TV signal manually.

Set Up the Display

This procedure is also optional. After you've connected your Windows Vista PC to the Internet and set up a TV signal, it's time to set up the display. Depending on the type of display that is connected to your Windows Vista PC, there may be several steps you must undertake to configure your display. Follow these steps to begin setting up your display for Media Center:

1. Open Media Center from the Start menu. Scroll down to Tasks, and then scroll left to Settings.

2. Scroll down to General, and select it.

3. Select Windows Media Center Setup.

4. Scroll down to Configure Your TV Or Monitor, and select it. Watch the initial video about setting up the display, and then click Next.

5. If Media Center is displayed on the preferred display, select Yes, I See The Wizard On My Preferred Display, and click Next. Media Center needs to make sure that you're viewing the picture on your preferred display. Your preferred display is the one that you plan to use the most (see Figure 4-7). This is important, because Media Center configures your preferred display to look the best it can, and if Media Center is on the wrong display, it may not make the display you plan to use the most look as good as possible.

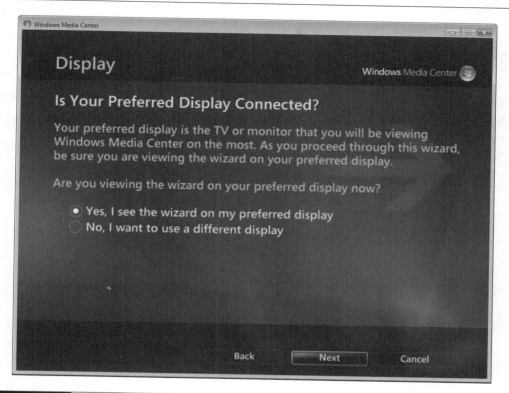

FIGURE 4-7   Make sure you're viewing Media Center on your preferred display.

6. Select your display type, as shown in Figure 4-8:

   a. Monitor (choose this if you have an old tube-based monitor)

   b. Built-in Display (choose this if you have a laptop)

   c. Flat Panel (choose this if you have an LCD TV)

   d. Television (choose this if you have an old tube-based television)

   e. Projector (choose this if you have any kind of projector or DLP technology).

7. Click Next. There are more steps after you click Next, but they vary based on your display type. To learn more about the options for each display type, read on.

Media Center takes one of two approaches to optimize your display picture and make it look as great as possible. In some situations, Media Center can automatically optimize the display. Other times, it uses the Display Calibration Wizard to help make your display look better. It all depends on the display type you selected earlier and how it is connected to your Media Center PC.

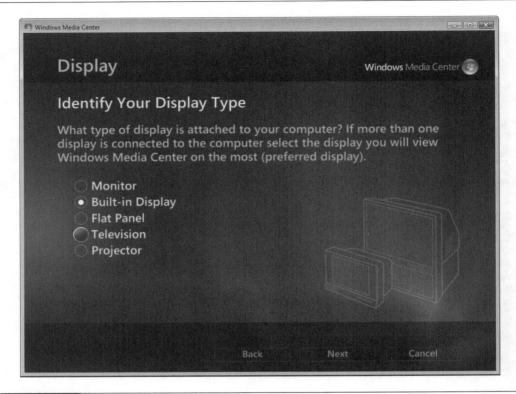

FIGURE 4-8 Select your display type.

If you're using Media Center on a laptop with a built-in display, there isn't much additional setup to be done; however, if you're using a monitor, flat panel, television, or projector, you may be able to make your picture look even better, depending on how your display is connected.

If your display is connected via composite, S-Video, or component, Media Center automatically optimizes your display picture. If your display picture is connected via DVI, VGA, or HDMI, you'll need to use the Display Calibration Wizard (see Table 4-1).

Connection Type	Use the Display Calibration Wizard?
Composite or S-Video	No—Media Center automatically optimizes the picture.
DVI, VGA, or HDMI	Select the picture width, confirm the resolution, and then adjust the display settings with the Display Calibration Wizard.
Component (YPbPr)	Select the picture width, confirm the resolution, and then Media Center automatically optimizes the picture.

TABLE 4-1 Display Calibration Wizard Options

To access the Display Calibration Wizard, just follow the steps in the Set Up Display Wizard. After you identify your display type, Media Center asks you to select the connection type. If your display is not built-in and is connected via DVI, VGA, or HDMI, Media Center asks a few more questions and eventually starts the Display Calibration Wizard. Read on to learn more about the Display Calibration Wizard.

About the Display Calibration Wizard

The Display Calibration Wizard is a part of Media Center that helps you optimize the picture outputted from your computer so that it appears as good as possible on your display. The Display Calibration Wizard (see Figure 4-9) consists of five tasks:

- Onscreen Centering & Sizing
- Aspect Ratio
- Brightness (Black & Shadow)
- Contrast (White)
- RGB Color Balance

The Display Calibration Wizard is available for separate display units connected to your computer via a DVI, VGA, or HDMI cable. To optimize the picture as much as possible, use each of the five tasks. Note that some tasks may not be applicable to your display if it does not have the appropriate controls.

Onscreen Centering & Sizing

Onscreen Centering & Sizing helps you make sure that you can see the entire picture on your display. Some displays may cut off corners, edges, or entire parts of the picture. Use the

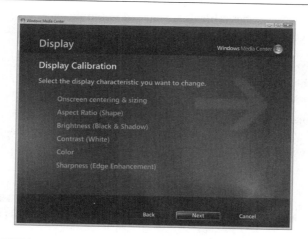

FIGURE 4-9   Display Calibration Wizard

Onscreen Centering & Sizing task if you think you might not be seeing the entire picture. Follow these steps to use Onscreen Centering & Sizing:

1. Select Onscreen Centering & Sizing. Locate the relevant controls on your display, and then select Watch Video (see Figure 4-9).

2. Compare the innermost video with the video you see around the edges of the screen. Resize and adjust your picture using the controls on your display until you can see all of the video.

3. Make sure your picture matches the inset window, especially along the edges. When you're done, press the Back button on your Media Center remote control. Then click the Next button.

Aspect Ratio

Aspect Ratio helps you adjust your picture to the right shape so that it does not appear deformed or inaccurate. Use the Aspect Ratio task if some edges in the picture look unnecessarily curved or inaccurate. Follow these steps to adjust the Aspect Ratio:

1. Select Aspect Ratio. Locate the relevant controls on your display, and then select Watch Video.

2. Adjust the picture as the ball rolls across the screen. Make sure that the ball looks round and that the blue cube of chalk that is slightly off-center is square.

3. Back button on your Media Center remote control. Then click the Next button.

Brightness (Black & Shadow)

Brightness (Black & Shadow) helps you adjust the brightness on your display so that colors are reproduced as accurately as possible. If the brightness is set too high, the picture may appear washed out. If the brightness is set too low, you may not be able to see some details in the picture. You should use the Brightness (Black & Shadow) task if the picture appears washed out or too dark. Brightness controls may also be called Black Level controls.

1. Select Brightness. Locate the relevant controls on your display, and then select Watch Video.

2. Adjust the brightness on the screen until the moving X in the upper-left corner of the screen disappears.

3. Make sure you can distinguish the shirt from the suit. The suit should be black, not gray. If you see a moving X, turn the brightness down until the X disappears. When you're done, press the Back button on your Media Center remote control. Then click the Next button.

Contrast (White)

Contrast (White) helps you adjust the contrast on your display so that you see all of the vivid details possible. If the contrast is set too low, you may miss out on vivid details in high-definition videos and DVDs and in ordinary television. Use the Contrast (White) task to adjust the contrast to a level that reproduces the picture as clearly as possible. Contrast controls may also be called Picture controls.

1. Select Contrast. Locate the relevant control on your screen. Select Watch Video.

2. Turn the contrast up and adjust the picture using the controls on your display until you can't see the buttons on the shirt any more.

3. Set the contrast as high as possible without losing the wrinkles and buttons on the shirt. When you're done, press the Back button on your Media Center remote control. Then click the Next button.

RGB Color Balance

RGB Color Balance helps you adjust how accurately colors are reproduced. Not all displays include an RGB Color Balance control. If your display doesn't include one, look for a color temperature setting. If your display has one, set it to 6500k.

1. Select RGB Color Balance. Locate the relevant controls on your display. Select Watch Video.

2. Adjust your picture using the controls on your display until you do not see any colors in the gray bars. When you're done, press the Back button on your Media Center remote control. Then click the Next button.

When you're done with the Display Calibration Wizard, click Next. Congratulations—your picture is now optimized to look as good as possible on your display!

Join a Wireless Network

Windows Media Center, like Windows Media Player 11, has many enhanced Internet features. The feature you'll probably find most important in Media Center is the electronic program guide: a two-week on-screen television guide that shows times, descriptions, and other information about every show on every television channel in your area. In order to get the electronic program guide in Media Center, you must be connected to the Internet. Other features in Media Center that require Internet access include the Movie Guide, Sports Guide, and parts of the Program Library.

Fortunately, connecting to the Internet is an easy process, even if you use a wireless network. Connecting your Media Center PC to a wired network is recommended, but if you have no other choice, 802.11a and 802.11n are the best wireless choices.

Make sure that your wireless networks are secure and protected with Wi-Fi Protected Access (WPA). WPA requires that you enter a password to connect to the wireless network. When you join a protected wireless network, Media Center asks for the wireless protection key. For more information about how to secure your wireless equipment, read the device's manual or consult the business you purchased the wireless equipment from.

You can configure your Media Center PC to use a wireless network for Internet access by following these steps:

1. Open Media Center, scroll down to Tasks, and then scroll left to Settings.

2. Select General, and then select Windows Media Center Setup. Finally, select Join Wireless Network.

3. Any changes that you make during the Media Center wireless network setup will overwrite your existing Windows Vista wireless network settings. If you've already connected to a wireless network with Windows Vista then you don't need to join the same wireless network a second time while using Media Center.

4. If you've already joined a wireless network, select No under Would You Like To Use The Join Wireless Network Wizard?, and then click Next to exit. If you haven't connected to a wireless network and still need to, select Yes, and then click Next to continue.

5. The next screen reminds you that you must already have set up wireless network before you can join it. Select Yes. Click Next.

6. Media Center searches the local airwaves to find compatible wireless networks. This may take up to a minute (see Figure 4-10). You should see the same list of wireless networks that you see in Windows Vista. Select a wireless network, and then click Next.

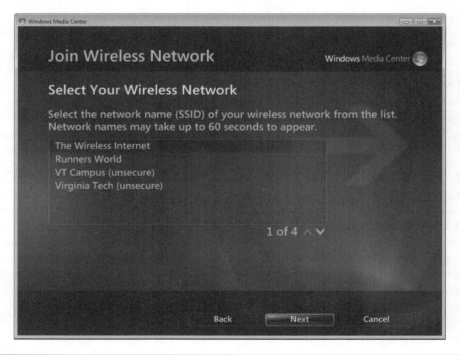

FIGURE 4-10   Join wireless networks using Media Center.

7. If the wireless network is protected, you'll need to enter the network key now. You can't connect to the wireless network without the wireless key (see Figure 4-11). If your wireless key contains letters, you may want to do this with a keyboard rather than with a remote control. After you enter the key, click Next.

Note that connecting to a wireless network is an action that requires administrator privileges and requires that you approve the connection first. You can tell that administrator privileges are required by the shield icon that is displayed next to the Next button. After you click Next, you'll get a User Account Control (UAC) prompt to approve the action. Click Continue.

Your Windows Vista PC should now be connected to a network! You're ready to start using all of the Internet-enabled features in Media Center, such as the Guide and Program Library.

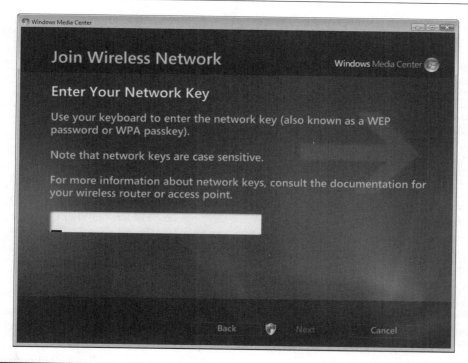

FIGURE 4-11 Enter the wireless network key.

Set Up the Library

Windows Media Center has a music library, video library, and picture library. You can browse any of these libraries to find music to listen to, videos to watch, or pictures to look at. You use Windows Media Player 11 to manage your libraries in detail. But if you just want to sit back, relax, and show your friends and family some vacation pictures, home movies, or just listen to your favorite song, nothing else can do it as easy as Media Center can.

Windows Vista includes Windows Media Player 11 to help you manage your media. Windows Media Player 11 automatically searches your personal Pictures, Videos, and Music folders for media and adds it to the media library. Media Center integrates with Windows Media Player 11 to provide a much more visually appealing and easy way to navigate the media library. Before you can navigate your libraries in Media Center, you've got to add some media to them to get started! Although this step is optional, it is easy to do—Windows Media Player 11 almost does it for you.

First, think about where you store your media. On your own computer, it is best to store all media in the respective personal folder: Music, Pictures, or Video. These folders can be accessed from the Start menu or from the Favorite Links list on the left side of the Documents folder. No one else can access your personal folders except for the system administrator. Even if someone else opens up Media Center on their own personal account, they can't see your libraries.

If you have media that you want to access saved on other computers, you can share it over the network and add it to the folders that Windows Media Player 11 and Media Center include in the libraries.

To add or remove folders to your libraries, follow these steps:

1. Open Media Center, scroll down to Tasks, and then scroll left to Settings.

2. Scroll down, and select Library Setup.

There are two options: Add A Folder To Watch or Stop Watching A Folder (see Figure 4-12). If you choose to add a folder to watch, there are three options: Folders On Your Computer, Shared Folders From Another Computer, or Both. Shared Folders From Another Computer simply refers to folders that are shared publicly from another computer on the network. The most important part to remember is that the shared network folders must be able to be read by other users on the network. If they're not accessible on the network, Media Center won't be able to watch them.

If you select Folders On Your Computer, you'll be able to select any folder from your local hard drive. Browse the hard drive using the remote control or the keyboard, if you are sitting at the computer. Select the folders that you want to add to the library, and then click Finish when you are done. Media Center will advise you that you can wait while the folders

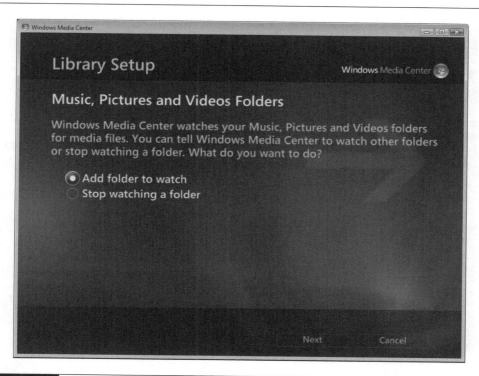

FIGURE 4-12   You can add a folder for Vista to watch or stop watching a folder.

are being added to the library or you can click OK to perform other tasks while Media Center adds the folders.

You can also configure Media Center to stop watching a folder from the library setup. To stop watching a folder, just clear the check mark next to the folder, and then click Next (see Figure 4-13).

NOTE   *Adding or removing watched folders is the same as adding or removing folders from inside of Windows Media Player 11's folder-monitoring feature. Windows Media Player 11 and Windows Media Center share the media library.*

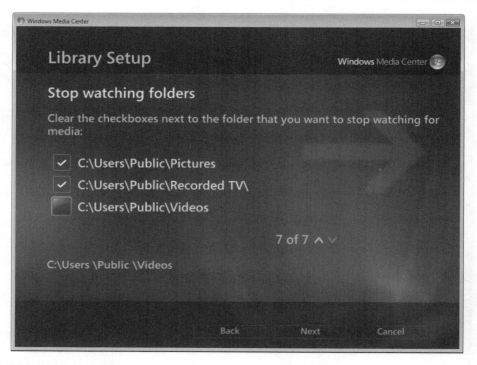

FIGURE 4-13
Stop watching a folder.

Chapter 5

Take Advantage of Advanced Settings

How to...

- Change startup and Window behavior
- Set up parental controls
- Optimize Media Center
- Change automatic download options
- Configure closed-captioning

Windows Media Center is a straightforward, simple, and powerful application to use. Almost anybody can pick up a Media Center remote control and go from total novice to expert very quickly. With Windows Media Center, before you know it, you'll be navigating your Media Library like a professional. Media Center doesn't sacrifice customizability for ease of use, however. There are plenty of advanced settings that you can tweak to make Media Center works just the way you want it to. In this chapter, we'll review several advanced settings that you can use to change how Media Center behaves so that you can use it even better.

NOTE   *All of these settings are set correctly when you first use Media Center. You don't need to change any of them to make Media Center work properly; doing so is entirely optional.*

Change Startup and Windows Behavior

Windows Media Center is flexible enough that you can tailor it to your exact lifestyle. Some people use Media Center in the living room on a large television; others use it close up while sitting at a desk. Whichever way you use Media Center, there are several ways to change the way it behaves so that it fits your lifestyle better. Let's take a look at several options that change how Media Center behaves while you use it, as well as when your computer starts up.

To change advanced settings, you first need to open Media Center and locate the advanced options under Tasks:

1. Press the green Windows logo button on the Media Center remote control, or press it on your keyboard if you have a Media Center–compatible keyboard. You can also click Start, click All Programs, and then click Windows Media Center.

2. In Media Center, scroll down to Tasks, and then scroll left to Settings.

3. Select General. You'll see several options:

   a. Startup And Window Behavior

   b. Visual And Sound Effects

   c. Program Library Options

   d. Windows Media Center Setup

   e. Parental Controls

   f. Automatic Download Options

   g. Optimization

   h. About Windows Media Center

   i. Privacy

In the next few sections, we'll be looking at some of these options, so don't go anywhere!

Startup and Window Behavior

In Media Center, click Tasks, click Settings, and then click General. Click Startup And Window Behavior. The first option, Windows Media Center Window Always On Top (see Figure 5-1), keeps the Windows Media Center window displayed over all other windows on your screen. This is useful when you use Windows Media Center while working with another application—for example, if you are using Microsoft Office Outlook to read e-mail while also watching television or listening to music with Windows Media Center. While you read messages, Windows Media Center remains visible and on top at all times.

5

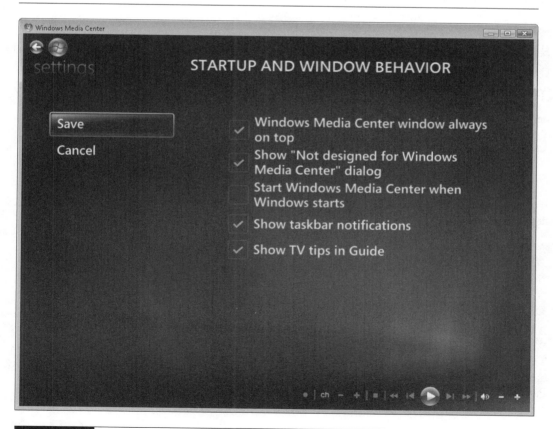

FIGURE 5-1   Configuring startup and window behavior

Show "Not Designed For Windows Media Center" Message

Sometimes when you launch Windows Media Center add-ons or view Web sites inside of Windows Media Center, you'll run across items that are not designed for Windows Media Center or are not designed for the version of Windows Media Center that you're using. When this happens, Windows Media Center warns you by displaying a message that you must acknowledge. If you frequently use add-ons or Web sites that are not designed for Windows Media Center and do not want the message to be displayed any more, simply clear the Show "Not Designed For Windows Media Center" Dialog Box check box.

Start Windows Media Center When Windows Starts

Some people have a dedicated Windows Media Center PC that is kept in the living room connected to an entertainment system. Sometimes, the system may need to be restarted. If you use your Media Center PC in this manner, it will benefit you to enable the Show Windows Media Center When Windows Starts option. This causes Media Center to automatically start as soon as you log on. That way, you worry less about having to start Windows Media Center and can start enjoying your Media Center PC as soon as Windows starts.

Show Taskbar Notifications

Occasionally, Media Center may need to notify you of an important event, such as not being able to record a scheduled television show or loss of television signal. When the need arises, Media Center notifies you by displaying a notification in your taskbar. Sometimes, you might already be aware of these situations, and the notification won't help you too much. If you run into this sort of situation, you can simply disable taskbar notifications by clearing the Show Taskbar Notifications option.

Show TV Tips in the Guide

If you want to see TV tips when using the Guide, select this option. Note that it's selected by default and offers all kinds of information when you use the Guide.

NOTE   *After making changes to the Startup And Window Behavior options, don't forget to click Save!*

Set Up Parental Controls

If you have young children, then this section may be the most important one for you to read. Windows Media Center supports parental controls for television shows, movies, and DVDs. This means that you can restrict these items by television rating or movie rating. You can also block television shows, movies, and DVDs that are not rated. You can also password-protect the Parental Controls area so that only those with the appropriate access code can bypass the parental control restrictions or access the parental control settings area of Media Center.

To access the Parental Controls area of Media Center:

1. Start Media Center, select Tasks, and then click Settings.
2. Select General, and then select Parental Controls. The Parental Controls setup screen is shown in Figure 5-2.

Before you can configure parental controls, you'll need to create an access code. This is a four-digit number that Media Center requires to protect the Parental Controls area and also to bypass parental controls when they are enacted. After you enter a four-digit number, you'll need to enter it a second time to confirm it. Media Center automatically continues after you enter the four digits a second time to confirm the access code. Make sure you keep your access code in a safe place—you don't want to lose it! But if you really do, the Help file should be able to "help" you.

There are four options in the Parental Controls area: TV Ratings, Movie/DVD Ratings, Change Access Code, and Reset Parental Controls. Let's take a look at each option in detail.

TV Ratings

To access TV ratings, first you must select Turn On TV Blocking. Once this is selected, you'll be able to select and access the rest of the TV Ratings parental controls. With TV Ratings, shown in

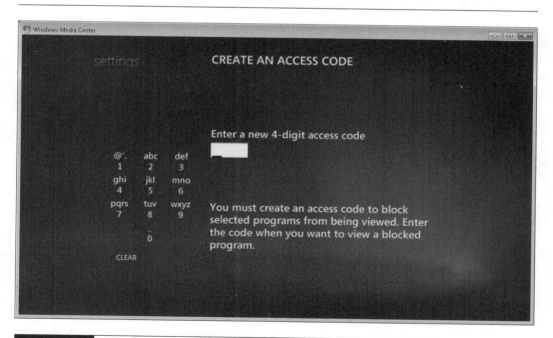

FIGURE 5-2   Parental controls setup screen

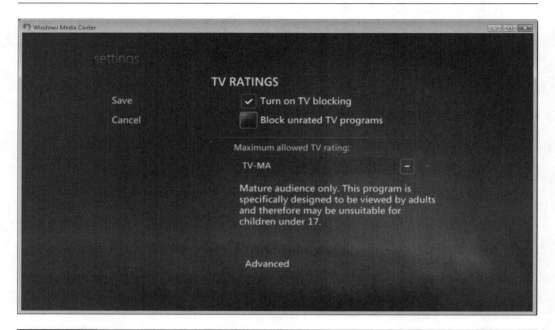

FIGURE 5-3 TV Ratings parental controls

Figure 5-3, you can block unrated television shows. This means that when a television show that is unrated broadcasts on the channel that is currently being watched, Media Center prompts for the parental controls access code in order to show it. To block unrated TV programs, select the relevant option.

You can also set the maximum allowed TV rating that Media Center shows without asking for the parental controls access code. There are seven possible TV ratings to select from, as listed in Table 5-1.

If you want to adjust TV Ratings parental controls more finely beyond TV-MA, at the bottom of the screen is an Advanced Settings link. Scroll down, select it, and then click OK or press ENTER.

There are five criteria that you can use to fine-tune TV Ratings parental controls, as listed in Table 5-2.

After you've made changes, select Save to go back to the original TV Ratings parental controls area, shown in Figure 5-4. To go back one more time to the general parental controls area, select Save again.

Rating	Description
TV-MA	Mature audience only. This program is specifically designed to be viewed by adults and therefore may be unsuitable for children under 17.
TV-14	Parents strongly cautioned. This program contains some material that many parents would find unsuitable for children under 14 years of age.
TV-PG	Parental guidance suggested. This program contains material that parents may find unsuitable for younger children.
TV-G	General audience. Most parents would find this program suitable for all ages.
TV-Y7	Directed to older children. This program is designed for children ages 7 and older.
TV-Y	All children. This program is designed to be appropriate for all children.
None	All rated programs will be blocked.

TABLE 5-1   Television Ratings

Movie/DVD Ratings

To access the Movie/DVD Ratings area, first you must select Turn On Movie Blocking. Once this is selected, you'll be able to select and access the rest of the movie-blocking parental controls.

With Movie/DVD Ratings, you can block unrated movies. This means that when a movie that is unrated broadcasts on the channel that is currently being watched or is inserted into your DVD drive, Media Center prompts for the parental controls access code in order to show it. To block unrated movies, select the relevant option.

Option	Allow/Block	Description	Ratings
Fantasy Violence	Allowed Blocked	Sexual Content	TV-MA TV-14 TV-PG Blocked
Suggestive Dialogue	TV-14 TV-PG Blocked	Violence	TV-MA TV-14 TV-PG Blocked
Offensive Language	TV-MA TV-14 TV-PG Blocked		

TABLE 5-2   Advanced Television Ratings

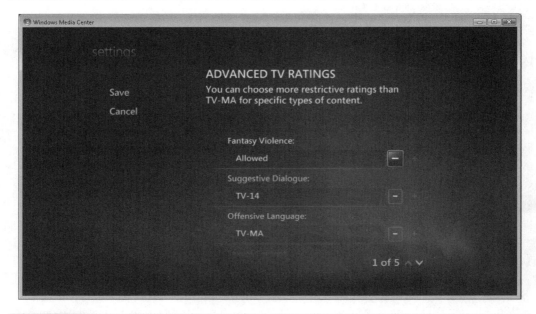

FIGURE 5-4 Advanced TV parental controls settings

You can also set the maximum allowed movie rating that Media Center shows without asking for the parental controls access code. There are six possible movie ratings to select from, as listed in Table 5-3.

Change Access Code

If you want to change your access code to something easier to remember—or perhaps it has gotten into the wrong hands—just select Change Access Code. You'll be prompted to enter a new four-digit access code and are then prompted to enter it a second time to confirm it, just like when you made the first four-digit access code.

Rating	Description
NC-17	Not intended for anyone 17 and under.
R	Restricted. Under 17 requires an accompanying parent or adult guardian.
PG-13	Parents strongly cautioned. Some material may be inappropriate for children under 13.
PG	Parental guidance suggested. Some material may not be appropriate for children.
G	General audience. Appropriate for all ages.
None	All rated movies will be blocked.

TABLE 5-3 Movie Ratings

Reset Parental Controls

If you want to start all over again and erase your access code and all associated settings, select Reset Parental Controls. When you do this, all of your settings and parental controls access code will be erased. This will turn off all parental controls, and you'll be able to watch anything without having to enter a code.

Optimize Media Center

If Media Center runs continuously for more than a day, performance may decrease. Media Center may not feel as snappy as it once was, and some tasks may take longer to perform. Fortunately, Media Center has a built-in way to optimize itself so that it always responds quickly and efficiently.

You can schedule Media Center to optimize itself every day at a specific time. While Media Center is optimizing, you won't be able to use it and any Media Center extenders won't be able to connect to your Media Center PC. The optimization process exits the Media Center process ehshell.exe program and starts it again. If optimization detects that Media Center is being used, it will delay optimizing the system.

To optimize Media Center:

1. In Media Center, scroll down to Tasks, and then scroll left to Settings.

2. Select General, and then select Optimization.

3. Select Perform Optimization, shown in Figure 5-5.

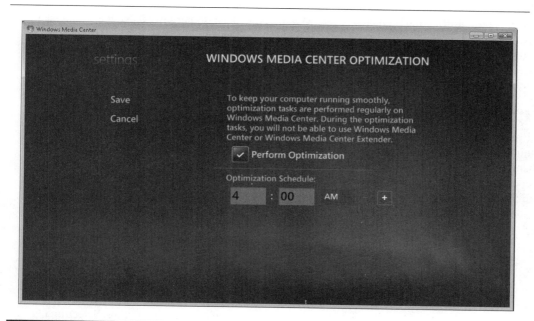

FIGURE 5-5   Optimize Media Center

4. Under Optimization Schedule, enter a time that Media Center should begin optimizing.

5. Click Save.

Change Automatic Download Options

Media Center integrates with Internet services to download information associated with music, television shows, and movies. For example, Media Center downloads album art for music albums, DVD chapter information for movies, and an entire electronic program guide to show you what is on television. Media Center can download this information automatically when you insert a DVD, or you can do it manually.

To access Automatic Download Options:

1. In Media Center, scroll down to Tasks, then scroll left to Settings.

2. Select General, and then select Automatic Download Options.

By default, Media Center downloads information for CDs, DVDs and movies, and the electronic program guide (after you have configured the electronic program guide). If you want to stop Media Center from downloading information automatically, clear the Retrieve CD Album Art, Media Information For DVDs And Movies, And Internet Services From The Internet option. This isn't recommended, however, as it may impair certain features in Media Center.

Media Center automatically downloads information when you are connected to the Internet. If you do not have an "always-on" Internet connection, it may make more sense to change Media Center so that it only downloads information manually. To prevent Media Center from downloading information manually, select Manual Download. Otherwise, leave the setting as it is set by default or change it to Download When Connected.

If you want to force Media Center to connect to the Internet and download information immediately, select Download Now.

Configure Closed Captioning

Closed captioning is a technology that displays a written transcript, or caption, of television audio on the screen with the video. This is helpful for people with impairments that may prevent them from being able to hear television audio clearly. Many people who have no hearing impairment turn on closed captioning anyway for situations where the television might be muted, but they still want to keep track of what is going on in the television show.

To turn on closed captioning:

1. In Media Center, scroll down to Tasks, and then scroll left to Settings.

2. Select TV, and then select Closed Captioning (see Figure 5-6).

There are two options: Caption Display and Basic Captioning. Caption Display controls when closed captioning should be disabled. There are three options. Selecting On displays closed captioning whenever it is available. Selecting Off never shows closed captioning. Selecting On When Muted shows closed captioning only when the audio is muted.

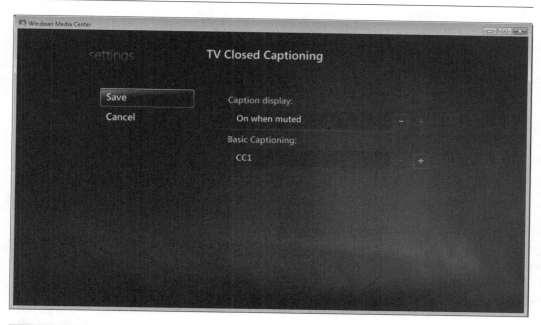

FIGURE 5-6   Closed captioning settings

There are two channels that may carry closed captioning data with a television channel. A long time ago, it was thought that television shows may want to include captioning in more than one language. Analog television, therefore, supports two closed captioning channels: CC1 and CC2. CC1 typically carries English closed captioning text. CC2 may carry closed captioning text for an alternate language, such as Spanish. In the Basic Captioning section of Media Center, you can select whether captions from CC1 or CC2 should be disabled. More than likely, you'll want to select CC1.

Basic Captioning

■ **Caption Display**   Media Center has built in closed captioning capability, much like most televisions do. You can select between turning closed captioning on, off, or having it display only while the audio is muted.

   ■ **On**   Shows closed captioning whenever it is available.

   ■ **Off**   Never shows closed captioning.

   ■ **On when muted**   Only shows closed captioning when the audio is muted.

■ **Basic Captioning** There are two channels that may carry closed captioning data with a television channel. A long time ago it was thought that television shows may want to include captioning in more than one language. Analog television therefore supports two closed captioning channels – CC1 and CC2. CC1 typically carries English closed captioning data. CC2 may carry closed captioning text for an alternate language, such as Spanish. In the Basic Captioning section of Media Center you can select whether captions from CC1 or CC2 should be disabled. More than likely, you'll want to select CC1.

Chapter 6

Navigate Media Center

How to...

- Browse Media Center's categories with a mouse, keyboard, and remote control
- Locate what you want in Media Center
- Use Media Center's navigation buttons
- Use Media Center's control buttons
- Learn keyboard shortcuts

Browsing Basics

With Media Center set up, it's finally time to start exploring what it has to offer. You can browse Media Center menus and options using your mouse and keyboard, a remote control, or a combination of these. You can also start Media Center using these tools or from inside the Vista interface.

Open Media Center

Look for the Media Center icon on your keyboard or remote control. The icon is shown in Figure 6-1. You'll see the icon on almost any remote control you'll receive with a computer and on some keyboards. If you can't find the icon on any hardware, you can open Media Center using the computer and your mouse. Just click Start, click All Programs, and click Windows Media Center.

You can also make the Media Center icon available in the Quick Launch area, pin the link to the application to the Start menu, or create a shortcut to it on the desktop.

To make Media Center accessible from the Quick Launch area of the taskbar:

1. Right-click an empty area of the taskbar.
2. From the pop-up list, point to Toolbars, and select Quick Launch.
3. Click Start.
4. Click All Programs.
5. Right-click Windows Media Center.
6. Select Add To Quick Launch.

FIGURE 6-1 Media Center icon

To pin Media Center to the Start menu:

1. Click Start, and right-click Windows Media Center.

2. Select Pin To Start Menu.

3. To unpin, right-click the new shortcut, and select Unpin From Start Menu.

To create a shortcut to Media Center on the desktop:

1. Click Start, and right-click Windows Media Center.

2. Point to Send To, and select Desktop (Create Shortcut).

Using Mice, Keyboards, and Remote Controls

Mice, keyboards, and remote controls differ depending on the model, but for the most part, using them is straightforward and basically the same across the board. Spend a few minutes with your remote control (if you have one) to make sure you can locate the Play, Rewind, Fast Forward, Pause, Record, and other buttons. Look for the Back and Forward buttons and/or buttons with arrows that you can use to move through the menus.

If you don't have a remote control, take a look at your keyboard. You may be surprised to see buttons on the keyboard for Media, Play, Stop, Pause, Record, and similar options. If you don't see these, no worries! You can use the arrow keys on the keyboard and click with your mouse to move through menus in Media Center.

Using the Arrow Keys

When browsing Media Center, you can use your mouse, keyboard, and/or remote control to work through the categories and subcategories using the four arrow keys that appear when you position your mouse over the interface. You'll use these arrows to access the applications you want to use.

To help you get started, try browsing through and selecting categories in these ways:

■ Hover the mouse over any of the four arrows (but do not click the arrow) to move through the categories without stopping on any. Figure 6-2 shows the top arrow and the continual browsing action.

■ Click the mouse on any of the four arrows to browse through categories one at a time. Each click of the mouse moves through the available categories.

■ Hold down the arrow keys on the keyboard or remote control to move through the categories without stopping on any.

■ Click the arrow keys on the keyboard or remote control to move through the categories one by one, stopping on each.

■ Click any category or subcategory to access that option immediately.

■ Click the Back button in the upper-left corner of the Media Center interface (it won't appear until you move the mouse there or press the proper button on the remote control) to return to the previous screen.

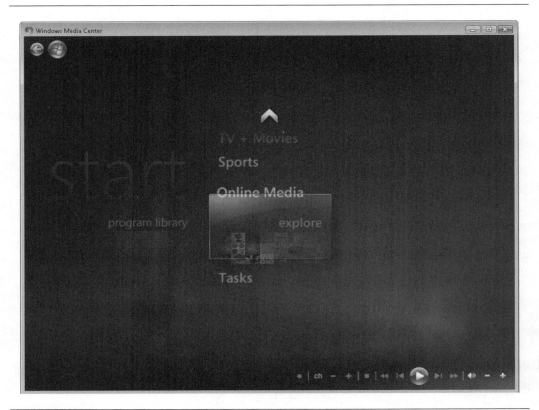

FIGURE 6-2 Hover the mouse over any of the four arrows (the top one is shown here) to browse through categories without stopping.

TV + Movies

Select TV + Movies. By default, Recorded TV is selected. Click the left arrow to move to More TV, the subcategory farthest to the left of the options (see Figure 6-3).

Using the arrow keys to move from left to right in the subcategories, you'll have access to the following, which will be further detailed in Chapter 7:

- **More TV**   Access Internet TV, including channels from Showtime, Fox Sports, Comedy Central, The Learning Channel, Movielink, and more.
- **Recorded TV**   View the TV shows you've previously recorded.
- **Live TV**   View live TV.
- **Guide**   View the Guide, which offers scheduled programming, and use it to record a show or series.

FIGURE 6-3   Locate TV + Movies and then More TV

- ■ **Movies Guide**   View movies that are currently playing, on next, top rated, or by genre.
- ■ **Play DVD**   Watch a DVD that's in the DVD-ROM drive.
- ■ **Search**   Search for media by title, keyword, category, actor, or director.

Sports

Select Sports. By default, On Now is selected. Click the left arrow to move to More Sports, the subcategory farthest to the left of the options. Using the arrow keys to move from left to right in the subcategories, you'll have access to the following:

- ■ **More Sports**   Access sports shows on the Internet, including channels from Fox Sports, Reuters, Yahoo! Sports, and more.
- ■ **On Now**   Find out what sports programs are on now, from archery to fishing to rugby to soccer.

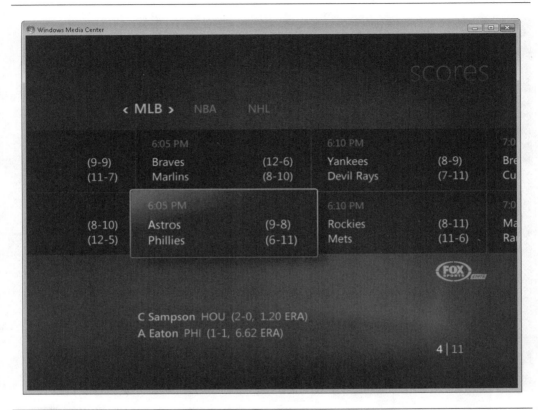

FIGURE 6-4 Media Center | Sports | Scores offers up-to-the minute information

- **On Later** Find out what sports programs are on later, and configure them to record if desired.
- **Scores** Get up-to-the-minute scores on currently running games. Figure 6-4 shows an example.
- **Players** Add players to track your favorites and fantasy league players for baseball, basketball, hockey, and more.

Online Media

Select Online Media. By default, Recorded TV is selected. Click the left arrow to move to Program Library, the subcategory farthest to the left of the options. Using the arrow keys to move from left to right in the subcategories, you'll have access to the following, which will be further detailed in the Chapter 10:

- **Program Library**   View items in your Media Library, including games, music, radio, pictures, news, sports, tasks, and more.
- **Explore**   Browse online media options, including Nickelodeon, MTV, Vongo, Movielink, Discovery Channel, NPR News, and more.

Tasks

Select Tasks. By default, Shutdown is selected. Click the left arrow to move to Settings, the subcategory farthest to the left of the options. Using the arrow keys to move from left to right in the subcategories, you'll have access to the following, which will be further detailed in various chapters throughout this book:

- **Settings**   Access to change Media Center–wide settings, including settings for TV, pictures, music, DVDs, extenders, and more.
- **Shutdown**   Choose from Close (to close Media Center), Log Off (to log off from the computer), Shut Down, Restart, and Sleep.
- **Burn CD/DVD**   Access options to burn various types of audio and data CDs and DVDs, depending on your PC's hardware and media.
- **Sync**   Click to sync a portable media device, such as a Zune. (Connect the device first.)
- **Add Extender**   Work through the Media Center Extender Setup Wizard to connect an extender to the computer, configure computer settings, and test the performance of the network.
- **Media Only**   Enabling Media Only keeps Windows Media Center displayed in Full Screen mode. In this mode, the Minimize and Close buttons are hidden.

Pictures + Video

Select Pictures + Video. By default, Picture Library is selected. Click the left arrow to move to More Pictures, the subcategory farthest to the left of the options. Using the arrow keys to move from left to right in the subcategories, you'll have access to the following, which will be further detailed in Chapters 15 and 16:

- **More Pictures**   Access pictures from the Internet from Yahoo! Photos and AOL Pictures. You can use these options to sign in to your own account and select an album to view. You can view your own photos (ones you've uploaded) or your friends' and family's.
- **Picture Library**   View the images on your computer, accessible network drives, CDs and DVDs, and third-party picture libraries. Figure 6-5 shows an example.

FIGURE 6-5 A sampling of all that the picture library can hold

- **Play All** Automatically view a slideshow of the pictures on your PC.
- **Video Library** Access folders on the PC or network drives that contain videos.

Music

Select Music. By default, Music Library is selected. Click the left arrow to move to More Music, the subcategory farthest to the left of the options. Using the arrow keys to move from left to right in the subcategories, you'll have access to the following, which will be further detailed in Chapters 11,12, and 13:

- **More Music** Access music on the Internet, including (but not limited to) MTV, Country Radio, VH1, and XM Radio.

- ■ **Music Library** Access your own playlists created in Media Player 11, or search for music by composer, year, album, artist, and more. You can also access other data, including recent e-mail, recent documents, and recently changed data.

- ■ **Play All** Play the music in your music library. You can view the queue, change visualizations, play a slideshow, shuffle music, repeat songs, and even buy music.

- ■ **Radio** Access local radio stations and configure radio presets.

- ■ **Search** Use the Search|Music option to enter letters from your keyboard, mouse, or remote control to search for the music you want. Figure 6-6 shows these options.

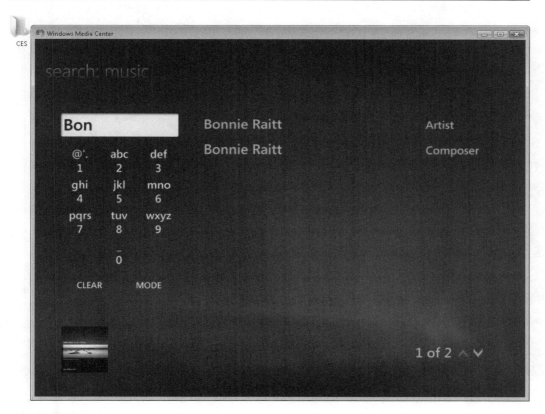

FIGURE 6-6   Search for the music you want to play

Now Playing + Queue

When you select Now Playing or Now Playing + Queue (whatever the case may be), you'll have access to information on what is currently playing. In Figure 6-7, music is playing and the song is part of a queue.

However, if a TV show were on, the options would differ. Since TV doesn't play in a queue, the Now Playing screen looks like what's shown in Figure 6-8.

FIGURE 6-7 Now playing music in a queue

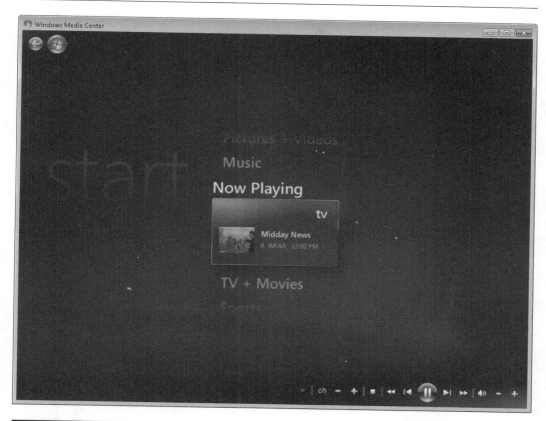

FIGURE 6-8   Now playing live TV

Navigation Buttons

No matter what type of media you're playing, whether it's music, movies, videos, or pictures, you'll have access to the navigation buttons in the lower-right corner of the Media Center interface (see Figure 6-9). You can use these navigation buttons to manage, browse, and move through the media you're playing.

In Figure 6-9, from left to right: The first button is the record button. It's red. Click this button to record what's currently playing or to stop a recording in progress. The second and third buttons are for changing the channel, down and up, respectively. The square button stops and closes live TV. The next two buttons are for rewinding (the first button rewinds

Navigation buttons

FIGURE 6-9 Navigation buttons

using speed intervals—one click to rewind slowly, two to rewind a bit faster, three to rewind even faster, and four to rewind as fast as possible; the second button is used to rewind in 30-second intervals); the middle is to play and pause; and the following two are for fast-forwarding (the first button fast-forwards using speed intervals—one click to fast-forward slowly, two to fast-forward a bit quicker, three to fast-forward even quicker, and four to fast-forward as quickly as possible; the second button is used to fast-forward in 30-second intervals). The volume button is for muting, and the last two buttons on the right are for decreasing and increasing volume, respectively.

Navigation Tips and Tricks

There are lots of keyboard shortcuts for navigating Media Center. Tables 6-1 through 6-4 offer a few of them.

To	Press
Move up	UP ARROW
Move down	DOWN ARROW
Move left	LEFT ARROW
Move right	RIGHT ARROW
Select	ENTER or SPACEBAR
Jump back one page at a time	PAGE UP
Jump ahead one page at a time	PAGE DOWN
Start Media Center	Windows logo key-ALT-ENTER
Go back to the previous screen or backspace a single character in Search	BACKSPACE

TABLE 6-1   Navigation Keyboard Shortcuts in Media Center

To	Press
Change to a specific channel	The number for the channel you want
Move up one channel	EQUAL (=) or CTRL-EQUAL
Move down one channel	MINUS (−) or CTRL-MINUS

TABLE 6-2   Keyboard Shortcuts to Change Channels in Media Center

To go to TV and DVD menus for	Press	To go to TV and DVD menus for	Press
Guide	CTRL-G	Recorded TV	CTRL-O
Record	CTRL-R	DVD Audio	CTRL-SHIFT-A
Details	CTRL-D	DVD Subtitle	CTRL-U
DVD Menu	CTRL-SHIFT-M		

TABLE 6-3   Keyboard Shortcuts for TV and DVD Menus

6

To	Press	To	Press
Pause	CTRL-P	Rewind	CTRL-SHIFT-B
Play	CTRL-SHIFT-P	Fast-Forward	CTRL-SHIFT-F
Stop	CTRL-SHIFT-S	Mute	F8
Replay	CTRL-B	Volume Down	F9
Skip	CTRL-F	Volume Up	F10

TABLE 6-4 Keyboard Shortcuts for Playback Controls

Note that you'll likely also find shortcuts on the keyboard, including buttons for TV, music, photos, etc., as well as on your remote control. Many of the keyboard shortcuts listed here will work on your remote control, too—play around with all of the arrows, page up and page down buttons, and other buttons on your remote.

Part III

Play, Customize, and Manage TV, DVDs, and Online Media

Chapter 7

Explore Live and Recorded Television, Movies, and the Guide

How to...

- Watch live TV
- Watch recorded television shows
- Navigate the Guide and Mini Guide
- Use the Movies Guide
- Use More TV or play a DVD

Like Windows Media Player 11, Windows Media Center organizes your digital memories so that you can display them for anyone from the convenience of your desk or the comfort of your living room sofa. While both Windows Media Player 11 and Media Center keep track of your music and organize your pictures, there are several things that Windows Media Player 11 can't do, like play and record live television or display a full-screen guide of what's on television at the moment. And that's where Media Center steps in.

By now you should be familiar with your Windows Vista PC and the different hardware components that enhance Windows Media Center—like a TV tuner, the basic hardware included with some Windows Vista PCs that translates a television signal into a signal that a computer understands. In this chapter, you'll learn how to put Media Center to work so that you can watch live or recorded television, find and record your favorite television shows using the Guide, and even look up a movie and find cast, director, and rating information.

Watch Live TV

The most important feature in Windows Media Center is the ability to watch live TV. Not all Windows Vista PCs may be able to do this, however—your computer must have a television tuner. If your computer is equipped to view live TV and is connected to a television signal, you're good to go! You can enjoy television from your Windows Vista PC in a way unlike you've never experienced before. To watch live TV in Media Center:

1. On the remote control, press the Live TV button to start watching live TV. On the Start screen, you can also scroll down to TV + Movies, then scroll right to Live TV, and then press OK (see Figure 7-1).

2. There are several parts to the Live TV screen. On the entire screen you'll see the television show currently airing on the television station. In the lower-left corner of the screen is the information bar, or Mini Guide, which you'll see when you click there. The right side of the screen is where menus are displayed when you right click in that area (see Figure 7-2).

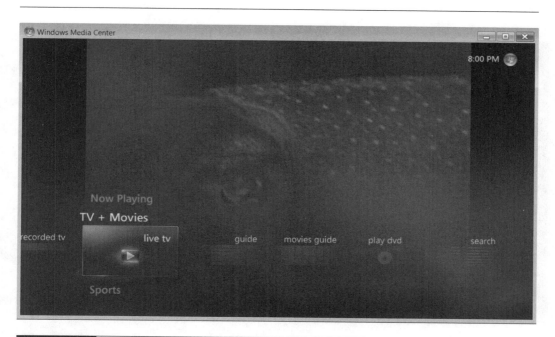

FIGURE 7-1 Select Live TV from TV + Movies

3. To see more information about the current television show, press the More button. This displays an information bar in the left corner of the screen and a menu in the right corner of the screen. On the menu there are six options:

- **Program Info** Displays the Program Info screen. You'll learn more about the Program Info screen soon.

- **Record** Starts recording the television show.

- **Record Series** Starts recording the television show and schedules the entire television series to be recorded.

- **Zoom** Alters how the picture is displayed. If the picture looks stretched or just incorrect, use Zoom to fix it.

- **Mini Guide** Shows a miniature television guide on your screen. You'll learn more about the Mini Guide soon.

- **Settings** Opens Media Center settings.

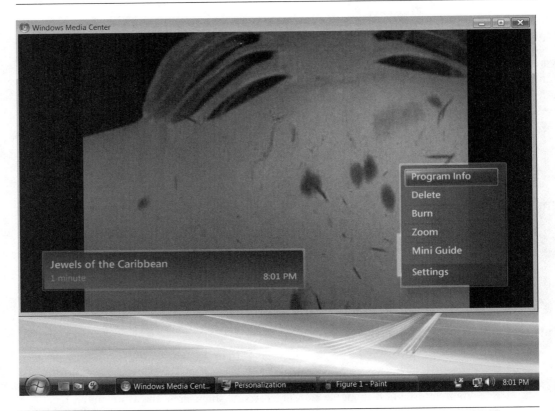

FIGURE 7-2

FIGURE 7-2 Information displayed on the Live TV screen

To change the television channel, press the Channel Up and Channel Down buttons on your remote control. There may be a slight delay in changing television channels, depending on your television signal source—changing channels takes slightly longer if your television signal comes from a set-top box. You can also enter the channel number using the remote control or a keyboard.

You can pause live television with Media Center, too (see Figure 7-3). This means that you're free from programming schedules set by television producers—free to get up and get that cup of coffee, answer the phone, or run to the grocery store. Any time you want to stop live television, just press the Pause button. To resume watching television where you left off, press the Play button.

You can pause up to 30 minutes of live TV. After 30 minutes, live TV starts playing again. This is because Media Center saves up to 30 minutes of a television show on the hard drive as you watch it. When you close Media Center or change the television channel, the 30 minutes of saved television is automatically deleted.

If you don't like watching commercials on television, one popular strategy is to start watching a television show and then immediately pause it. Wait about five or ten minutes. Then press Play to start playing it. You'll have about five or ten minutes of time that you can fast-forward through as

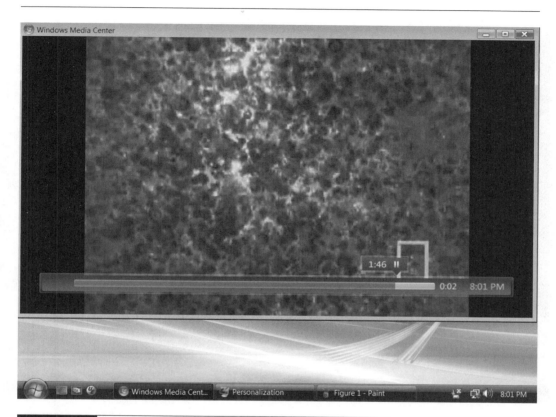

FIGURE 7-3   Paused television

you watch the television show. Use this time to skip commercials when they air. You can also record the television show and then skip the commercials as you watch it later. You'll learn more about recording soon.

To rewind television, press the Rewind button (see Figure 7-4). As with Pause, you can only rewind up to 30 minutes of television on the current station. If you change the channel to a different television station, the 30 minutes that was temporarily stored is erased. You can only rewind up to the last 30 minutes of the current television channel that you're watching. Use the Replay button to move back seven seconds.

To fast-forward television, press the Fast-Forward button. To fast-forward more quickly, press the button multiple times. When you press the Play button, fast-forwarding stops and resumes playing. To skip forward 29 seconds, press the Skip button.

Press Stop to turn off live TV and return to whatever you were doing in Media Center. For example, if you were browsing the Guide, when you press Stop, live TV will stop playing and the Guide will appear.

FIGURE 7-4   Rewind television

Navigate the Guide and Mini Guide

You don't need to have a reason to use Media Center—if you're looking to sit down, relax, and just find a television show to watch, Media Center has you covered. It downloads two weeks of television listings and displays them in the television guide. To access the guide, follow these instructions:

1. On the remote control, press the Guide button to display the Guide. You can also press the green button, scroll down to TV + Movies, and scroll right to Guide.

2. Now use the arrow buttons on the remote control to browse up and down and left to right on the Guide. To move into the future and see what television shows are going to be on, press the right arrow button. You can't view television shows in the past; the Guide only shows you what is on at the moment and in the future. Notice that the Guide is split into three areas: Categories (on the left), TV Channels (next to Categories), and Television Shows (this occupies most of the space on the screen). See Figure 7-5.

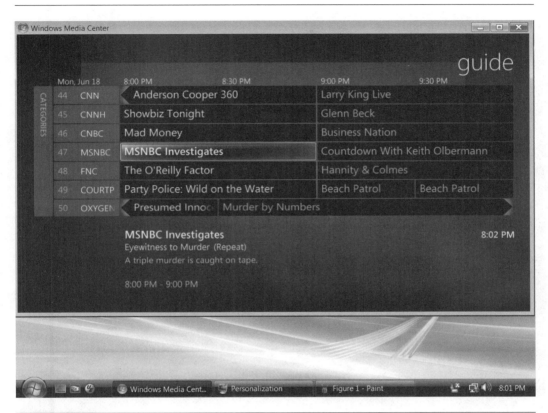

FIGURE 7-5   Media Center Guide

TIP   *To skip forward in increments of three hours on the Guide, press the Forward (FWD) button on the remote control. To skip ahead 12 hours, press the Skip button.*

3. You can select almost anything on the Guide that you can move to with the arrow buttons. For example, press the right arrow button to move the selection right on the guide. You'll notice that as you move the selection from television show to television show that a description is shown on the bottom of the screen. If you've selected a movie, sometimes a rating is also displayed. You'll learn more about how to browse movies in Media Center that are showing on television soon.

4. If you want more information about a television show that airs in the future, select it, and then press OK. If you select a television show that is currently airing, Media Center changes the television channel so that you can view it.

5. When you select a television show on the Guide that airs in the future and press OK, the next screen is called the Program Info screen, and it shows four options: Record, Record Series, Advanced Record, and Other Showings. For more information about the Program Info screen, see the section "Program Info" later in the chapter.

> TIP
>
> *You can also select a television show and press the More button on your Media Center remote control to display a similar menu with the options Program Info, Record, Record Series, and Categories.*

Program Info

The Program Info screen (see Figure 7-6) is where you go to schedule a recording, view more information about a show, and find other times that the show airs. You can get to the Program

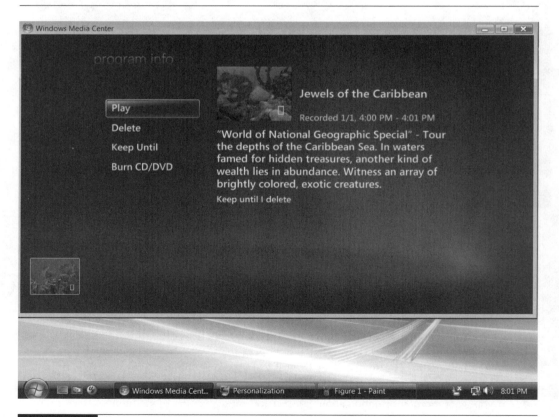

FIGURE 7-6   Program information

Info screen from the Guide or directly from the television show on Live TV. There are four options in Program Info:

- **Record**   Select Record to schedule this specific television show to record when it airs. Television shows that are scheduled to record have a red dot to the right of their Guide entries.

- **Record Series**   If the television show is a series, you'll see this option. Select Record Series to record every episode of that specific television show that airs. You'll see multiple red dots displayed to the right of the show's Guide entry if Media Center is set up to record every episode of a specific television show. For more information, see the section "Record and Record Series."

- **Other Showings**   If the television show is a series and airs more than one episode, Other Showings shows you all of the future airings of a particular television show within the next two weeks, broken down by each day.

- **Advanced Record**   Here you can tweak some more advanced recording settings. These settings include Frequency, Stop, Quality, and Keep. Advanced Record lets you configure many additional options for that particular television show. The following section provides more information about what you can change using Advanced Record.

Advanced Record

Advanced Record lets you tweak all of the little details of a television show recording. If you're trying to record a television show that usually runs over its scheduled end time, use Advanced Record (see Figure 7-7) to make Media Center record that last five or ten minutes. You can also schedule when and if Media Center automatically deletes the television show and whether or not to record all the episodes in a series.

- **Frequency**   Frequency controls whether Media Center should record just one show or an entire series. This is the same setting that was displayed on the previous screen with Record Series. If you select Record Series on the Frequency option, you'll notice four new options at the bottom of the screen: Keep Up To, Channels, Airtime, and Show Type. You can use these options to further control how Media Center will record future episodes of the television show that air. Once Media Center records the television show, it'll be stored for a certain period of time. You can control how long it is stored with the Keep option.

- **Stop**   Not all television shows end at their scheduled time. Sometimes a television show might end a little later than when the Guide says it will. If this is the case, and you know that the time on the Guide is inaccurate, you can use the Stop option to control when Media Center stops recording a television show. There are nine options for Stop: On Time, 5 Minutes After, 10 Minutes After, 15 Minutes After, 30 Minutes After, 1 hour After, 90 Minutes After, 2 Hours After, and 3 Hours After.

- **Quality**   Media Center has four quality levels for recorded television shows. If you are low on disk space, you may want to alter the quality that Media Center is recording the show at. You can pick from Fair, Good, Better, and Best.

7

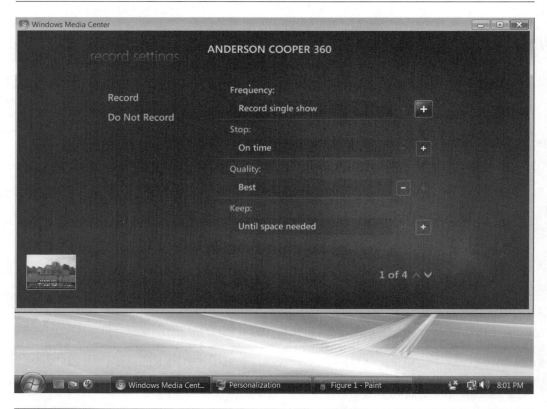

TIP

Fair quality uses 1 gigabyte (GB) per hour. Good quality uses 2 GB per hour. Better quality uses 2.5 GB per hour. Best quality uses 3 GB per hour.

■ **Keep**   If you're running low on hard disk space, or if you record a television series that airs often, you should take a look at the Keep options. Keep controls how long the recorded television file stays on your hard drive. There are four choices: Until Space Needed, For 1 Week, Until I Watch, and Until I Delete.

■ **Keep Up To**   If you record a television series that is popular and airs many times a day on different television stations, you'll quickly become overwhelmed with the dozens of recorded television files on your Windows Vista PC. Rather than overwhelm your hard drive with a file for each episode that might air, you can configure Media Center only to keep a specific number of recordings. With Keep Up To, you can select 1 Recording Through 7 Recordings, 10 Recordings, and As Many As Possible.

- **Channels**   Many television series air on multiple television channels. If the television show that you select airs on multiple channels within the next two weeks, you can record the series only on the station you selected or on multiple stations.

- **Airtime**   Popular television series air several times a day on multiple stations and at multiple times. If you want to narrow down what episodes Media Center records, you can pick among three settings: Around A Specific Time, Anytime, and Anytime, Once Per Day.

- **Show Type**   Media Center is able to distinguish between episodes of television shows that are airing for the first time and episodes of television shows that are reruns. If you only want Media Center to record new episodes, you can set Show Type to make sure that Media Center doesn't re-record old episodes. There are three settings for Show Type: Live, First Run, and First Run & Rerun.

Record and Record Series

When you select a television show or series that you've scheduled to record, you'll notice that the Program Info screen changes slightly. That is, rather than having the four usual options described in the preceding paragraphs (Record, Record Series, Advanced Record, and Other Showings), there are now several new options for a television series that is set to record:

- Record Settings

- Do Not Record

- Keep Until (for television series only)

- Series Info (for television series only)

- Other Showings

Record Settings (see Figures 7-8 and 7-9) accesses a new screen that lets you choose between configuring settings for the specific instance of the television show that you've selected and editing settings for the entire television series. For example, if you only want to edit the quality setting for the one television show you've selected and not the entire series, select Record Settings, and then select Settings For This Episode Only. If you want to change a recording setting for the entire series, select Record Settings, and then select Settings For The Entire Series.

Do Not Record cancels the scheduled recording for the current episode or the entire series, depending on what you selected in Record Settings and when you opened the Program Info section.

Keep Until shows the settings for keeping the television show or series. There are several options: Do Not Change, Keep Until Space Needed, Keep Until (a specific date), Keep Until I Watch, and Keep Until I Delete.

NOTE   *Media Center may automatically start to delete old recorded television shows to make room for new ones unless you select Keep Until I Delete. These settings are controlled by the recording default settings. To access and change the recording default settings, scroll down to Tasks, and then scroll left to Settings. Then select TV, select Recorder, and select Recording Defaults.*

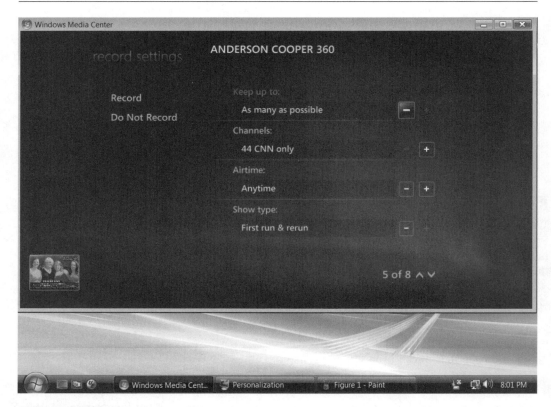

Record Series settings

Series Info only appears for television series, and it shows you all of the episodes that are scheduled to record for that specific television series, along with what the current channel, record, and keep settings are. To access the record settings for the entire series, select Series Info, and then select Series Settings. To cancel the recording of the entire television series, select Cancel Series. These are the same options that you access through Record Settings when you select Settings For The Entire Series.

Other Showings shows you other episodes of the same television show or television series that are airing within the next two weeks.

Recording Conflicts

A recording conflict occurs when two television shows are scheduled to record at the same time. If you only have one television tuner, you can only watch one show at a time. If you have two television tuners, then you won't see a recording conflict occur.

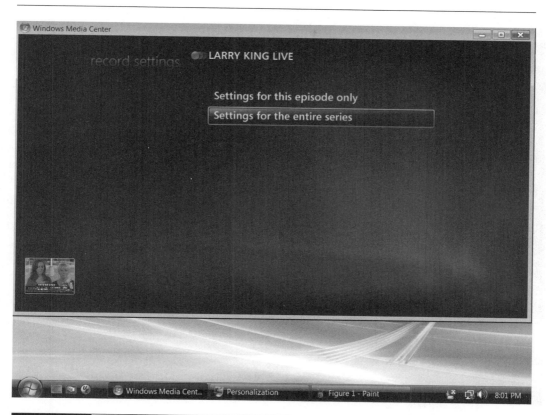

FIGURE 7-9   Record Settings

Navigate the Guide by Category

You can also filter and navigate the Guide by television show category. On the left side of the Guide you'll notice a categories bar that extends vertically along the side of the channel listing. To select it, press the left arrow button until Categories is highlighted, and then press OK (see Figure 7-10).

The Categories menu consists of seven categories that you can use to narrow down what the Guide shows: All, Most Viewed, Movies, Sports, Kids, News, and Special. As you move over each category option and highlight it, notice that the Guide filters immediately. If you want to keep the filter, press OK on the category; you can also press Back to go back to the Guide.

FIGURE 7-10   Navigate the Guide by category

Navigate the Guide by Television Channel

By default, the Guide shows a lot of information—every television show that is airing within the next two weeks for every television station. You can control the Guide so that it shows less information, therefore making it easier to find the television shows you want to watch—think of it as making the haystack smaller so that it takes less time to find the needle. When you filter the Guide, you make it easier to find that precious gem of a television show or movie that you didn't know existed or didn't know was airing.

To filter the Guide by television channel, press the left or right arrow button on the Guide until a television channel is selected, and then press OK (see Figure 7-11). The television channels are displayed to the right of the categories bar on the Guide and to the left of the television show listings—for example, 58 USAP, 59 SCIFIP, and 60 COMEDY.

When you select a television station, Media Center shows a smaller Guide just for that station. If you press the right or left arrow button, the smaller Guide changes stations. You can tell what station you're on at the moment by looking in the upper-right corner of the screen, where it says,

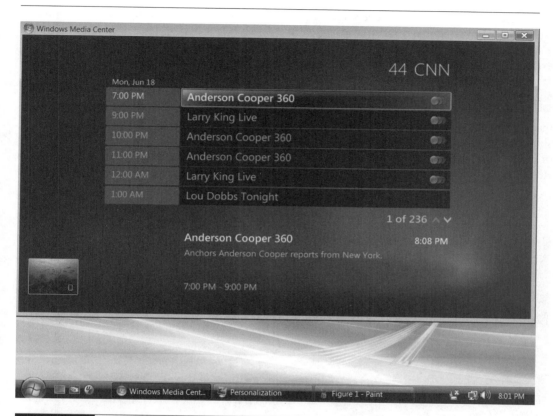

FIGURE 7-11   Navigate the Guide by television channel

for example, 60 COMEDY. Scroll down to see other shows listed in the Guide for that television channel.

When you select the television channel on the Guide, Media Center shows a brief summary of what airs in the future for that television channel on the bottom of the screen.

Navigate with the Mini Guide

When you change channels, or when you first start live TV, Media Center displays an information bar in the lower-left corner of the screen. The information bar shows the current television station name, television channel, television show title, start and end times for the television show, and the current time.

The information bar is actually much more than a simple notification—you can use it to browse the Guide from the convenience of the corner of your display. It's called the Mini Guide. Press the up or down arrow button on the remote control to expand the information bar and display the Mini Guide. You can also press the More button, and then select and press OK on

Mini Guide. The Mini Guide displays a description of the television show in addition to all of the other information previously mentioned.

The Mini Guide (see Figure 7-12) behaves in exactly the same way as the ordinary Guide. Press the up and down arrow buttons to change the television channel information that is displayed. Press the right and left arrow buttons to see what television shows are coming up—none of these actions actually changes the television show that you're watching.

If you're watching a television show and you are curious about what is coming up, rather than display the full Guide, you can browse with the Mini Guide. When you find a television show that you like, press OK to change the channel to the television show, if it is currently airing, or press OK to open the Program Info screen for the show. If you want to record it, just press the Record button on the remote control, and Media Center will schedule the recording for you.

FIGURE 7-12 The Mini Guide

Watch Recorded Television

When you record a television show, it is saved in your Recorded TV folder. To watch a recorded television show, scroll down to TV + Movies, and scroll right to Recorded TV, and then press OK (see Figure 7-13).

Media Center shows a thumbnail preview of all of your recorded television shows in order of date recorded. If you want to sort by title instead, press the up arrow button to select the date recorded, press the right arrow button to select the title, and finally, press the down arrow button to go back to the recorded television shows.

To show a menu of additional options for recorded television, press the More button. The Additional Options menu (see Figure 7-14) appears with the following entries:

- **Program Info**   Displays the Program Info screen.
- **Play**   Starts playing the television show immediately.

7

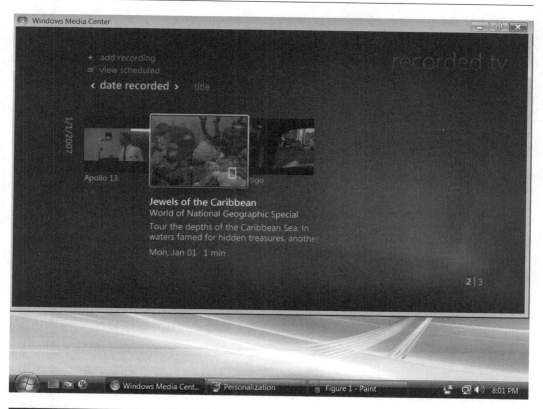

FIGURE 7-13   Recorded television

FIGURE 7-14   Additional options for recorded television

- ■ **Delete**   Deletes the recorded television show.
- ■ **Burn**   Burns the recorded television show to a DVD.
- ■ **View List**   Shows all of the recorded television show files in a list, without images.
- ■ **Settings**   Shows links to Settings, including General, TV, Pictures, Music, DVD, Extender, and Library Setup.

There are even more things you can do from the Recorded TV menu. At the top of Media Center there are two options: one to add a recording and another to view all scheduled recordings. To access these two options, press the up arrow button twice until you see the text selected.

Use Add Recording to find a program on the Guide or to search for a program to record. You can search by title, keyword, category, movie actor, or movie director.

You can also create a custom (also called manual) recording (see Figure 7-15) for a particular channel and time, or even keyword, such as actor name, director name, movie title, program title, or generic keyword.

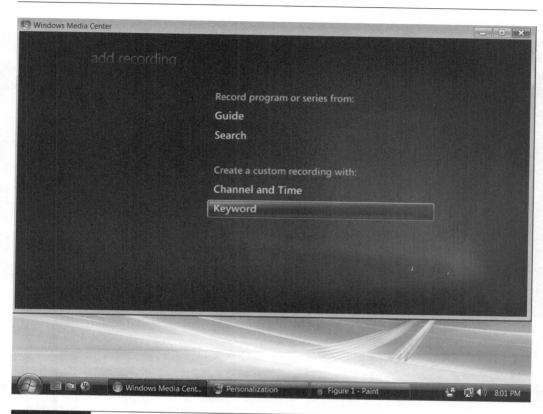

FIGURE 7-15   Custom recording options

Use the Movies Guide

Windows Media Center includes a Movies Guide. This helps you find movies that are on television at the moment or in the future. It can even show you top-rated movies or let you search by genre.

To access the Movies Guide (see Figure 7-16):

1. Scroll down to TV + Movies.
2. Scroll right to Movies Guide, and press OK.

This amazing feature of Media Center uses the Internet to download additional information about the movie, such as ratings, a description, and even a listing of the cast.

When you first open the Movies Guide, Media Center shows a list of genres. You can select a particular genre to browse for movies or change to another view that you can use to find movies that are currently showing on television, movies that will be starting soon, or movies by top-star rating. To change the view, press the up button, and then move left or right.

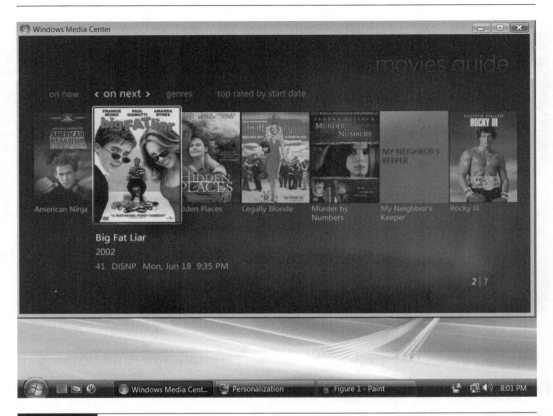

FIGURE 7-16   The Movies Guide

TIP

If you browse by genre, you can look up almost any movie—even movies that aren't showing on television right now. You can even record a particular movie in the future, should it show up on television.

For additional options, press the More button. If you press the More button while you're looking at a movie in the Movies Guide, a menu appears with these options (see Figure 7-17):

- **Movie Details**   Use Movie Details to find out more information about a movie, such as a description, rating, and director. You can even find reviews, similar movies, and cast information.

- **Record**   Records the movie with a single click.

- **View Large**   Changes the way movies are displayed. View Large shows large previews of a movie so that you can scroll left or right to see each one.

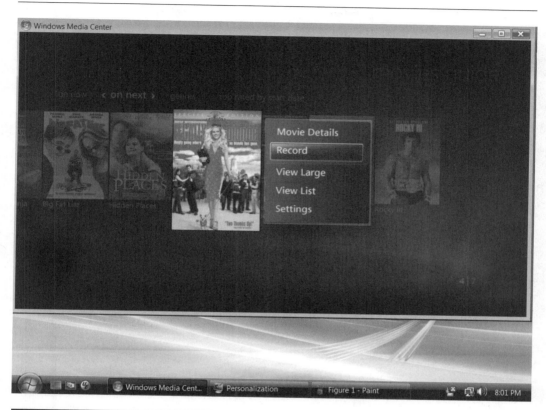

FIGURE 7-17   Additional movie options

- ■ **View List**   Changes the way movies are displayed. View List doesn't show you previews of movies; instead, it just shows a list of titles that you can scroll through.
- ■ **Settings**   Use this option to access Media Center settings, including General, TV, Pictures, Music, DVD, Extender, and Library Setup.

Use More TV or Play a DVD

More TV (see Figure 7-18) is a feature of Windows Media Center that uses the Internet to connect with television networks so that you can watch extras, view additional content, or even watch more episodes of a television show from the comfort of your Media Center PC. To access More TV:

1. Scroll down to TV + Movies.
2. Scroll left to More TV, and press OK.

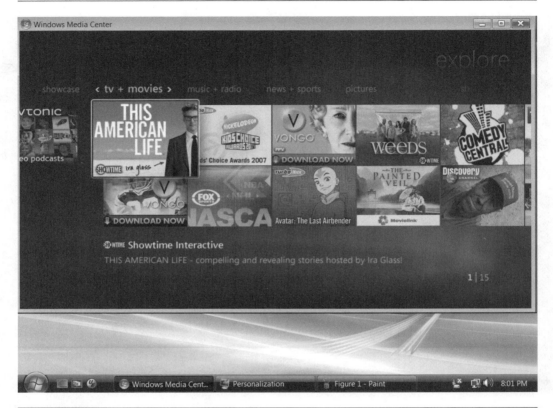

FIGURE 7-18　More TV options

When you select More TV, Media Center connects to the Internet to find the latest Web sites from television networks that have been integrated to add extra content to Media Center. Some examples include Nickelodeon, Showtime, Fox Sports, Comedy Central, Discovery Channel, and TLC.

You can also use More TV to access additional content for:

- **Music and radio**　VH1, NPR, AOL Radio, MTV, XM
- **News and sports**　Fox Sports, NPR News, Reuters, Yahoo! Sports
- **Pictures**　Yahoo! Photos and AOL Pictures

Since More TV uses the Internet to find additional content, the preceding list can change at any time, so it is important to check back often with More TV to see if your favorite television network is listed.

Play a DVD

Media Center can do more than just play television and music or show pictures. As with Windows Media Player 11, you can also play DVDs. To play a DVD, just insert a one into your DVD drive. If Media Center is already open, it automatically starts playing the DVD. You can always play it manually: Scroll down to TV + Movies, and scroll right to Play DVD.

Media Center downloads additional information from the Internet to make browsing the DVD easier. To display this additional information, press the More button. Media Center shows a menu with these options:

- ■ **Zoom**   Alters how the picture is displayed. If the picture looks stretched or just incorrect, use Zoom to fix it.

- ■ **Movie Details**   Shows more information about the DVD, such as the rating, release year, and total run time.

- ■ **Title Menu**   Returns to the title menu.

- ■ **Eject**   Ejects the DVD from your DVD drive.

- ■ **Settings**   Use this option to access Media Center settings, including General, TV, Pictures, Music, DVD, Extender, and Library Setup.

If you press the More button while watching a DVD, Media Center displays the name of the current chapter that is playing. All of the ordinary television controls work while you are watching a DVD. You can rewind, fast-forward, replay, or skip. Skip moves forward to the next chapter. Replay moves to the previous chapter.

If you press Stop, Media Center returns to the screen it was on before you played the DVD.

7

Chapter 8

Record Live TV

How to...

- ■ Record a TV show
- ■ Record a TV series
- ■ Configure advanced recording settings
- ■ Manage recorded TV
- ■ Burn recorded TV to a DVD

Let's get to the main reason why you purchased Windows Vista with Media Center. You want to watch, pause, and record live TV so you can skip the commercials! That's exactly what you'll learn here: how to record a TV show or a TV series, how to configure basic and advanced recording settings, and how to manage the media you want to keep.

Record TV

When recording a TV show, you have more than one option. For instance, you can click the Record button in Media Center to record what's currently playing, select a future show in the Guide and press the Record button on the remote, right-click any show and select Record from the drop-down list using your mouse, or press CTRL-R on the keyboard after selecting the desired show in the Guide. You can also record a series of shows and make changes to the default recording settings. You'll learn about all of this and more in this section.

Record a Single TV Show

There are two scenarios for recording a single TV show (and not the entire series). You can record it at the moment it airs, or you can schedule it to record the next time it is on.

To record a live TV show while watching it in Media Center:

1. Open Media Center and select Live TV.

2. Use the navigation buttons, keyboard, or remote control to move through the channels to locate the program you want to record.

3. When the program begins, or anytime it's playing, click the red Record button, shown in Figure 8-1. You'll see this if using the mouse or keyboard. If you are using the remote control, click the Record button on the remote instead.

4. You can click the Stop button to stop recording if desired. (The Stop button is the square button at the bottom of the screen, or the Stop button on the remote control.)

FIGURE 8-1   The first button on the left is the Record button (it's the round, red one).

To record a show that's currently playing without viewing it live:

1. Open Media Center and select Guide.

2. Use the navigation buttons, keyboard, or remote control to move through the channels shown in the Guide to locate the program you want to record. In Figure 8-2, we've chosen *Star Trek: Deep Space Nine*.

3. Right-click the program name, and click Record if using a mouse, or press the Record button on the remote control (see Figure 8-3).

You can right-click again and select Stop Recording if desired, or press Stop or the appropriate button on the remote control.

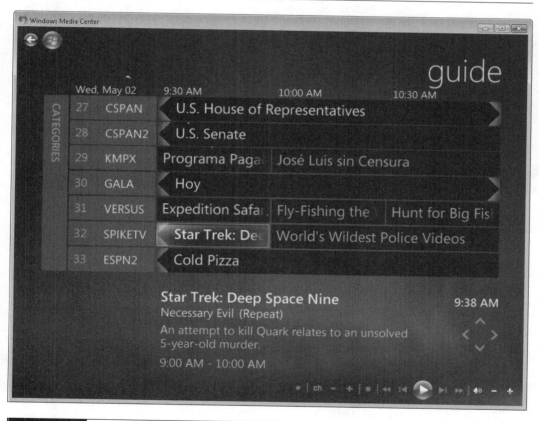

FIGURE 8-2   Locate the program you want to record using the Guide.

FIGURE 8-3   Right-click the show you want to record and select Record.

To record a TV show that is schedule to air in the future:

1. Open Media Center and select Guide.

2. Use the navigation buttons, keyboard, or remote control to move through the channels to locate the program you want to record.

3. Right-click the program, and from the drop-down list, select Record. Note that if you were to decide not to record the future program, the steps to cancel it are similar, except the option is Do Not Record.

Record a Series of Shows

You can also record an entire television series. As detailed in the previous section, recordings can be configured while a TV show is airing live or while you're watching it in Media Center by using the Guide. Or, you can use the Guide to schedule a recording for future airings.

However you get to the show you want to record the series for, the steps are the same for recording the series as they are for recording a single show. As shown in Figure 8-4, you'll locate the show, right-click it, and then select Record Series.

After selecting Record Series, you'll see the screen shown in Figure 8-5 *if* a conflict is found. A conflict occurs when two shows are schedule to record at the same time and you only have one TV tuner installed. If this occurs, you'll need to make a decision about what shows you want to record.

You can choose from the following:

■ **Record All Episodes Of New Series**   All episodes of the selected series will record.

■ **Record Only When No Conflict Exists**   Only episodes of this series that do not conflict with other previously configured recordings will record.

■ **Select Which Instances To Record**   You choose what programs will and will not be recorded by going through each one separately and selecting which instance to record for each conflict.

FIGURE 8-4   To record an entire series, select Record Series.

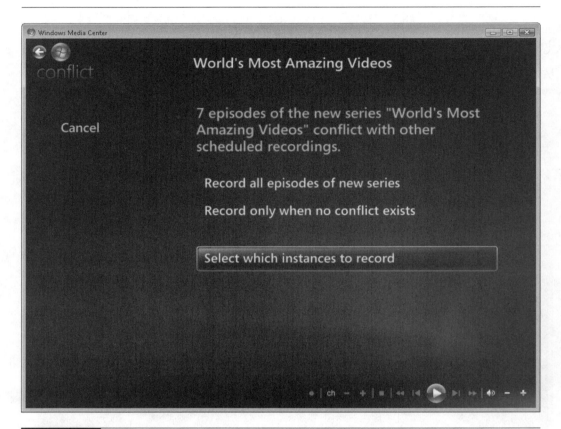

FIGURE 8-5 Conflicts occur when two shows are configured to record at the same time.

To resolve a conflict by selecting the latter option, Select Which Instances To Record:

1. Click Select Which Instances To Record.
2. Click Resolve Conflict if it appears. You might only see this option if you select a specific episode of the series, however, so keep that in mind.
3. When prompted, select the show to record for each conflict. A conflict resolution screen is shown in Figure 8-6.
4. Click Done.

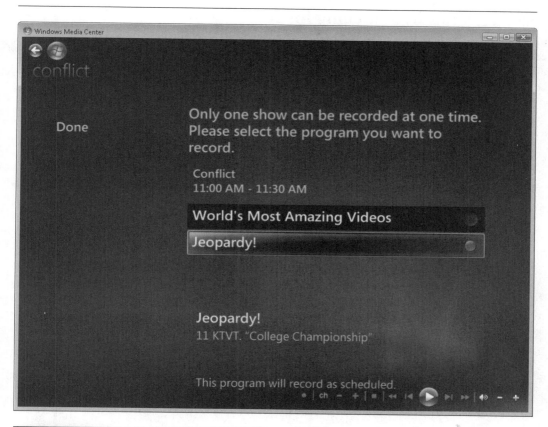

FIGURE 8-6   Resolve conflicts manually.

If you have difficulty resolving conflicts, or if there are just too many to deal with, you may have to review what's being recorded and delete series recordings you no longer want. To review the series you are recording:

1. In Media Center, under TV + Movies, select Recorded TV.
2. Select View Scheduled.
3. Select Series.
4. Right-click and select Cancel Series if desired.
5. Click Yes to confirm the cancellation.
6. Or, if you prefer, select Change Priorities to set which show has precedence over others. In the latter case, use the arrows to move shows to the top or bottom of the list. Click Done.

Record a Show by Searching for It

You can create a recording from TV + Movies and Recorded TV. Using the Add Recording feature, you can browse for the program you want to record from the Guide or you can search by title, keyword, actor, director, and more. Since you already know how to add a recording using the Guide, here you'll add a recording by searching using your own criteria.

To add a recording by searching for your own criteria:

1. From Media Center, select TV + Movies, select Recorded TV, and select Add Recording.
2. Select Search, as shown in Figure 8-7.
3. Select from the following:
   - ■ Title
   - ■ Keyword

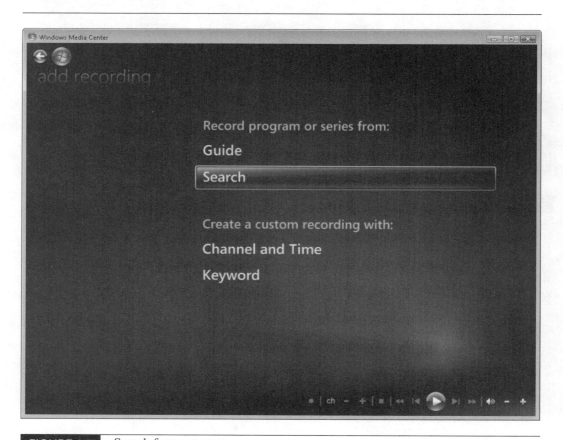

FIGURE 8-7   Search for a program.

- ■ Categories
- ■ Movie Actor
- ■ Movie Director

4. Use the keyboard, remote control, or mouse to type the search criteria (see Figure 8-8).

5. Select the show from the choices on the right.

6. Choose the show to record, and select Record or Record Series. To configure advanced recording settings, as detailed in the next section, click Advanced Record.

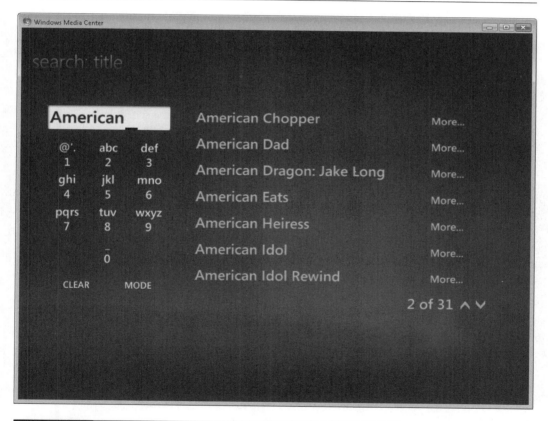

FIGURE 8-8   Search for what you want to record.

Configure Recording Settings

When you record a show or a series of shows, Media Center applies the default settings. These settings may or may not be what you want. Default settings include that the series or show will:

- Record every time shown, including first runs and reruns
- Be recorded with the best possible quality
- Be kept until space is needed and as many episodes as possible
- Stop on time
- Record only from the channel configured initially
- Record anytime it's aired

You may not want to keep these default settings. Options you might want to change include:

- Recording only the first airing, not reruns. You should only record reruns when you've missed shows you think might be aired again.
- Recording using fair, good, or better, instead of best. The lower the quality, the less hard drive space you'll use.
- Stopping a show after it's scheduled to end. You should extend the scheduled recording if you think the game you're recording will go into overtime, for instance.
- How long a recorded show is kept. You can choose from Until I Delete, Until I Watch, Latest Recordings, or Until Space Needed.
- How many shows to keep. You can choose from As Many As Possible or 1, 2, 3, 4, 5, 6, 7, or 10.
- On what channel the show records. In our example, Jeopardy airs on a local channel and on the Game Show Network and we'd like to record both (one is a new showing and one is a repeat).
- What types of shows are recorded: live only, first runs only, or first runs and reruns.

To make changes to any of these settings:

1. In Media Center, select TV + Movies, and select Recorded TV.
2. Select View Scheduled.
3. Select Series.
4. Right-click the series you want to manage, and select Series Info.
5. Select Series Settings.
6. Make changes as desired using the plus (+) and minus (−) keys (see Figure 8-9).
7. Click Save.

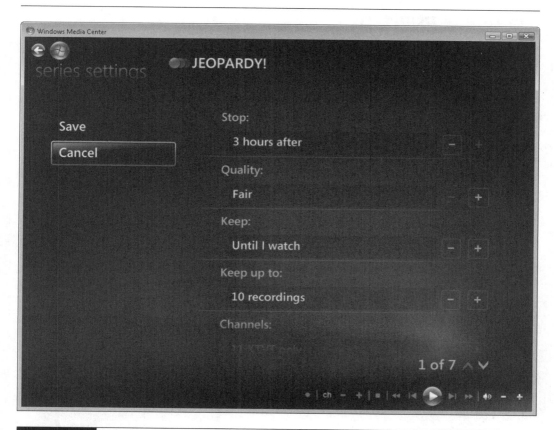

FIGURE 8-9   Change default recording settings.

NOTE   *You can make changes to a single show, too. One way is to locate the show in the Guide, right-click it, select Program Info, and select Record Settings.*

Manage Recorded TV

The problem with Media Center's default recording settings is that you can fill up your hard drive with recorded media rather quickly. If you don't stay on top of things, before you know it, you won't have any hard drive space left at all! I changed my default settings to keep recorded TV shows until I watch them—that way, I never have to worry about deleting them. However, this won't work for everyone, especially if your goal is to create your own DVD set of every *Simpsons* episode ever created. That being said, it's important that you know how to delete recorded shows and how to manage the media you want to keep for the long term.

Know How to Delete

To find what's been recorded in Media Center, select TV + Movies, and then select Recorded TV. Figure 8-10 shows an example. To delete any program, right-click it, and select Delete. Click Yes to verify.

It's difficult to delete recorded TV from here if you've got a lot to delete, however. If you have a lot of programs to delete, it's best to locate them in the Recorded TV folder and delete them there. From this folder, you can select multiple recordings by holding down the CTRL key while selecting noncontiguous recordings or by holding down the SHIFT key when selecting contiguous ones. The Recorded TV folder is located in C:\Users\Public\Recoreded TV, where C: is the root drive.

If you need help finding this folder:

1. Click Start, and click Computer.

2. Double-click Local Disk.

FIGURE 8-10   View items by date recorded or by title, and right-click to delete.

3. Double-click Users.

4. Double-click Public.

5. Double-click Recorded TV.

Know Where to Save Media

Some computers come with several "partitions." Partitions are areas of the hard drive sectioned off for a specific purpose. Your computer may have come with a partition for saving media. In addition, you may have installed Windows Vista on a PC without much free hard drive space and added a secondary drive for storing your media. Whatever the case, you need to be sure you know exactly where your media is being stored, specifically recorded TV.

To find out where your recorded TV shows are stored:

1. Open Media Center, and select Tasks.

2. Select Settings.

3. Select TV. Select Recorder.

4. Select Recorder Storage. An example of Recorder Storage settings is shown in Figure 8-11.

5. Use the plus and minus buttons to move through the available options. In Figure 8-11, recordings are saved to the C: drive, which is 186 gigabytes (GB). You should choose the larger drive or partition if one is available. In addition, you may want to set a maximum TV limit and change the recording quality.

6. Click Save when finished.

NOTE

If you want to add or remove a folder that Windows Media Center searches when looking for recorded TV (perhaps an external drive or network folder on another Windows Vista PC), in step 3 in the procedure, instead of selecting Recorded Storage, select More TV Locations. You can add a folder to watch from there. You may have set this up already when configuring Media Center for the first time.

Know How to Back Up Media

Now that you have media, how will you back it up? And what do you want to back up? There are as many ways to back up media as there are to back up your "regular" data. The only problem with media is that it's much larger. You'll have to take size into account when backing up this type of data.

One way to back up media is to purchase a large external hard drive. You can get a 300-GB drive for around $100 U.S. now if you wait for a sale. That's a good size for saving media. Once it's connected, you can simply drag the Recorded TV folder to a folder on that drive. Another way is to back up what you want to DVDs (more on that in the next section). You can also use Windows Vista's Backup And Restore Center (see Figure 8-12). Using Backup And Restore is detailed in Chapter 22.

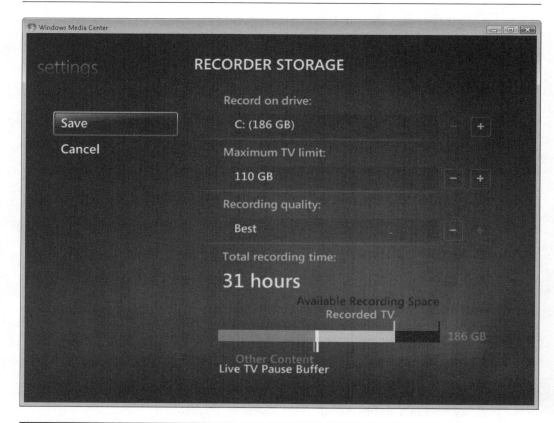

FIGURE 8-11   Recorder Storage lets you configure where and how much hard drive space to set aside for recordings.

Burn a Saved Program to a DVD

There will come a time when you want to save a program or a group of programs to a CD or DVD for posterity. Perhaps the recordings are of your favorite *Star Trek* shows, past recordings of *ER*, or your college team's championship game. Whatever you want to burn to a CD or DVD, it must be recorded first.

The best choice to make when recording media is to use a DVD-RW disc and burner. It's even better if you have a dual-layer drive. With dual-layer hardware, you can record around 9 GB of data on one DVD. With a regular DVD burner, the limit is 4.7 GB. CDs only offer 700 megabytes (MB), hardly enough to do anything with, so we'll suggest avoiding that option. With rewritable DVDs, you can reuse them as many times as you want without wasting space.

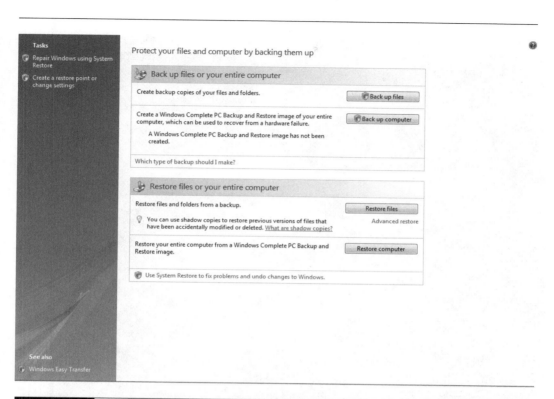

FIGURE 8-12   Vista's Backup And Restore Center is a great way to back up media.

To record a single show or a group of shows (or even a movie) to a DVD-RW:

1. Put a blank disc in your DVD burner. If Windows Vista prompts you to take an action, close the window without making any choice.

2. Open Media Center, select TV + Movies, select Recorded TV, and locate the show you want to burn to the DVD.

3. Right-click the show's icon, and select Burn.

4. Select Video DVD. This choice lets you play the DVD in a DVD player later. Click Next.

5. Type a name for the DVD using the keyboard, mouse, or remote control. Click Next. Figure 8-13 shows the interface.

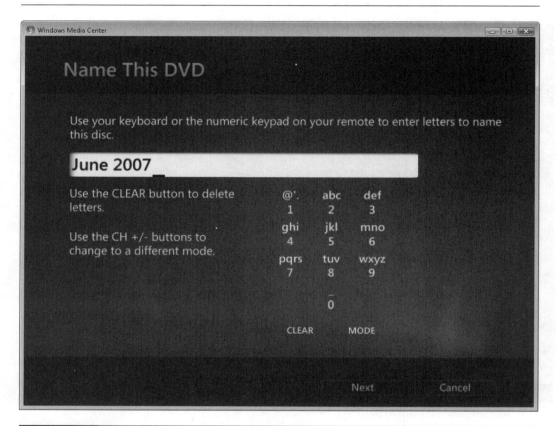

FIGURE 8-13   Type the name of the DVD.

6. In the Review And Edit List window, click Add More if you want to add more media. You can choose from recorded TV or your Video Library. Click Next, and select another show to add. Click Next to continue. If you aren't adding more media, continue to step 7.

7. When finished, click Burn DVD.

8. Click Yes to verify.

It may take a while for the DVD to burn. Click OK to do something else while the process completes.

Chapter 9

Working with DVDs

How to...

■ Watch a DVD you own

■ Troubleshoot DVD playback

■ Configure Media Player for optimal DVD playback

■ Turn on closed captioning

■ Configure remote control options

■ Save and play e-mail attachments

Don't let the title of this chapter fool you; there's a lot more going on here than us telling you how to put a DVD in your drive and watch it in Media Center! There's configuring optimal playback, enabling closed captioning, and working with video e-mail attachments, just to name a few. Let's get started!

Play a DVD You Own

You'd think that playing a DVD that you own in Media Center would be straightforward. Unfortunately, that's not always the case. For starters, a DVD might play in Windows Media Player when you insert it. That isn't what you want. You want to use Media Center! So first, you'll need to tell Windows Vista that you want to play all DVDs in Media Center and not in Media Player.

Once that's done, you might find that the DVD you want to watch still won't play in Media Center. This is likely because your DVD player does not support the type of DVD you want to play. This could be due to a number of reasons, including but not limited to having installed a third-party DVD application that interferes with Windows Vista, having a DVD drive that does not play certain kinds of DVDs, or having a disabled DVD drive. You'll learn more about these problems shortly.

Change AutoPlay Settings

Before playing that first DVD, change the AutoPlay settings so that the DVDs you insert will play in Media Center, not Media Player. To change AutoPlay settings:

1. Click Start, and click Control Panel.

2. Under Hardware And Sound, click Play CDs Or Other Media Automatically. (Note that we are in Control Panel Home view.)

3. In the AutoPlay window, shown in Figure 9-1, scroll through the options, and change settings as desired. You might want to select Windows Media Center for every option!

4. Click Save.

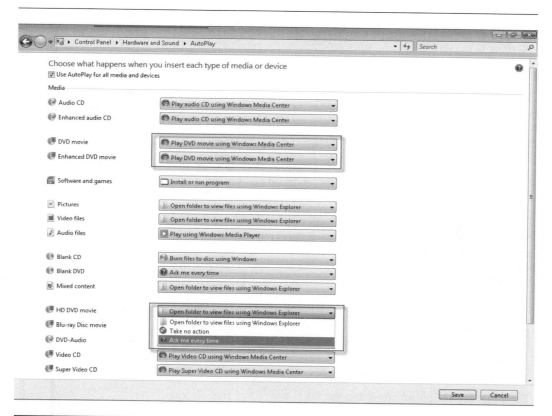

FIGURE 9-1   Select Windows Media Center for playing DVD movies.

If there's going to be a problem playing DVDs, you will likely find it here. Take a look at Figure 9-1. Although there is a choice to play a DVD movie in Windows Media Center, notice that option isn't available for playing HD (high-definition) DVD movies. You may find the same problem with Blu-ray Disc movies, DVD audio discs, or Super Video CDs. If there's no option to play it, you don't have the required hardware.

Playing DVDs

Playing a DVD is indeed quite simple, as long as your DVD player is supported by Windows Vista. To find out if you can play DVDs, complete the steps in the "Change AutoPlay Settings" section, and then insert the DVD you want to play in the DVD player.

One of two things will happen:

- The DVD will play in Media Center.
- Nothing will happen.

If the DVD plays, you can navigate the DVD in Media Center using the same navigation buttons you use for other Media Center tasks. Although you can move the mouse to the lower-right area of the screen to access these buttons, most likely, you'll use your mouse. If the DVD does not play, work through the next section, "Troubleshooting."

TIP *Under the Tasks option is the Media Only choice. You can enable Media Only when watching DVDs. In this mode, the Minimize and Close buttons are hidden, so you only view the media.*

Troubleshooting

There are several reasons why a DVD won't play. Most of the time, it's because your DVD player doesn't support the type of DVD you've inserted. As shown in Figure 9-1, some PCs can play DVD movies, but not HD DVDs. Try inserting a non-HD DVD first to see if that's the problem. If the DVD still won't play, there could be other issues.

Although not a common problem, your DVD drive could be disabled. To see if the DVD drive is disabled and enable it:

1. Click Start, and click Computer.
2. Right-click the DVD drive, and select Properties.
3. From the Hardware tab, select the DVD drive, and click Properties.
4. From the General tab, click Change Settings, and click Continue.
5. Click the Driver tab.
6. If Enable is shown, as in Figure 9-2, you'll need to click it to enable the drive. If it says Disable, do nothing.
7. Click OK twice, and then restart your PC if prompted.

If this is not the issue, check the AutoPlay settings again, and verify that no third-party DVD application is selected, as this can interfere with Windows Vista. You should also try disabling or uninstalling the offending program.

NOTE *You do not need a DVD decoder to play DVDs in Windows Vista Premium or Ultimate edition. It is included with the operating system.*

Another issue may be your computer resolution. You can try changing the resolution to a lower setting. You can access these settings by right-clicking an empty area of the desktop and selecting Personalize. Select Display Settings. Make changes as needed.

FIGURE 9-2   If Enable is shown, click it to enable the DVD drive.

9

Finally, if you still can't play DVDs, try opening Media Center, inserting a DVD, selecting TV + Movies, and selecting Play DVD. You may receive an error message with a helpful hint to solving the problem.

Configure DVD Settings for Optimal Playback

You'll want to configure settings for optimal playback. There are a lot of settings that you can change by selecting Tasks and then selecting Settings. Settings specifically for DVDs include selecting the DVD language, enabling closed captioning, and setting options for your remote control. You can configure these settings as desired to personalize Media Center.

DVD Language

To make changes to the DVD language settings, in Media Center, click Tasks, and click Settings. Select DVD, and select DVD Language.

DVD Language settings include the following:

- **Subtitle**   Select the subtitle language using the plus and minus buttons. This doesn't mean you can select Chinese or Croatian and the subtitles will magically appear. They have to be included in the DVD. But if your DVD supports it, you can select just about any language you like.

- **Audio Track**   Select the audio track language using the plus and minus buttons. The same restriction with regards to languages applies as with subtitles (in other words, if it isn't supported, you can't use it).

- **Menu**   Select the menu language using the plus and minus buttons. Again, the same restriction with regards to language applies.

When changes are complete, click Save.

Closed Captioning

To make changes to closed captioning settings, in Media Center, click Tasks, and click Settings. Select DVD, and select Closed Captioning. There are two options:

- **Caption Display**   Choices include On When Muted, On, and Off.

- **Captioning Channel**   Settings include CC1 though CC4, although you may not have all of these as options. Accept the default, and only try the other settings if the default does not work for you. Generally, captions in the program's language are CC1; other caption languages are on other choices.

When changes are complete, click Save.

Remote Control Options

To make changes to the remote control settings, in Media Center, click Tasks, and click Settings. Select DVD, and select Remote Control Options. There are two options, shown in Figure 9-3:

- **Program Skip And Replay Buttons To**   Choices include Skip Chapters, Skip Forward And Back, and Change Angles.

- **Program Channel Up And Down Buttons To**   Choices include Skip Chapters, Skip Forward And Back, and Change Angles.

When changes are complete, click Save.

NOTE   *DVD producers often record different angles of the same scene. Changing the angle lets you view the selected scene from a different perspective.*

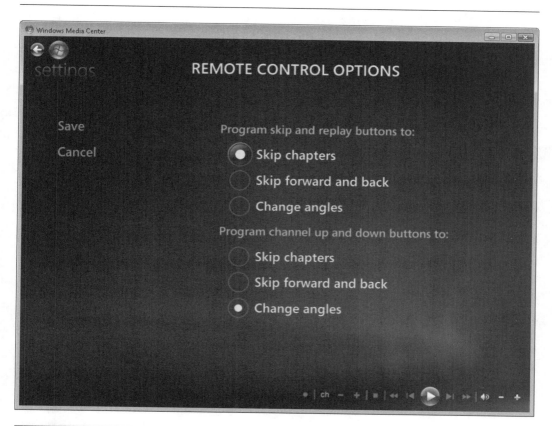

FIGURE 9-3   Configure remote control options.

Save and Play E-mail Attachments

By default, when you open an e-mail attachment that contains a video, it plays in Windows Media Player. But what if you'd rather save those attachments and watch them in Media Center or have a specific type of file, like a .wmv file, always open and play in Media Center? It's possible!

First decide what types of files you get in e-mails. Most of the videos we get end in .wmv. That's a Windows Media Video file. To configure that file type to always play in Media Center instead of in Media Player:

1. Open an e-mail that contains the type of file you want to open with Media Center. Save the attachment to your hard drive.

2. Locate the file, and right-click it. Select Open With.

3. Select Choose Default Program.

4. Select Media Center, and click OK. This is shown in Figure 9-4. (You might have to browse for Media Center if it isn't listed here.)

5. Select Always Use The Selected Program To Open This Kind Of File.

6. Click OK.

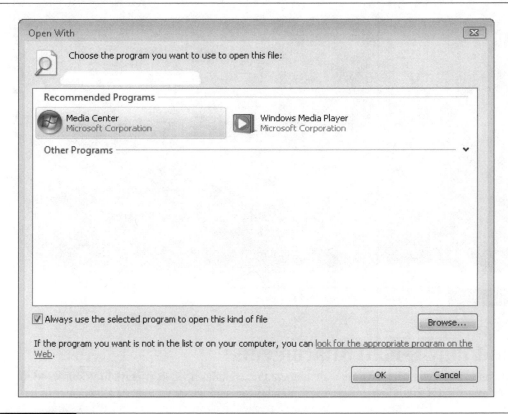

FIGURE 9-4   Select a program to open the file with.

Chapter 10

Download and Watch Online Media

How to...

- Choose a subscription service
- Sign up for a subscription service
- Install required components for obtaining and watching online media
- Download and watch your first online movie
- Understand online media's limitations
- Explore other online media

Options for obtaining media—specifically movies—are on the rise. You can have movies mailed to you, rent them from a video store, or both. You can buy DVDs from your local drugstore or megastore, too. And now there's another way. You can download them from the Internet and watch them on your PC.

Internet media is a little different from physical media. Unlike Netflix or similar services, you can't rent and then keep a movie indefinitely. You have a window of opportunity for watching the movie, and then it's disabled. And even when you can purchase a movie and watch it as many times as you want, you still can't burn it to a DVD and take it to a friend's house. (Some companies let you make a backup copy, but these copies won't play on traditional DVD players.) And last but certainly not least, you have to install software on your computer to obtain and manage the media, and the idea of this often scares people away.

In this chapter, we'll work through all of this. You'll learn how to find a provider, how to sign up, and how to install any required software. You'll also learn what it takes to download and watch a movie from the Internet. You'll learn about online media limitations, such as the inability to burn what you've obtained to a DVD and watch it in a DVD player or at someone else's home, and if you can take it with you on your own portable media player. Finally, you'll learn about additional online media options, including Internet TV, music and radio, news and sports, special events, podcasts, and more.

Sign Up for a Media Subscription Service

Deciding on and signing up for a media subscription service is the first step in obtaining media online. There are a few choices, but my favorites are Movielink and Vongo. Both let you rent or purchase movies and almost always offer a free trial. You can access both from Media Center's Explore option on the Online Media menu.

Because prices and options change, as do free trials and offers, I won't detail the cost here for these two options or any others. It will be up to you to check out each option and find a service that suits your needs. However, all options let you select a plan, ranging from unlimited selections per month to a one-time amount for a single movie on demand. You'll have to choose one, depending on how often you think you'll obtain online media. We suggest trying the full subscription option; not only do you get unlimited access to movies, but you also often have access to video specials, concerts, and other media.

For all services, movies are near-DVD quality; you can use your remote control to browse, preview, download, and watch movies; watch while you download; and control movies just as you would with a physical DVD. You can even watch movies on Internet TVs, laptops, some portable players, and Xbox 360s.

Install Required Software Components

Once you've decided on a service and a plan, you'll need to download the software required by the Web site. Special software is required to keep users from downloading movies and burning them to DVDs or otherwise violating the terms of use. In Media Center's Online Media menu, choose Explore. Select the service that you want to use, and look for the Download link. We'll introduce the Vongo installation and setup, but you should keep in mind that you can choose other online services.

After opening the Vongo Web site and clicking Download, you'll follow the directions to download the software. Generally, it's fairly easy. Just click Install Vongo, click Run when prompted, and follow the instructions in the wizard provided. (You may be prompted by Windows Vista to click Continue and log on with administrator credentials.) When we downloaded and installed Vongo, the entire process with a broadband connection took less than five minutes.

After installation is complete, Media Center will display the Vongo screen, where you can sign up for a free trial and/or launch Vongo. Launching Vongo requires you to register and then log on before you can continue, so either way, be prepared to register. You can register for a free trial if you desire. Figure 10-1 shows the home page for Vongo.

Register and Log On

Registration requires a few steps and takes a bit longer than installation. However, like the installation process, you only have to do it once. Before starting the registration process, make sure you have the following information in place:

- E-mail address
- User name
- First and last name
- Password
- Security question and answer
- Optional secondary e-mail address
- Type of subscription
- Credit card number and billing address

Registration generally takes place through your Web browser, probably Internet Explorer. Once you're registered, you'll need to go back to Media Center. This is a little confusing if you've never done it before, because once registered, there's no way to start downloading movies! That is not done from Internet Explorer—it's done from Media Center!

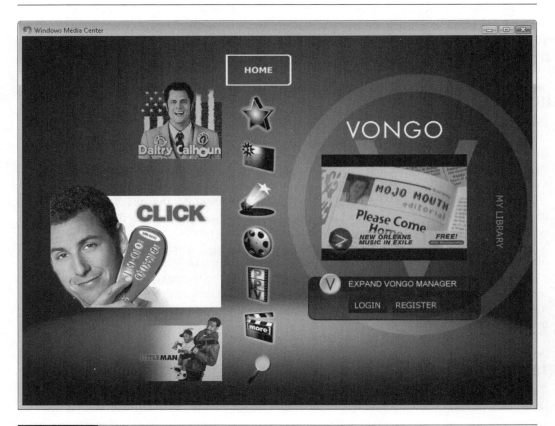

FIGURE 10-1 Vongo's home page

TIP *Although you can register and choose to only purchase movies on demand, if you choose the subscription service, you'll have access to a lot of media that's free and included with the fee you pay, including concerts, television shows, and more.*

Open Media Center, if it isn't already open, and click Online Media And Program Library. You'll see Vongo (or any other subscription option) there, as shown in Figure 10-2.

Click the Vongo icon to begin. Once the Vongo home page is displayed, click the login button, type your user name and password, and browse through the movies to find one you want to watch. Figure 10-3 shows the login screen.

You may be prompted to register a device like a remote control, keyboard, or mouse. To add a device that's not already shown in the list, look for the option to add a device, click it, and then use the device to register it with Vongo.

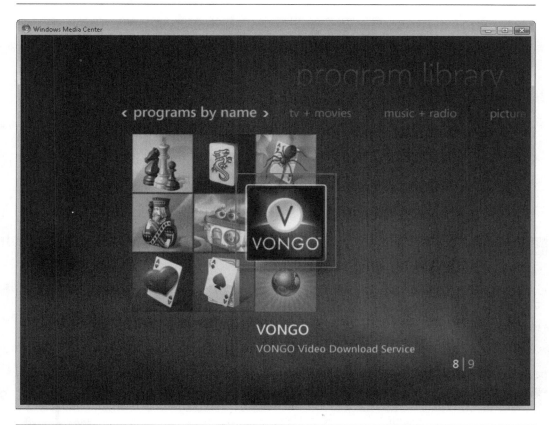

FIGURE 10-2   Vongo is now available in the Online Media and in the Program Library.

Download a Movie and Watch It on Your PC

You can now start browsing for a movie or show to download and watch. Interfaces vary among subscription options, so while we can't go into depth here, look for the following after logging on to your media choice:

- Options selected just for you based on your age, sex, and other information you provided during registration
- Top picks among registered users
- New media recently added to the Web site
- Movies

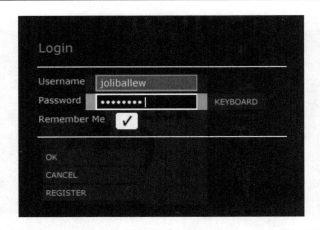

FIGURE 10-3   Log on using your user name and password.

- Pay per view
- Search options

Once you've found something to watch, select it and read the details. Figure 10-4 shows a pay-per-view option. Notice you can preview the movie, download it, or see more download options. What you see may differ, depending on the service and subscription plan you choose.

You can watch the preview of the movie, and watch the movie while it's downloading if you desire. In Figure 10-5, note that our movie is downloading and there's a Watch Now option.

> **TIP**   *If you purchase a movie through a pay-per-view option, you generally have 24 hours to view it after clicking Play.*

Understand Options for Viewing the Movie

Terms of service differ among online media companies, but for the most part, you may not capture, reproduce, transfer, sell, modify, republish, upload, edit, transmit, publicly display, distribute, or otherwise exploit in whole or in part any content downloaded from the Web site. Basically, that means you can watch it and that's it. However, things are turning around a little.

With a subscription to Vongo (as well as some other sites), you can access over 2,500 movies and videos that include bonus material not available otherwise and watch them as many times as you want, as often as you want, all commercial-free, during the download viewing period. You can also usually download movies to three or so different devices. This means you can download movies to a laptop and take the laptop with you if you want to go portable.

FIGURE 10-4 Select a movie and view details.

You can also use an approved portable Media Center device. Vongo offers customers the ability to transfer movies to a media device called a Gigabeat from Toshiba. With it, you can take your movies with you, making personal video access a reality. This is a step in the right direction for online media services, as most people will eventually want to take their media with them, and subscription services are trying hard to make this an option.

Due to licensing restrictions, you may not copy any movie to a storage device. This includes but is not limited to a CD or DVD, Universal Serial Bus (USB) key, external hard drive, and network drive.

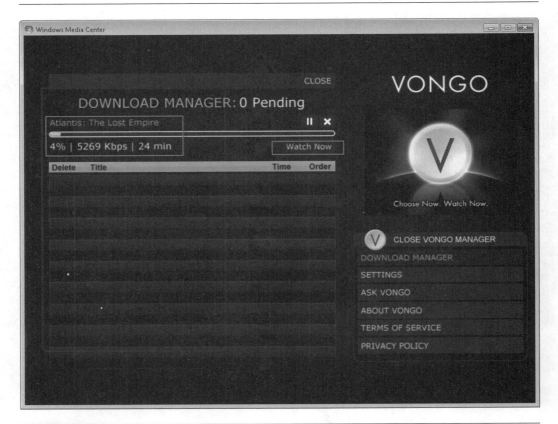

FIGURE 10-5 Download and watch a movie at the same time.

Finally, although you cannot burn the movie to a DVD, you can watch movies on a television, external monitor, or liquid crystal display (LCD) projector. There are several methods of connecting an external monitor, including but not limited to:

- Standard (Composite) Video Output and Audio Output
- S-Video Output
- DVI (Digital Visual Interface)
- VGA (Video Graphics Array)

There's much more information on external viewing in Chapter 20.

Other Online Media Types

Other online media options include subscription TV, music and radio, news and sports, podcasts, and more. You don't have to go to Vongo or Movielink for these either. Additional types of online media can be accessed from the Online Media menu by selecting Explore. One option, the Discovery Channel, is shown in Figure 10-6. You can also see Yahoo! Sports, XM Radio, NPR News, and more.

If you happen to stumble across a show you like, you may be able to record the program from the Online Media options. Figure 10-7 shows an example. By clicking Record Program (not shown in the figure because it's underneath the dialog box), you can configure a recording easily. For the most part, television programs are free to access and record.

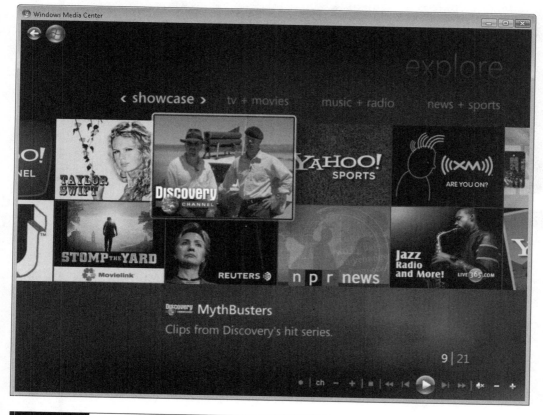

FIGURE 10-6   Additional online media options

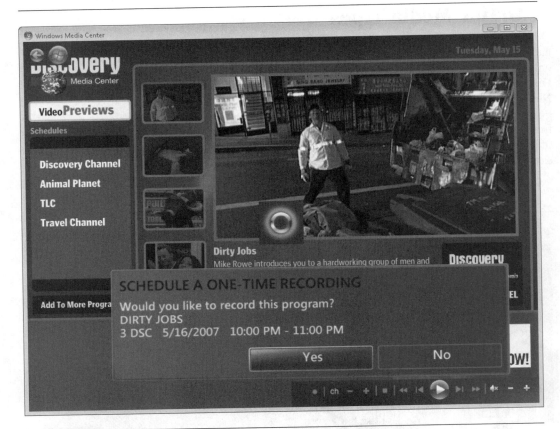

FIGURE 10-7   Access and record TV shows.

Beyond movies and TV, however, you can also access news. Here you can listen to headlines as well as commencement addresses and shows like *Talk of the Nation*.

Although there's more to discover and more offered every month, you can also access XM Radio, Live 365 Radio, MSN TV Today, Comedy Central, MTV.com, and much, much more.

Chapter 11

Create a Personal Music Library

How to...

- Navigate Media Center's music options
- Play a sample song or album
- Rip your CD collection with Media Player 11
- Import media from sources other than CDs
- Move media versus copying media
- Edit songs in your Music Library
- Work with the queue

Using your computer to play music is becoming an increasingly popular pastime among people of all ages. With Media Center's Music option, you can customize one place to organize all of your music-related media. This chapter shows you how to customize your own personal music library using both Media Center and Media Player 11. Among other topics, you'll learn about working with the different Media Center Music options as well as how to play and rip music.

Navigate Media Center's Music Options

Media Center's Music category is a "one-stop shop" for all of your music files. You can view everything you've downloaded using Windows Media Player and everything you've ripped (uploaded) from your personal CD collection—all directly within Media Center's Music category.

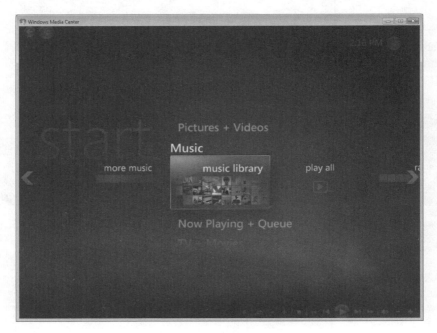

Media Center has several music options (all of which we're going to cover in more detail in this chapter), including:

- Music Library
- Play All
- Radio
- Search
- More Music

Music Library

Inside the Music Library, you'll enjoy instant access to all of the songs available on your computer. The songs Media Center offers initially include anything stored in the Sample Music folder. However, once you begin to add your own personal music, the Music Library expands. To access Media Center's Music Library, you simply click the Music Library icon under Music from the Media Center Start screen. By default, the Music Library displays as shown in Figure 11-1, with available music displayed by album.

The Albums view, shown in Figure 11-1, is just one of many views. Inside the Music Library, using the category options across the top of the window, you can view your music by:

- **Albums**   The Albums view displays each album's cover art (if available) and, when selected with the mouse, shows the artist, number of tracks, total music time, and year the album was released. This view closely matches the Years and Album Artists views.

- **Artists**   The Artists view displays each artist with songs in your Music Library and, when selected with the mouse, shows the number of tracks and total music time.

- **Genres**   The Genres view displays each genre category (such as Jazz or Rock) represented in your Music Library and, when highlighted with the mouse, shows the numbers of tracks in each genre and total music time.

- **Songs**   The Songs view displays each song saved in your Music Library and, when selected with the mouse, shows the artist, total music time, and year the song was released.

- **Playlists**   The Playlists view displays several auto-playlists including music played in the last month and music played the most, as well as any custom playlists you create.

- **Composers**   The Composers view displays each composer with songs in your Music Library and, when selected with the mouse, shows the number of tracks and total music time.

- **Years**   The Years view displays each album's cover art (if available) grouped by years and, when selected with the mouse, shows the artist, number of tracks, total music time, and year the album was released. This view closely matches the Albums and Album Artists views.

- **Album Artists**   The Album Artists view displays each album's cover art (if available) grouped by album artist and, when highlighted with the mouse, shows the album name, artist, number of tracks, total music time, and year the album was released. This view closely matches the Albums and Years views.

11

FIGURE 11-1   The Music Library

NOTE *Once you begin using the Music Library's views to display your available music, each time you open Media Center, you'll be presented with the most recent view you used instead of the default Albums view.*

By clicking any song or album reference from the Music Library, you will eventually drill down to an album thumbnail view. Once you see an album thumbnail (in any view), click the album cover graphic to display the Album Details screen, shown in Figure 11-2.

In the Album Details screen, you have several options for working with the selected music, including:

- **Play Album**   Switches Media Center to the Now Playing screen and begins playing the selected music.

- **Add To Queue**   The queue is a list of music you want to play. This way, when one song or album finishes, the next album or song in the queue will begin. When you click Add To Queue, the album or song is added to the queue and, if no other music is playing, the music begins.

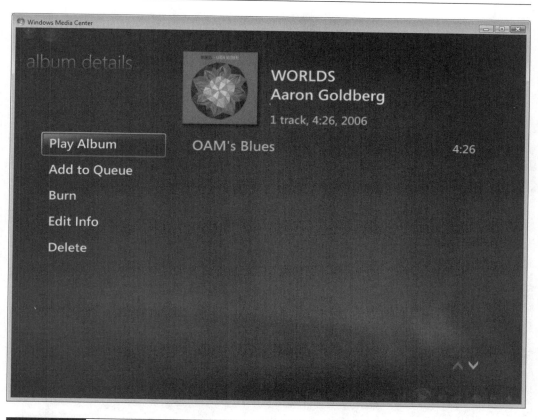

FIGURE 11-2 View album details

- **Burn** When you click the Burn option, Media Center immediately begins the process of copying the selected song or album to your CD or DVD. Make sure you have a writeable CD or DVD in your computer before clicking this option.

- **Edit Info** The Edit Info option allows you to modify the album title, artist name, and genre of the selected album.

- **Delete** Be careful with this one. The Delete option permanently removes the selected media from the Music Library and, ultimately, from your computer.

TIP *When viewing the thumbnails, you can right-click anywhere on the Media Center screen to display a shortcut list with several options. Among those options are typically three different views: Large, Small, and List. Use these views to customize the way the music is displayed.*

Play All

If you're ready to start listening to music right away and you really don't have a preference as to which songs you'll hear, the Play All option is the one to choose.

Clicking Play All immediately opens the Now Playing window and begins playing all of the music accessible by Media Center in random order (as the default state is "Shuffle"). However, once the music begins, there are several options available in this window, including:

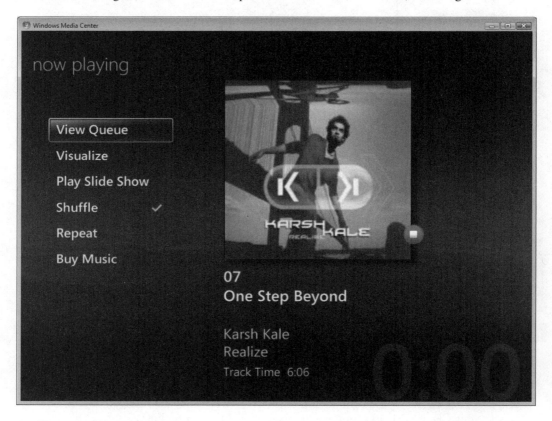

- ■ **View Queue**   The View Queue option allows you to see the order in which the songs will be played.

- ■ **Visualize**   The Visualize feature creates cool, moving graphics on your computer monitor that move to the beat of the music that is currently playing. You can easily change the displayed graphic either by pressing the UP ARROW or DOWN ARROW key on the keyboard or clicking the Ch + or − commands.

- ■ **Play Slide Show**   The Play Slide Show option displays photos stored in your Picture Library in random order as a slideshow.

- **Shuffle** Shuffle can only be in one of two states: on or off. By default, Shuffle is enabled, as shown with a check mark next to it. However, you can disable the Shuffle feature by clicking this option to remove the check mark.

- **Repeat** Just like Shuffle, the Repeat feature can only be in one of two states: on or off. By default, Repeat is disabled, shown without a check mark. However, you can enable the Repeat feature by clicking this option to show a check mark.

- **Buy Music** The Buy Music option takes you to the Windows Media Center Web site where you can browse for music to purchase.

Radio

Radio has been around for years—even before television. And with the growing popularity of the Internet, radio on the Internet is fast becoming a hot trend. So hot, in fact, that there are now way too many Internet radio stations to list here. But Media Center does offer a few to get you started listening right away. For best results, you'll need an "always on" Internet connection to listen to Internet radio. Figure 11-3 shows how to do this.

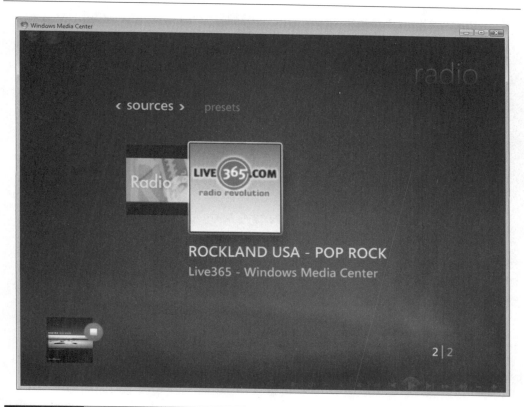

FIGURE 11-3 Access radio stations using the Radio options.

NOTE
You can also listen to your local radio stations if you have a radio antenna attached to your computer.

Before you'll see any Internet radio stations added to your Radio list, you'll need to choose the stations you want to see. Available radio stations can be found under Online Media, which lists many stations, including (to name just a few):

- AOL Radio
- Live365.com
- Napster's TV on the Radio
- XM Radio

When viewing the thumbnails, you can right-click to display a shortcut list with three options:

- **Delete**   Removes the selected radio station link.
- **View List**   Displays the available radio stations in List view without their associated thumbnails.
- **Settings**   Opens the Media Center Settings window, where you can customize Media Center.

How to ...   Add Internet Radio Stations

You can add Internet radio stations to display when you choose the Radio option. To add Internet radio stations, follow these steps:

1. From the Media Center main screen, navigate to Online Media.
2. Click Explore under Online Media.
3. In the navigation bar at the top, choose Music + Radio.
4. Choose the radio station you want to add (for example, click AOL).
5. Follow the individual radio station prompts to add a link. Each station will have different options. Some of the stations can be listened to through the Online Media option, but others can add links to the Radio section.

Once you've added your favorite Internet stations under Online Media, you can switch back to Radio (found under Music) to see each station's associated tile.

To listen to a station, simply click the associated station thumbnail. This displays the Radio Now Playing window, shown in Figure 11-4.

Once you start listening to the radio, the options you see will depend on the radio provider. However, the options are typically navigated through the individual radio provider's interface (which isn't Media Center–specific).

Nevertheless, one option you'll want to look for (particularly if you opened a radio station from anywhere other than the Radio category under Music) is the Add To My Radio link shown in Figure 11-4. Clicking this link will add a shortcut to this radio station so that you can quickly access it again, this time under the Radio category.

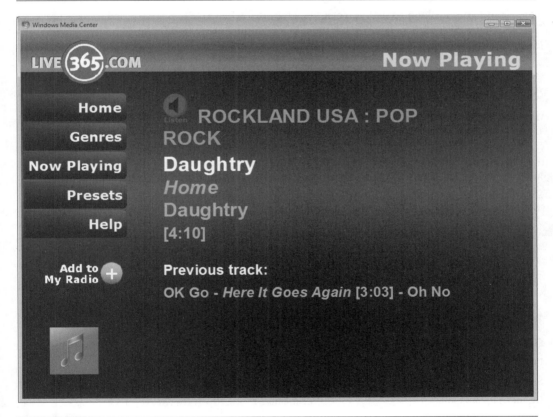

FIGURE 11-4   Radio – Now Playing Window

11

When you access sites outside of Media Center, you may see the "Not Designed For Windows Media Center" warning shown in the following illustration. Initially, choose View Now, as the site may display fine in Media Center.

However, if you run into an issue, you can always choose View Later. This creates a shortcut to the site on your desktop so that you can view the sites when you're not enclosed in the Media Center window. Shortcuts you create by clicking View Later are stored in the Windows Media Center Shortcuts folder.

Speaking of shortcuts, if keyboard shortcuts are your thing, refer to Table 11-1.

Search

After you've been using Media Center for any amount of time to store and listen to your music, you may find it becomes increasingly difficult to locate a specific song. That's where the Search feature comes in handy. From the Search window (accessed by clicking Search under Music from the Media Center main screen), shown in Figure 11-5, you can type just the first few characters of the artist or song name. Each time you enter a new letter, the Search feature scans your music files and returns the closest matches, helping you to zero in on the specific track for which you're looking.

TIP   *If you use the mouse to click the search numbers or letters, clicking each button multiple times will cycle you through the different characters stored on an individual button. This is a lot like creating a text message on a cell phone. For example, to get the letter "c", you would click the number "1" button three times.*

To Do This	Use This Shortcut Key
Go to Radio	CTRL-A
Pause or resume live radio	CTRL-P
Stop live radio	CTRL-SHIFT-S
Resume playing radio	CTRL-SHIFT-P
Skip back	CTRL-B
Skip forward	CTRL-F
Display the context menu	CTRL-D

TABLE 11-1   Radio-Related Keyboard Shortcuts

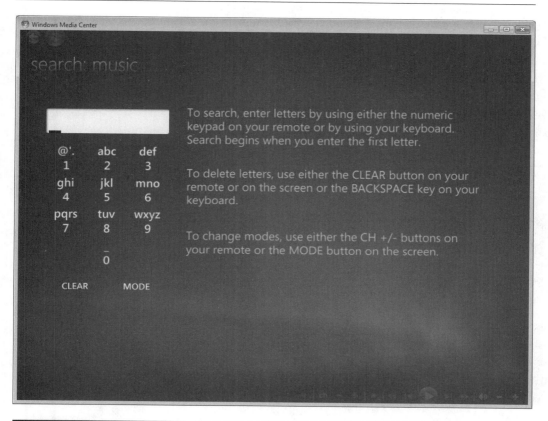

To search, enter letters by using either the numeric keypad on your remote or by using your keyboard. Search begins when you enter the first letter.

To delete letters, use either the CLEAR button on your remote or on the screen or the BACKSPACE key on your keyboard.

To change modes, use either the CH +/- buttons on your remote or the MODE button on the screen.

FIGURE 11-5   The Search window

The Search window is fairly intuitive, and if it isn't, the directions are right there on the screen for you. From this window, you have a few options:

- **Search**   To search for a specific artist or track, begin typing letters or numbers using the keyboard. If you prefer, you can use the mouse to click the numbers that correspond to the letters you want to type.

- **Clear**   Use the Clear button on the screen to remove characters you've entered in the Search box, one at a time.

- **Mode**   Use the Mode option to cycle through the three different character modes. For instance, you can switch between lowercase letters, uppercase letters, and symbols.

Once you locate the track or artist you've been looking for, simply click the related link. Doing so typically takes you to an album view and eventually the Album Details view shown in Figure 11-2.

More Music

In addition to the music that is available on your computer and the radio stations you may have seen earlier, you can access more music choices under the More Music window, shown in Figure 11-6.

FIGURE 11-6   The Online Media Explore window

Clicking More Music actually opens the same window you see when you click Explore under Online Media. The Explore window offers a navigation bar across the top with the following categories:

- Showcase
- TV + Movies
- Music + Radio
- News + Sports
- Pictures

Clicking any of the thumbnails shown in the Explore window typically opens a Web site outside of Media Center, but displays that site within the Media Center window. Each thumbnail is actually a link to a specific Web site. As such, it's difficult to predict what you'll see when you click each thumbnail. The best way to find out is to click the thumbnails that interest you. From any of the windows, you'll always have access to the Windows button located in the upper-left corner that will direct you safely back the Media Center main screen.

Play a Sample Song or Album

Media Center comes preloaded with several sample songs. These are great files to practice with when you're first learning to work with your music in Media Center. To play a sample song, follow these steps:

1. Click Music Library under the Music category on the Media Center main screen.

2. Display the music you want to listen to.

3. Choose Play Album or Play Song. The music starts playing, and the Now Playing screen shown in Figure 11-7 displays.

Once you access the Now Playing window, you already know about the options listed down the left side. But there is also a whole row of navigation elements shown across the lower-right edge of the window. This navigation bar is similar to the Play and Pause buttons you'll see when you watch TV inside Media Center. Luckily, the buttons in each case (watching TV and listening to music) perform similar functions.

11

FIGURE 11-7   The Now Playing window

The first few buttons (Record and Channel Down and Up) are grayed out and unavailable when listening to music. However, the remaining buttons work fine and are (in order):

- Stop
- Rewind
- Jump Back
- Play/Pause
- Jump Forward

- Fast Forward
- Mute
- Decrease Volume
- Increase Volume

Each of these buttons is shown in detail in Figure 11-8.

Sometimes, working with these music settings is easier using the keyboard. Table 11-2 lists some handy keyboard shortcuts for listening to your music in Media Center.

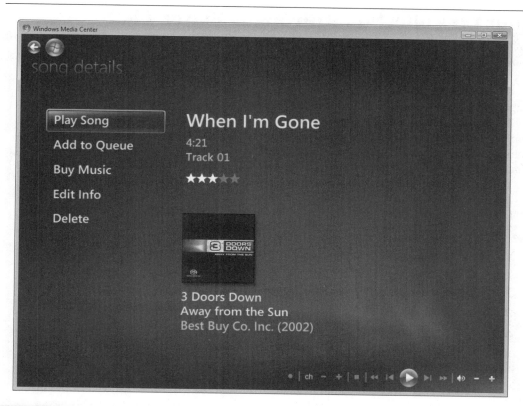

FIGURE 11-8   Song navigation buttons

To	Press	To	Press
Accept a selection	ENTER	Pause	CTRL-P
Play	CTRL-SHIFT-P	Mute	F8
Stop	CTRL-SHIFT-S	Volume down	F9
Replay	CTRL-B	Volume up	F10
Skip	CTRL-F		

TABLE 11-2   Music-Related Keyboard Shortcuts

Rip Your CD Collection with Media Player 11

While few of us still hold on to (let alone listen to) eight-tracks, cassettes, and vinyl records, many of us have physical CDs. You can copy the music on those CDs to your Media Center Music Library. The process of copying a physical CD to the computer is called *ripping*.

Of course, after the ripping process, the songs will remain on your CD. The bonus is that the songs you choose will also be available on your computer.

The music you see in Media Center is actually just a view of music stored elsewhere on your computer. And while you can burn music displayed in Media Center to a CD, there really isn't a viable option for ripping music stored on a CD to the computer. For this task, you'll want to use Windows Media Player 11.

Windows Media Player 11 is another media application, just like Media Center, that is included with Windows Vista. Just like Media Center, Windows Media Player comes preloaded with sample music, various default playlists, built-in genres, and preconfigured library categories.

To rip a CD, follow these steps:

1. Click the Start button and type **Media Player** in the Start Search box. This displays Windows Media Player in the Start menu under Programs.

2. Click Windows Media Player. This launches Windows Media Player.

3. Click the Rip tab.

4. Insert the CD you are ripping into the CD drive on your computer. The ripping process should start automatically, as shown in Figure 11-9. If you see the AutoPlay window, close the window without selecting an option.

NOTE *If the ripping process does not start automatically, after inserting the audio CD, click the drop-down arrow under the Rip tab, and choose Rip [CD Name] from the menu. Be patient—it may take a few seconds for Media Player to recognize the audio CD after it has been inserted.*

TIP *If you prefer to control when a CD rips and when it doesn't, you can change the rip settings by clicking the drop-down arrow under the Rip tab and choosing Rip CD Automatically When Inserted. Then, from the submenu, choose your ripping preference. For all options related to ripping CDs, click the Rip drop-down arrow, and choose More Options.*

Import Media from Sources Other Than CDs

Using CDs you already own is an easy way to make more music available in Media Center. But what if you have downloaded music stored in various locations on your computer?

In Media Center, you can control which folders (either locally on your computer or on your network) that Media Center looks in for your music files. This way, you're free to store music in any folder you choose and still have access to the music from within Media Center.

FIGURE 11-9   Windows Media Player 11

By default, Media Center is configured to automatically scan your personal and public Music folders—those are the folders that are already created when you install Windows Vista. But not everyone can be so organized. To add folders that Windows Media Center searches, follow these steps:

1. Click Settings under the Tasks category on the Media Center main screen.
2. Click Library Setup. This displays the Library Setup screen.
3. Click Add Folder To Watch, and then click Next.
4. Choose one of the following options:
   - Add Folders on this Computer
   - Add Shared Folders from Another Computer
   - Add Folders From Both Locations

5. Add a check mark next to any folder you want Media Center to "watch." An example is shown in Figure 11-10. When you've selected all necessary folders, click Next. Selecting a folder means that folder will be watched for musical content.

6. Click Finish. Depending on the strength of your network connection and the number of folders you choose to watch, it may take several seconds to several minutes for the new files to appear in the Music Library.

NOTE *To add files you have stored on a mapped network drive, choose Add Folders On This Computer instead of Add Shared Folders From Another Computer in step 4.*

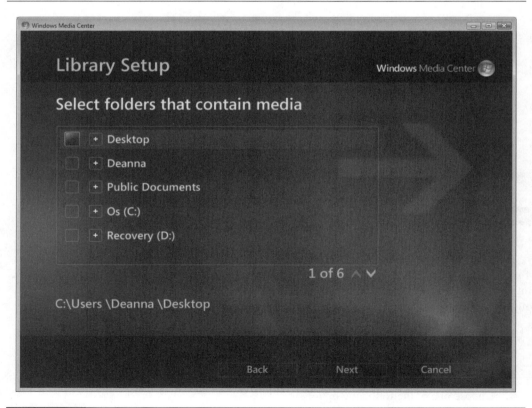

FIGURE 11-10 Choose folders for Media Center to watch.

Moving Media vs. Copying Media

Whenever possible, you don't want to duplicate music stored in one folder on your computer just to store it in a second folder on the same computer. Essentially, the only thing you'll achieve by doing this is consuming more of your hard drive space. And if you're considering copying media from your computer to a different computer, you should consider the wealth of copyright laws in place before you copy anything, anywhere.

As for moving, when you relocate a folder or music file, make sure you either place it a folder that Media Center already searches or that you add the folder in which you've placed the file to the folders Media Center searches, as shown in Figure 11-10.

To copy or move media, follow these steps:

1. Open your personal Music folder by clicking Start and then clicking Music (also known as My Music). This opens a Music folder similar to the one shown in Figure 11-11. (If your music is stored in a different folder, open that folder in this step.)

2. Navigate to the folder that contains the media file you want to move or copy.

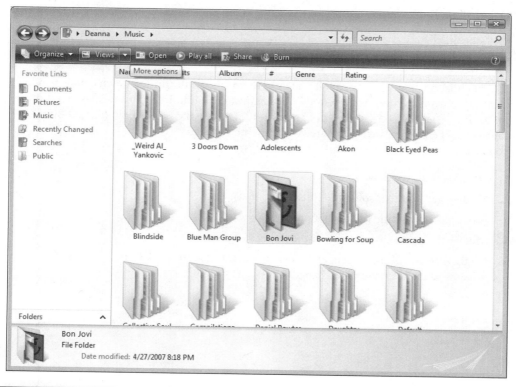

FIGURE 11-11   View your personal Music folder.

3. Right-click the folder or file you want to move or copy.

4. Choose Cut (to move) or Copy (to copy) from the shortcut menu that appears.

5. Right-click the folder you want to copy or move the media file to.

6. Choose Paste from the shortcut menu.

Edit Songs in Your Music Library

In order to make your music display in a way that is meaningful to you—particularly when you are viewing it based on titles or artists, or to assist you when using the Search feature—you can edit specific album elements.

Editable album elements include:

- Album title
- Album artist
- Genre

Editable song elements include:

- Song title
- Song artist
- Rating

To edit either an album or a song, all you need to do is view the drilled-down details window, like the one shown in Figure 11-2. From this screen, just click Edit Info. This displays the Edit Album (or Edit Song) window shown in Figure 11-12. Once in the Edit Album (or Edit Song) window, you can edit one, two, or all three of the elements listed.

To edit album (or song) details, follow these steps:

1. Open the Edit window.

2. Modify the album or song title (this is optional).

3. Modify the artist title (this is optional).

4. Modify the genre (for albums) or the rating (for songs).

5. On the left side of the screen, click Save when finished (or click Cancel to close the window without saving your changes).

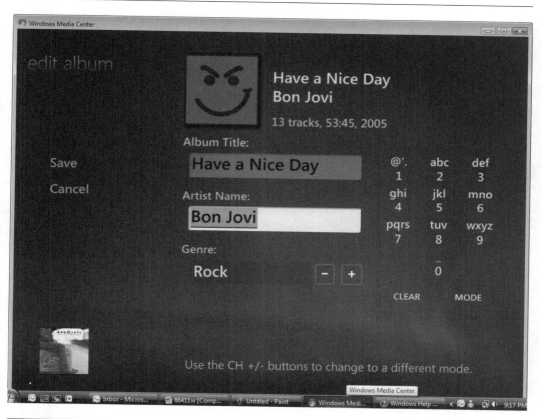

FIGURE 11-12 Edit album details.

NOTE *The Ratings option you see when editing an individual song helps populate the auto-playlist that displays the top-rated songs in your library. Think of ratings as your own personal measurement system for the music you enjoy listening to.*

TIP *You can quickly open the Edit window by right-clicking any album thumbnail or song name and choosing Edit from the shortcut menu.*

11

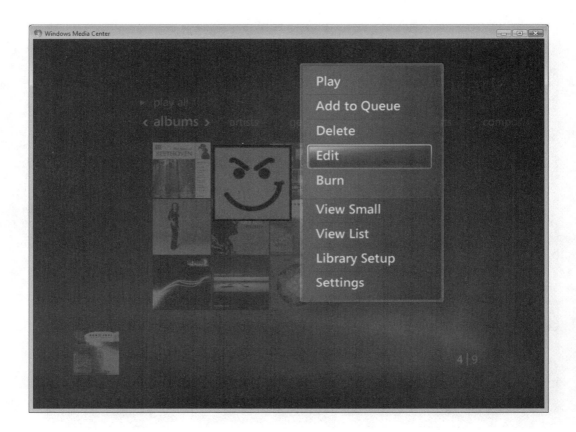

Working with the Queue

Now that you've learned how to navigate Media Center's music options and import your personal music collection, you're ready to learn about working with the music queue.

The queue is the list of songs you have scheduled to play and their order. For those days when you don't want to play all songs in your library, or even all songs on an individual album, you can create a queue of songs that Media Center plays.

To add songs to the queue, simply right-click a song (or an album) and choose Add To Queue—it's as simple as that. However, more powerful is your ability to modify the queue after it's been established and to save it as a playlist to which you can refer again and again, as shown in Figure 11-13.

FIGURE 11-13 The Edit queue

To view the queue, from the Media Center main screen, click the box under Now Playing + Queue. This opens the Now Playing window. In this window, you can then click View Queue from the navigation options displayed on the left side of the window. Doing so opens the Queue window shown in Figure 11-13, which offers the following options:

■ **Edit Queue** By clicking Edit Queue, you open an entirely new window in which you can remove individual songs from the queue and re-order the remaining songs to suit your preferences.

■ **Clear Queue** The Clear Queue option removes all songs currently in the queue, freeing it up for new songs you're ready to add.

■ **Save As Playlist**   This option allows you to save the current list of queue songs as a playlist you can play over and over again.

■ **Shuffle**   Shuffle can only be in one of two states: on or off. By default, Shuffle is enabled, as shown with a check mark. However, you can disable the Shuffle feature by clicking this option to remove the check mark.

■ **Repeat**   Just like Shuffle, the Repeat feature can only be in one of two states: on or off. By default, Repeat is disabled, as shown without a check mark. However, you can enable the Repeat feature by clicking this option to display a check mark.

■ **Burn**   When you click the Burn option, Media Center immediately begins the process of copying the selected queue to your CD or DVD. Make sure you have a writeable CD or DVD in your computer before clicking the Burn option.

Chapter 12

Buy or Rent Music Online

How to...

- ■ Select among music subscription services
- ■ Sign up for a service
- ■ Install required components
- ■ Download a song and listen to it on your PC
- ■ Listen to Internet radio

There are many ways to build your music library. You can rip your own CD collection, move existing media from other PCs, and even play the sample media that comes with Windows Vista, all of which was detailed in Chapter 11. Another way to build your collection is by subscribing to an online music service and "renting" the songs you want or purchasing songs or albums outright.

In this chapter, you'll learn how and where to get started with online music services. You'll see what you have to choose from, how to sign up, what software components are required, and how to download and listen to a song on your PC. (In Chapters 13 and 14 we'll expand on this, including managing the music you obtain and taking it with you on a portable player, among other things.) Also in this chapter, you'll learn what Internet radio is and what you'll need to access it.

Choose Between Media Center and Media Player 11

You can listen to music from inside Media Center or from Media Player 11. This includes music in your music library, including CDs you've ripped and music you've purchased or subscribed to. You can also access subscription music services from both Media Center and Media Player, then sign up, download songs, and listen to what you download from either one. At the moment, Media Player 11 is the better choice for obtaining subscription media, but Media Center has offerings, too.

NOTE *Just about anything you can configure or obtain in Media Player 11 will carry over to Media Center. This includes playlists and auto-playlists, which you'll learn more about in Chapter 13. That's why here and in the next few chapters we deal quite a bit with Media Player 11. Although Media Player is not part of Media Center, your Music Library is part of both. Thus, building a music collection in Media Player 11 is important to having a proper Music Library in Media Center.*

Understand Music Subscription Services

For the most part, all music subscription services offer the same thing. You generally have two choices: You can sign up for unlimited access to more music than you could listen to in a lifetime for around $10 U.S. a month, or you can choose to purchase songs outright for about a dollar a track or $10 U.S. per album. You can also do both. You can always change your subscription option at any time, and almost all services offer a free trial period of a week or so for subscription services. It's up to you, but we suggest opting for the free trial for two or more services and then selecting your favorite when the trials are over.

Incorporating on Online Music Service

Lately, more and more music subscription services are offering a Media Center option for downloading and listening to media using Media Center instead of Media Player 11. For instance, Napster, available from the More Music options in the Music category of Media Center, offers a free week-long trial and a free plug-in to make Media Center work with the service. With Napster incorporated into Media Center, you can search for media you want, have unlimited listening and downloading on your computer and TV, choose from custom playlists, and have direct access to the online music library from your PC.

AOL Music also offers a Media Center option called AOL's Music on Demand. With it, you can browse and listen to the music you want for free. The same is true of MTV. With MTV, you can search music videos and play them anytime you like. Both of these, as well as others, make a great choice for Windows Vista PCs used in family rooms in conjunction with a big-screen television. It's easy to browse through media using the remote control, and on a big screen, Media Center looks really cool! With free services, you can't download the music to your PC, however, or sync the music with a portable player or burn the songs to a CD. That's why it's often used in a family or recreation room. It's like having always-on live video feeds.

As noted earlier, there are more music subscription choices currently available in Media Player than there are in Media Center. Hopefully, this will change in the future, because Media Center should be the "center" of all media, and having music incorporated in that is the ultimate way to go. That being said, we still think it's best for you to explore both and decide what's right for you after experimenting with the trial offers of various companies. Keep in mind that music you obtain online is stored in your Music folder (as long as the store carries the PlaysForSure logo and uses Windows Media) and can be accessed from either Media Player or Media Center. So for the most part, it doesn't really matter where you get your music; it should be available in Media Center.

12

TIP   *Even if your downloaded music does not appear in the Music folder, you can tell Media Center to watch the folder it appears in or move the music to the Music folder manually.*

Sign Up for a Music Subscription Service

Before signing up for a service, it's best to review the available options. This includes the options in Media Center and in Media Player. Once you've decided which service you want and if you'd rather use Media Player or Media Center for obtaining media, you can work through the sign-up process.

Select a Provider and Application

To view your provider options in Media Center, open Media Center, select Music, and then choose More Music. Browse through the options to see what's available. You may find that free music-on-demand sites suit your needs and that you don't really need to subscribe to anything. You were introduced to this feature in Chapter 11.

Now open Media Player 11. To find this application, click Start, point to All Programs, and then click Windows Media Player. From the Media Guide tab, select Browse All Online Stores. As you can see in Figure 12-1, Napster is available in Media Player, along with several other options. Napster is also available in Media Center, and thus works quite well when used with both.

URGE is one of the more popular choices in Media Player. It offers millions of songs and unlimited downloads, thousands of playlists, radio stations, and exclusives from MTV, CH1, and CMT. As with other options, you can try it for free for a limited time. If you plan to use Media Player to obtain music, we'll suggest URGE. It is intuitive, easy to use, has its own built-in categories in Media Player, and offers tons of media options.

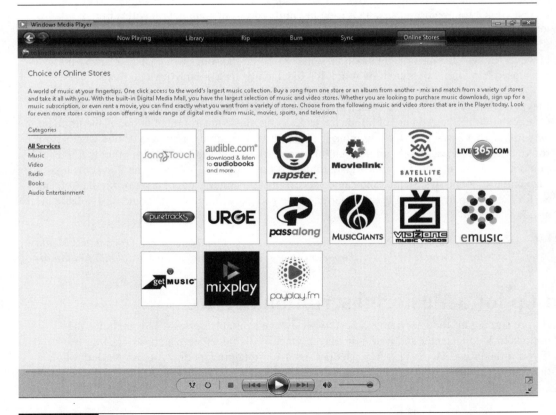

FIGURE 12-1 Media Player currently offers more subscription options than Media Center.

By the time this book goes to press, there will likely be more subscription options available both for Media Player and Media Center. So in this chapter, we're going to work with both to obtain media and help you decide what's best for you. As it stands now, we prefer to obtain music in Media Player and listen to it using Media Center. However, it is likely that Media Center will ultimately be the place to manage music and online media in the long run, and our opinions on this may change.

Install Required Software Components

Although required software varies from company to company and will continue to evolve as technologies improve, most online subscription services require you download and install *something*. It may be a simple ActiveX control or a plug-in, but whatever the case, you'll need to have administrator privileges to install it, and you'll have to install it to use the service.

As an example, and to help you get started, we'll walk you through getting signed up for Napster in Media Center. Signing up for any service in Media Player is just about the same, including the requirement to create a trial account and install a plug-in or other software. (From Media Player, select Online Stores from the Media Guide options, click Browse Online Stores, and select a store. Then skip to step 2 here to obtain Napster.)

To sign up for and install software required to work with Napster inside Media Center:

1. Open Media Center, click Music, and click More Music.

2. Locate Napster in the choices. Click it.

3. Select Get Napster! 7-Day Free Trial or whatever the trial option is at the time of publication.

4. Click Open Website to go to the Napster Web site and sign up. You'll need to use a keyboard and mouse for this, as the remote control won't work.

5. Fill in a member name, password, and e-mail address. Then continue to work through the sign-up wizard, providing required information. This will include a credit card number and billing address. Cancel during your trial period if you do not want your credit card to be charged.

6. Click Start Napster.

7. While still at the Napster Web site, click Get Napster. This is the software you'll need to use Napster with Media Center and Media Player.

8. Click Run when prompted.

9. Left-click Continue.

10. Work through the installation wizard.

11. Close and restart Media Center.

12

Download a Song or Album and Listen to It in Media Center

If you've chosen Napster or another subscription service that offers access from Media Center, you can use Media Center to log on, browse online media, download songs, and listen to them. Songs you download or purchase in Media Center will appear in your Music Library, and these songs can also be accessed later from Media Player. Let's look at the process.

Log On

The first step in obtaining music online from Media Center is to locate the link to the subscription service in the Music folder. Some companies may offer a new icon under Music; most must be accessed through the More Music option. Whatever the case, the first time you use the service, you must log on. You can select an option like Automatically Log Me In if offered, and skip this step next time. Figure 12-2 shows Napster's current login screen.

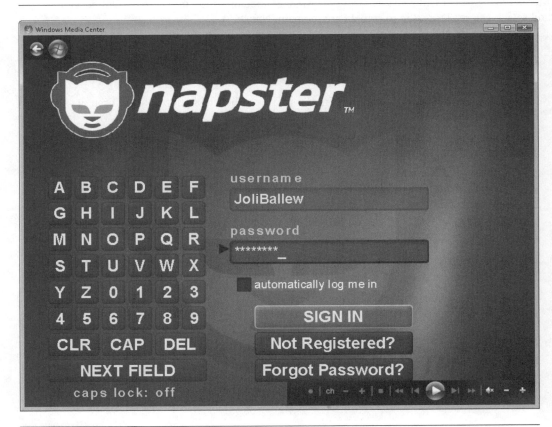

FIGURE 12-2   Log on with your user name and password.

Obtain Media

Once logged on, you can begin searching for the media you want. If you don't have a remote control, you might find the process a bit arduous. Without a remote you can use with Media Center (which was designed with a remote control in mind), you'll have to use the keyboard or mouse, and depending on the type and manufacturer, they may not work as you'd expect. If you can't get the mouse to work for browsing, try the arrow keys on your keyboard, along with the ENTER key for selecting.

Once you've found a song, video, or album you want to download or listen to, use the appropriate keys on the mouse, keyboard, or remote control to choose the appropriate option on the screen. Figure 12-3 shows a download in progress. Here, I'm downloading all songs on the album, and you can see the arrows denoting the download is in progress.

Although you can play media using the Play option on your remote control or keyboard or by clicking Play with the mouse, if it's a song you want to listen to often, it's ultimately better to locate and play the music from your Music Library. That's detailed next.

FIGURE 12-3   You can download songs inside Media Center.

Play Media in Music Library

Any music you've downloaded from inside Media Center can be located in the Music Library. Playing songs using the Music Library in Media Center lets you have easy access to all of the songs you've obtained. To play media in this manner:

1. Open Media Center, select Music, and select Music Library.

2. Use the mouse, keyboard, or remote control to select the category and song or artist. In Figure 12-4, Album Artists is selected as is the recently downloaded Kellie Pickler album.

3. Select the album or song.

4. From the options on the right, select Play Album to hear the entire album, or select any song to hear just that song.

FIGURE 12-4   Use Music Library to play songs you've obtained.

Download a Song or Album and Listen to It in Media Player 11

If you've chosen Napster, URGE, or another subscription service that offers access from Media Player, you can use Media Player to log on, browse online media, download songs, and listen to them. Songs you download or purchase in Media Player will appear in your Music Library, and these songs can also be accessed from Media Center. Let's look at the process.

Log On

Provided you've worked through the subscription process, the first step in obtaining music online from Media Player is to locate the link to the subscription service from the toolbar. Look on the toolbar and in the drop-down list for the available online services you belong to. Whatever you choose, the first time you use the service, you must log on. You can select an option like Automatically Log Me In if offered, and skip this step next time. Figure 12-5 shows an example. Here, we're members of both URGE and Napster, and URGE is showing in the main window.

FIGURE 12-5 You can use more than one service for obtaining media.

12

Browse for Media

Browsing is unique to a particular service, but for the most part, once you're logged on, you can immediately begin searching for the media you want. If you don't have a remote control, don't worry; Media Player works just fine with a mouse and keyboard.

Use the appropriate keys on the mouse or keyboard to browse the available media, and once you've found a song or album to listen to, download, or purchase, select the choice related to it. In Figure 12-6, I've located the soundtrack to *The Sopranos* from HBO. Notice that some of the tracks on the album are grayed out and thus not available for download. You'll run into this occasionally; music producers do this when they don't want specific songs to be available online. What I really want is the song "Woke Up This Morning," but it is not available for download (it's grayed out).

FIGURE 12-6   You can download songs inside Media Center.

Download or Purchase Media

To purchase media in Media Player 11, generally, all you have to do is right-click the media, select Buy, and then click Confirm, Yes, or some other option to verify that you really want to buy the song(s). Once you confirm that you want to purchase the music that's selected, the music will download and will be yours. Note that the songs that are not highlighted will not be downloaded. You can also right-click any song to access options. Figure 12-7 shows an example.

To download media and play it, simply click the song or right-click it, and select Play.

Play Media

Media Player was built for the purpose of obtaining, organizing, and playing music. This is a bit unlike Media Center, which adds television, videos, pictures, and more to the mix. Because Media Player is a music-themed application, you might find it better to use Media Player over Media Center when playing the music in your library. However, remember that whatever you do

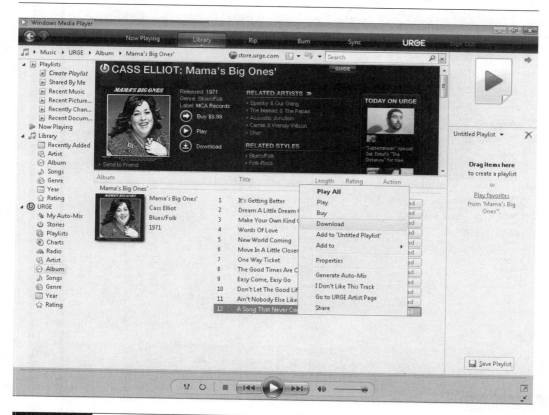

FIGURE 12-7 Right-clicking offers additional options.

in Media Player, such as creating playlists, downloading music, rating music, or whatever else, most of the configurations can also be found and accessed in Media Center. That means that if you create a playlist in Media Player, you can access it Media Center. We think Media Center looks much cooler on a big screen than Media Player, and we enjoy using the remote control from Media Center as well.

To play a song in Media Player, locate the song under the proper library in the Playlists pane. That's the pane on the left side, and it contains folders and subfolders that can be navigated easily. You can access songs, albums, and artists from more than one category.

As an example, under Recently Added in the Library list, shown in Figure 12-8, you can see the albums I downloaded while writing this chapter. They include Alicia Myers; The Band; Crosby, Stills, Nash, and Young; and others you can't see that are farther down the list.

However, these same albums can be found under Artist, Album, Genre, Year, and more. Figure 12-9 shows Alicia Myers in the Artist category in the Library list.

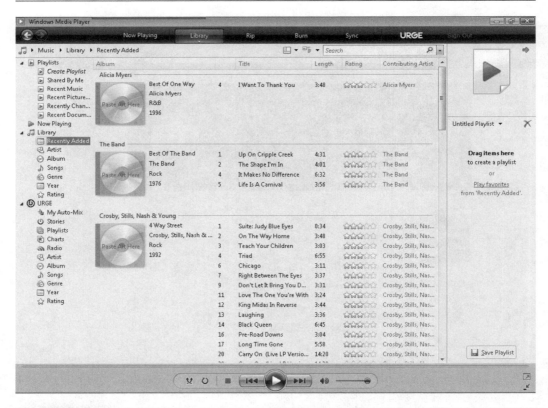

FIGURE 12-8 New downloads can be accessed from the Recently Added category.

FIGURE 12-9   You can access songs just about everywhere in Media Player.

> **TIP**   *You'll learn a lot more about Media Player and Media Center, including navigating their categories and interfaces, in the next few chapters.*

It's important to note that songs aren't duplicated so that they appear in multiple areas of Media Center or Media Player. They are downloaded once, and the references you see to them in various categories are, in reality, more like shortcuts to the song.

Listen to Internet Radio

You can listen to Internet radio from Media Center as well. There are lots of choices, including AOL Radio, Country Radio and More, XM Radio, NPR Talk, and more. These are generally free resources, and you can start listening by clicking the station you want in the More Music category under Music. Figure 12-10 shows AOL Radio, which we accessed from Media Center

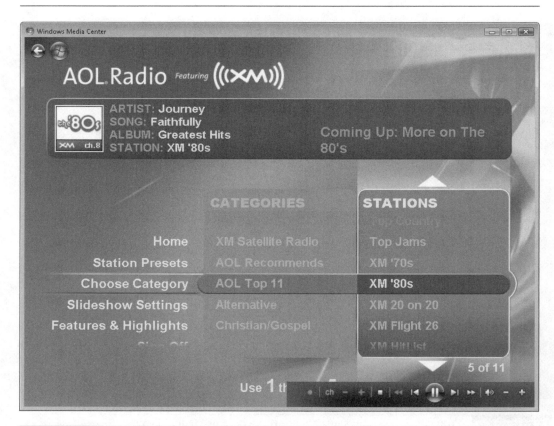

FIGURE 12-10 AOL Radio featuring XM is free.

by selecting Music, then selecting More Music, and finally selecting AOL Radio. After signing in with our AOL user name and password, we have unlimited access to all the AOL Radio options. Here, being stuck in the '80s, Joli listens to Journey.

You'll want to explore all of the free options in More Music, including radio stations. It may turn out that you don't need to subscribe to any music service!

Chapter 13

Manage Your Music

How to...

- Create playlists
- Add media to playlists and listen to playlists
- Use the Now Playing list
- Manage the Media Library

Windows Media Player 11 is a great tool for watching movies or organizing recorded television shows from Windows Media Center. It's also a great tool for organizing and playing media. With features like auto-playlists and the Now Playing list, it is easy to listen to music or to watch a series of television shows or even listen to entire music albums, and then synchronize them to a portable media device or burn them to a CD-ROM or DVD.

In this chapter, we'll take a look at what playlists are and how to create them, and then we'll cover how to manage your media using the Media Library. You'll learn how to make Windows Media Player 11 watch particular folders for new songs and movies, how to correct inaccurate song data, and how to find new song data using Internet resources. Note that the playlists, corrected data, and the folders you watch and create in Media Player 11 carry over to Media Center, and you can access and play those playlists there. That's why with music anyway, incorporating Media Player 11 is extremely important to creating, organizing, and managing your music library.

Create Playlists

Windows Media Player 11 automatically organizes and sorts all of your digital media so that it is easy to search through and enjoy (we'll cover more about how to search the Music Library later on in this chapter). With the Media Library, you can effortlessly look for music by artist, album, or other characteristics. Sometimes, however, it is more helpful to make your own groups of music, pictures, and video.

Playlists are lists of media—any type of media—including pictures, videos, or music. You can use playlists to group together similar media, like your favorite songs or videos, all of the songs from a particular artist or album, or just create a slideshow of pictures to show friends and family. Playlists are great for creating lists of media to synchronize to a music player or to copy to a CD-ROM. They are also excellent for creating lists of music to play at parties, at work, or for long drives. It is important to keep in mind that when you create a playlist and then play it, the playlist is played in order, unless you enable the Shuffle or Repeat options in Windows Media Player. There are two types of playlists in Windows Media Player 11. With an auto-playlist, you set the criteria of the media that should appear in it. You can specify artist, number of stars, number of times the media has been played, album, and many other criteria. When you open the playlist, Windows Media Player 11 searches the Media Library for media that matches the criteria you specified, which then appears in the playlists. Auto-playlists are useful for synchronizing media to a portable media player like the Zune. Whenever the portable media player is connected, Windows Media Player 11 refreshes the auto-playlist and all new content is synchronized.

Ordinary Playlists

An ordinary playlist is one that you populate with media yourself. You can add any type of media to a playlist and then play the playlist, synchronize it to a portable media device, or burn it to a CD-ROM.

Follow these steps to create an ordinary playlist or an auto-playlist:

1. Click the arrow under the Library button. (The arrow appears after you move your mouse over the Library button.)

2. Click Create Playlist or Create Auto Playlist. (You can press CTRL-N to create a new playlist). See Figure 13-1.

3. If you're creating an ordinary playlist, click Create Playlist, and then type a name for your playlist.

4. If you're creating an auto-playlist, click Create Auto Playlist, and then type a name for your auto-playlist. Next, you must select the criteria for the auto-playlist.

After you've created an ordinary playlist, it's time to start adding media to it! We'll cover how to add media to a playlist in the next section. For now, let's take a look at how to create two different auto-playlists: one that shows music added in the last month and another that shows music that is auto-rated with at least five stars.

Auto-Playlists

Auto-playlists are flexible and can be configured to display the exact music you want from your Media Library. Auto playlists differ from ordinary playlists in that with an Auto playlist you do not need to pick individual songs to add to the playlist—you set criteria (such as number of rated stars) and Media Player finds all the songs that match the criteria.

In this example, we'll create an Auto Playlist that shows music added in the last month.

1. To begin, first create a new auto-playlist.

2. Type **Auto Playlist Music Added in the Last Month** for the new auto-playlist's name.

3. Click [Click here to add criteria] under Music In My Library.

13

FIGURE 13-1   Create a playlist or an auto-playlist.

4. Click Date Added. Change Is After to Is Before (see Figure 13-2).

5. If you want to limit the auto-playlist to a certain number of songs, under And Apply The Following Restrictions To The Auto Playlist, click [Click Here to add criteria], and select Limit Number Of Items To. Click [Click to set], and enter the number of items you want to limit the playlist to.

6. Click OK to save the auto-playlist.

In the next example, you'll create an auto-playlist that shows music that has been auto-rated with five stars:

1. Create a new auto-playlist.

2. Type **Music Auto Rated With Five Stars** for the new auto-playlist's name.

3. Click [Click here to add criteria] under Music In My Library.

4. Click Auto Rating. Change 4 Stars to 5 Stars. Change Is At Least to Is (see Figure 13-3).

5. Click OK to save the auto-playlist.

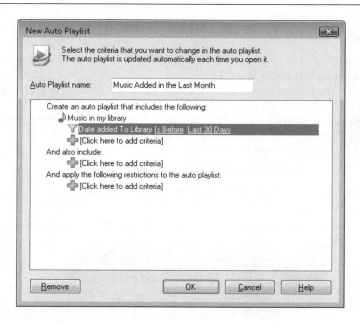

FIGURE 13-2   Creating a playlist that shows music added in the last month

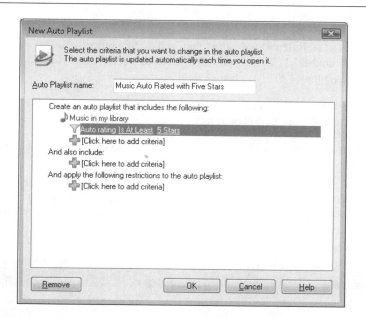

FIGURE 13-3 Music that is auto-rated with five stars

Add and Play Music in Playlists

Auto-playlists automatically search your library to find media that matches criteria you have set. Auto-playlists are a great way to find music you haven't heard in a while or to create CDs for a long drive. Playlists serve a different purpose, however. With a playlist, you can create your own list of media for a party, get-together, reunion, trip—wherever you want to be the DJ. Rather than having to browse the library every time you want to hear music, you can create pre-defined lists of music that fit particular moods or occasions. Then you can just play the playlist, walk away from the computer, and enjoy the occasion. Now that you see the potential uses for playlists, let's take a look at how to create one.

You might be thinking that creating a playlist could be difficult or time-consuming—that couldn't be any further from the truth! Creating a playlist is as easy as dragging a media file to Windows Media Player 11. Let's create a playlist and add a new song from the Media Library.

First, click the Library button at the top of Windows Media Player 11. Once you're in the Media Library:

1. Click Create Playlist under the Playlists heading on the list on the left side of the Media Library. Type a name for the playlist—for example, **Party Songs**. Now that the playlist has been created, it's time to add some music!

2. Under Library on the left side of Windows Media Player 11, click Artist. Browse through the list of artists until you find an appropriate artist that has a song to add to the playlist.

13

Want to add an entire artist? No problem! Right-click the artist, select Add To, and click the name of the playlist you just created, as shown in Figure 13-4.

3. If you want to get a little more detailed than just adding an entire artist, you can! Double-click an artist, double-click an album, right-click any song, go to Add To, and then click the name of the playlist that you just created.

That was only three steps to create your own custom playlist of songs! It only gets easier from here. Let's add songs from the Music folder of your hard drive.

1. On the left side of Windows Media Player 11, under Playlists, click the playlist that you just created.

2. Resize the Windows Media Player 11 window so that you can see other windows around or near it. Click the Start menu button, and then click Music. If you don't see Music, click Documents, and then click the Music link on the left side of the Documents window.

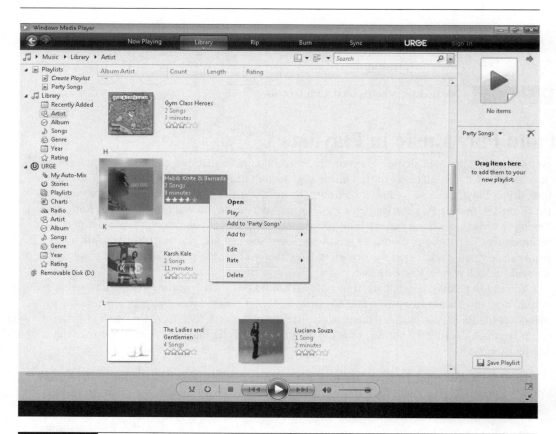

FIGURE 13-4   Adding an entire artist to a playlist

3. Make sure that the Music folder window isn't maximized. Now arrange the Windows Media Player 11 window and the Music folder window so that you can see both. Adding songs to the playlist is a simple drag-and-drop operation: Just click the folder or song that you want to add and drag it to the playlist in Windows Media Player 11.

Congratulations, you've just made a playlist! After you add a song to the playlist, the playlist is automatically saved. The next step is the easiest step. It's time to listen to a playlist. In Windows Media Player 11, right-click your playlist, and click Play. You can also just double-click the playlist. Read on to learn about a new type of list called the Now Playing list. The Now Playing list is like a playlist, but temporary.

TIP
Media Center plays playlists made in Windows Media Player. Just open Media Center, scroll down to Music, and then select Music Library. In Music Library, scroll up until Albums is selected, and then scroll right to Playlists and select it. Select the playlist you want to listen to, and then select Play.

Use the Now Playing List

The Now Playing list is a temporary playlist of media that you are listening to or watching. It can contain any media that a playlist contains, and the list is deleted when Windows Media Player 11 is closed. You can add media to the Now Playing list, and Windows Media Player 11 plays the temporary list in order until it reaches the end. You can use options such as Shuffle or Repeat to alter how the list is played. In other music applications, the Now Playing list is referred to as a *queue*.

To view the Now Playing list:

1. Click the arrow under the Now Playing button.
2. Click Show List Pane (see Figure 13-5).

The Now Playing list appears on the right side of Windows Media Player 11. At the top of the right side of Windows Media Player 11, the album art and title of the media that is currently playing is displayed. Under that is the text "Now Playing." When you click it, a menu appears. From this menu, you can clear the list, shuffle the list, sort the list, or save the Now Playing list as a playlist to listen to again later.

To edit the Now Playing list:

1. Click Now Playing on the Now Playing list on the right side of the screen. (You must follow the previous steps to view the Now Playing list first.)
2. Click Clear List to clear the contents of the Now Playing list.
3. Click Shuffle List Now to shuffle the contents of the Now Playing list.
4. Click Sort, and then select how you'd like to sort the Now Playing list.
5. Finally, if you'd like to save the Now Playing list so that you can resume listening to it later on, click Save Playlist As. Type a file name, and click Save.

13

FIGURE 13-5   The Now Playing list

Manage the Media Library

The Media Library is great tool that helps you find and organize media on your computer. Windows Media Player 11 automatically scans your Music, Pictures, and Videos folders for media and adds it the library. Then you can use the library to search for media and listen to or watch it. The Media Library is all about making your media easy to find. How easy it is to find, however, depends on how accurate the data is that is stored in the file identifying the artist, album, etc. In this section, we'll take a look at how to find and save new song information from the Internet and how to manually enter it in case it is not on the Internet.

Find Album Information for Songs

Music files store more information than just the audio that you hear when you play them. Other information, such as the artist, album, and release year, is often stored inside of the music file in a separate section that is next to the audio part of the file. This extra data is called tag data (some other applications may call it metadata). Windows Media Player 11 reads this tag data to figure out how to organize your Media Library. This is how Windows Media Player 11 knows the artist of a particular song or the album the song is from, for example.

Audio CDs cannot store tag data, however. In fact, audio CDs can only store audio for each song. If you rip an audio CD, all that Windows Media Player 11 knows about the CD is how many tracks are on it, the length of the tracks, and sometimes a unique number that identifies the audio CD. If you are connected to the Internet when you rip an audio CD in Windows Media Player 11, Media Player will access the Internet and look up the audio CD using the unique number in order to find the artist, album, and other information for each song. Sometimes, this information isn't on the Internet, however, or it isn't entirely accurate. In these cases, you may need to manually enter the information for each song.

Rather than have you manually enter the information for an entire audio CD, Windows Media Player 11 comes with a feature called Find Album Info. All you need to do is select the songs, search for the album or artist, and then click the right result. Windows Media Player 11 automatically saves the information to the tag data section of each song, and like magic, your Media Library is tagged, recognized, and then sorted.

Let's take a look at how to use the Find Album Info feature step by step.

1. First, select the song or group of songs that you want to look up.

2. Right-click the song or group of songs, and click Find Album Info.

3. If Windows Media Player 11 can find information for the song on the Internet, you'll see a screen that says "Select the album that matches," along with a list of albums that may match the song. Click the album that matches the song. Windows Media Player 11 automatically saves data from the album that relates to the song—like artist and album art—in your Media Library (see Figure 13-6).

4. If Windows Media Player 11 cannot find album information that matches the song on the Internet, you'll need to refine your search or manually enter the song information. To refine your search, click the Refine Your Search link, located at either the top of the window or the bottom of the window by the magnifying glass.

5. When you're done, click the Save button. Windows Media Player 11 saves the new information to the tag data for each song that you selected.

That's all you need to do! Now your songs should be tagged, and you can take advantage of the great organization features that the Media Library offers.

Edit Song Data

Almost all songs that you find in your Media Library have associated tag data, such as the artist, album, genre, and more. If you ripped a CD, the songs may not have this data associated with it because Windows Media Player 11 couldn't find it on the Internet. Sometimes, the tag data on the Internet is not accurate or is formatted incorrectly. If you like to keep an accurate, organized, tagged Media Library, this can be irritating and frustrating. Fortunately, Windows Media Player 11 includes all of the tools that you need to edit tag data on one or more songs at the same time. Some tools refer to this functionality as "batch editing."

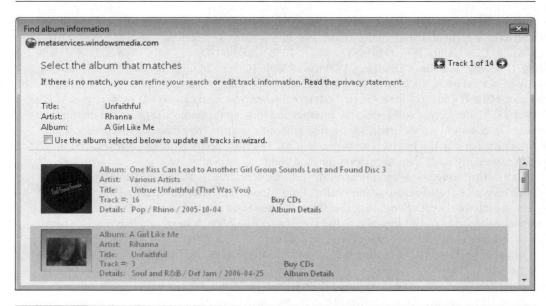

Find album information

metaservices.windowsmedia.com

Select the album that matches

Track 1 of 14

If there is no match, you can refine your search or edit track information. Read the privacy statement.

Title: Unfaithful
Artist: Rhanna
Album: A Girl Like Me

☐ Use the album selected below to update all tracks in wizard.

Album: One Kiss Can Lead to Another: Girl Group Sounds Lost and Found Disc 3
Artist: Various Artists
Title: Untrue Unfaithful (That Was You)
Track #: 16   Buy CDs
Details: Pop / Rhino / 2005-10-04   Album Details

Album: A Girl Like Me
Artist: Rihanna
Title: Unfaithful
Track #: 3   Buy CDs
Details: Soul and R&B / Def Jam / 2006-04-25   Album Details

FIGURE 13-6   Use Find Album Info to add album information.

If you have a song or group of songs and you'd like to edit the tag data yourself, follow these simple instructions:

1. First, select the song or group of songs that you want to look up.

2. Right-click the song or group of songs, and click Advanced Tag Editor.

3. If you only selected one song, you can simply click the fields that you want to edit, enter new data, and then click Apply or OK to continue.

If you selected more than one song, the fields will be unavailable, and you won't be able to change the tag data until you select the check box next to the field. When you select the check box next to the field, any data in it will be applied to all of the songs that you selected.

If you don't select the check box next to a field, no changes will be made. This is for your own protection. If you select an album of songs and open the Advanced Tag Editor and then enter a new title, the title of every song you selected will be overwritten. You only want to select the check boxes next to the fields that you want to apply to all of the songs that you selected.

For example, to edit the artist on a group of songs, follow these instructions:

1. First, select the song or group of songs that you want to look up.

2. Right-click the song or group of songs, and click Advanced Tag Editor.

3. Select the Artist check box on the Artist Info tab. Enter a new artist, and then click Apply or OK (see Figure 13-7).

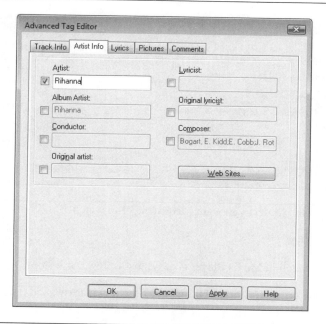

FIGURE 13-7   Editing artist information with the Advanced Tag Editor

The artist for all of the selected songs will change, but none of the other data will change. The Advanced Tag Editor is a powerful tool, but you have to be careful when you use it. You'll almost never want to select the check box next to the Title field—as we mentioned, doing this would overwrite the song title for every song that you've selected. You may find yourself wanting to change the artist or album on a group of songs, however. In the next section, we'll take a look at how to make Windows Media Player 11 automatically watch folders on your hard drive for new media and add it to your Media Library.

Add Folders to the Media Library

Windows Media Player 11 discovers your media automatically. You may have noticed this the first time you started the program. Windows Media Player 11 watches your personal folders for new media and adds it to the Media Library without you having to take any action. The personal folders that Windows Media Player 11 watches include Pictures, Videos, and Music. You can change settings in Media Player so that it watches every other personal folder that you have access to, in addition to your own personal folders.

For example, if you want to keep track of the pictures, videos, and music in the personal folders of your children, you can have Media Player automatically add media in those folders to your Media Library. Then you can just open Windows Media Player 11, browse to the library, and get a master view of all of the media on your computer.

13

FIGURE 13-8   Select the folders you want Media Player to watch.

Adding a folder to watch in Media Player is easy; just follow these steps:

1. Move the mouse over the Library button, click the down arrow, and then click More Options.

2. Under Update Library By Monitoring Folders, click Monitor Folders.

To change which folders Media Player monitors, under Select The Folders To Monitor, choose between My Personal Folders and My Folders And Those Of Others That I Can Access (see Figure 13-8).

There are also several advanced options associated with monitoring folders. To view the advanced options, click Advanced Options.

If you want Windows Media Player 11 to re-add songs to the Media Library that have been previously deleted from it, select Add Files Previously Deleted From Library.

As Media Player monitors folders and adds media to the library, it can collect data about the volume of sound inside of the file. This may be useful for playing music in quieter environments. When Windows Media Player 11 has volume-leveling data, it can prevent sudden jumps in volume.

Chapter 14

Enjoy Music on the Go and at Home

How to...

- Select the media type for burning CDs and DVDs
- Burn a CD in Media Player 11
- Burn a CD in Media Center
- Synchronize a mobile device with Windows Media Player 11
- Configure privacy options in Media Center
- Configure privacy options in Media Player 11

Windows Vista includes Windows Media Center and Windows Media Player 11—both complete solutions for all of your digital media needs. You'll generally use Windows Media Player 11 while working at your computer and Windows Media Center when watching media from afar: on the couch, sofa, or while with a group of friends or family. Whatever you choose, both Windows Media Player 11 and Windows Media Center are capable of letting you browse media in the Media Library, burn media, and configure privacy settings.

In this chapter, we'll discuss types of media you can burn to, how to burn a CD using Windows Media Player 11, and how to burn a playlist using Media Center. Then you'll learn how to synchronize a mobile device, such as a personal digital assistant (PDA) or MP3 player so that you can take your music with you. Finally, you'll learn how to configure privacy options in Media Player and Media Center.

Select a Media Type

In Windows Media Player 11 and Windows Media Center, you can copy (also known as *burn*) the contents of your Media Library to a CD or DVD. This process is called burning a CD, because the laser in your CD-ROM drive literally alters the surface and chemicals ("burning") on a media disc so that data can be read by other devices, like your living room DVD player or video game console. This means that you can select entire artists, albums, songs, or playlists (including auto-playlists) and burn them to a media disc such as a CD or DVD.

Before you can burn anything, however, you must decide what type of media you want to burn and what you want to do with it. Do you want to burn pictures to a CD so that you can mail it to family members? Do you want to burn a video of a child's concert to a DVD so that they can show it to their friends?

If you just want to copy pictures or videos to a CD or DVD, then you want to create a data CD or data DVD. If you want to copy music files, such as MP3s or WMAs to a CD or DVD, then you want to create a data CD or data DVD. If you only want to copy audio to play in a car stereo, DVD player, or another device, then you want to create an audio CD. Table 14-1 summarizes the differences between Data CDs, Data DVDs, and Audio CDs.

Media Type	Best Uses
Data CD/Data DVD	Stores any kind of data, such as files located on your hard drive, Universal Serial Bus (USB) data stick, or other CDs or DVDs
Audio CD	Stores audio that plays on a CD player or DVD player

TABLE 14-1   Types of Media Discs

A data CD or data DVD stores data, just like your hard drive does. If you want to copy picture files or video files to a media disc so that you can reopen the files on another computer, you want to use a data CD or data DVD. Some DVD players and CD players have the ability to understand the way a computer stores files, and they can actually read a data DVD or data CD. Make sure that you consider where you plan to use any data CDs or data DVDs when you create them. Refer to Table 14-2 if you are not sure about what kind of media to use for certain content.

Devices that can understand data CDs or data DVDs typically have stickers or logos on the front of them that show what types of files they understand.

For example, many car stereo CD players understand WMA and MP3 formats now and have WMA and MP3 logos on the front. There are also many DVD players that understand MPEG video files and WMV video files.

Like hard drives, Audio CDs, Data CDs, and Data DVDs can only store a finite amount of information—a maximum amount of audio or data that can fit on the disc. Table 14-3 summarizes the typical storage capacities of Audio CDs, Data CDs, and Data DVDs.

Burn Music to a CD or DVD Using Media Player 11

By now, you should know what kind of media you want to burn to a CD or DVD and on what kind of media disc to burn it: a data CD or DVD or an audio CD.

1. First, open the drive tray, insert a blank CD or DVD, and close the drive tray. Make sure you are aware what kind of media your computer supports.

14

Content Type	Best Media To Use
Pictures and/or Videos	Data CD/Data DVD
Music files	Data CD/Data DVD
Audio	Audio CD

TABLE 14-2   Types of Data Appropriate for Data Media Discs

Media Type	Storage Capacity
Audio CD	Holds up to 74 minutes of audio
Data CD or DVD	Holds up to 700 megabytes (MB) or 4.7 gigabytes (GB)

TABLE 14-3 Media Disc Capacities

2. After you close the drive tray, Windows Vista reads the disc. If the disc is blank and formatted, the AutoPlay window will open. Click Burn An Audio CD Using Windows Media Player (see Figure 14-1).

NOTE *If this dialog box doesn't appear, open Windows Media Player 11, and click the Burn button.*

3. Click the Burn button again.
4. Click the type of media disc you need: Audio CD or Data CD or DVD.
5. Drag files from your Windows Media Player 11 library to your Burn List. You can drag entire artists, albums, or playlists to the Burn List (see Figure 14-2).

FIGURE 14-1 AutoPlay dialog box in Windows Vista

FIGURE 14-2   Burn List

6. Click the arrow at the top of the Burn List to show a drop-down menu that can sort the Burn List or shuffle it (see Figure 14-3). After you've added media to the Burn List, sort or shuffle it as desired.

7. Click Start Burn to immediately begin copying your media to your media disc. Windows Media Player 11 won't ask you to confirm your selection.

NOTE   *If you're using a CD-R or DVD-R, you can't cancel the burn once it has started without destroying the media disc, so make sure you've made your final decisions before you click Start Burn!*

There are a number of other options that you can use to customize how media is burned, which the following sections describe.

14

FIGURE 14-3   The Burn List options

Burn Options

Burning media to a disc in Windows Media Player 11 is as easy as point and click—you never need to set any options to begin burning. All you need to do is insert a media disc, drag files to the Burn List, and click Start Burn. Despite this, there are several advanced options in Windows Media Player 11 that you can use to customize burning. Most of these you won't need to change except for special circumstances.

To access the burn options, click the Burn button, and then click More Options (see Figure 14-4).

General

■ **Burn Speed**   Media discs are rated at a particular speed for burning. If you try to burn a media disc at a speed that is faster than the disc's maximum burn speed, the data may not

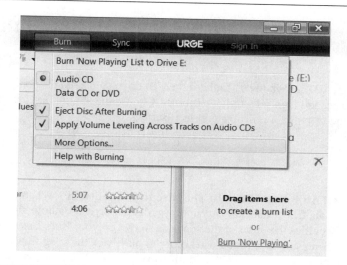

FIGURE 14-4   Burn options

copy to the disc correctly. Most of the time, Windows Media Player 11 is able to detect the disc's maximum burn speed. If you find that Windows Media Player 11 is creating CDs or DVDs that cannot be read, you may want to try slowing down the burn speed. By default, Fastest is selected.

- **Eject Disc After Burning**   After burning a disc, Windows Media Player 11 automatically ejects it. If your computer is in an unusual place where there might not be room for the drive tray to open, or if you keep other items near your computer in front of the drive bay, this may not be convenient. To stop Windows Media Player 11 from automatically ejecting the disc after burning, clear the option. It is selected by default.

Audio CDs

- **Apply Volume Leveling Across Tracks On CDs**   If you're burning songs that are recorded at different volume levels, this option helps keep the volume the same across the entire CD. That way, you don't have to adjust the volume between songs, in case one song is louder or quieter than the next. If you have an audio system that does this for you, or if you don't mind the sudden volume changes between songs, then clear this option. It is selected by default.

14

How to ...   **Burn a Music CD in Media Center**

You can also burn a CD in Windows Media Center. To do this, insert a disc open Media Center, select Music, and then select Music Library. Choose the album, playlist, or any other group of songs, and from the Details page, select Burn.

Data Discs

■ **Add A List Of All Burned Files To The Disc In This Format**   When you burn a series of songs to a data CD or data DVD, Windows Media Player 11 automatically creates a playlist that specifies the order of the songs as shown on your Burn List. Without this playlist file, there is no way to tell what order to play back the song files in. There are two different playlist formats: WPL and M3U. By default, Windows Media Player 11 creates a WPL playlist file. Many devices support M3U files. If you are going to play back a data CD or data DVD on a DVD player, for example, that doesn't support WPL playlists, change this to M3U.

■ **Use Media Information To Arrange Files In Folders On The Disc**   When you burn media to a media disc, Windows Media Player 11 can try to organize it into folders for you, or it can burn all of the files onto the disc without putting them into any folders at all. With this option selected, Windows Media Player 11 uses the artist and album data stored in music files to create a folder structure on your data CD or data DVD that is similar to this:

\Music\Artist Name\Artist Album
\Video\
\TV\

If no information is available about the song's artist or album, it is stored in:

\Music\Unknown Artist\Unknown Album

You can always add your own information or search the Internet to store information in a music file about the artist or album.

■ **Fit More Music On The Disc By Converting To A Lower Bit Rate**   Data CDs and data DVDs can only store a finite amount of data. The number of songs that you can fit on a data CD or data DVD depends on how the song is encoded. A data CD or data DVD can hold more low-quality songs than it can high-quality songs. Windows Media Player 11 can convert songs to a particular quality level—that way, you can fit more songs (or less) on one data CD or data DVD. This option also converts all MP3 or WAV files to WMA format, since the WMA format is smaller. This option may cause some songs to be converted to lower-quality audio, and the burn process will take longer, since some songs may need to be converted. This option is not selected by default.

Next, you'll learn how to synchronize a mobile device like a music or video player with Windows Media Player 11. That way, all you need to do is connect it to your computer. Media Player does the rest of the work, automatically copying the newest and most popular songs to the media device.

Synchronize a Mobile Device with Windows Media Player 11

Windows Media Player 11's Media Library is the place to go for searching and organizing all of your music, pictures, and videos. You can use Media Player to play any file from your Media Library while you're at your computer, or you can use Media Center to play any file from your Media Library with an Xbox 360 in the living room, or even from the den, with Windows Media Center on your PC. Sometimes, however, you're not always at home, or you may not have a computer with you every place you go. This is where a mobile device like a music or video player can be useful. With such a device, you can take your media library with you anywhere.

Windows Media Player 11 automatically detects when you connect a media device to your computer. Once this happens, you can configure Media Player to automatically copy your favorite music or video files based on your latest listening habits. Let's take a closer look at how to set up Windows Media Player 11 for use with your media device.

The first time you connect a media device to your computer, Windows Media Player 11 may ask to search your computer for library files if you haven't added any to the library yet (see Figure 14-5). If you have files on your computer that you want to add to your Media Library, you should do this first.

Next, Windows Media Player 11 asks you to name the media device. This name is only for use with Media Player so that you can distinguish between the different media devices that are connected to your computer (see Figure 14-6). You can change this name later, so don't worry about it too much.

Once you've connected your media device to your computer and have named it, it's time to set up synchronization.

Set Up Synchronization

Synchronization is the process of copying a set of media to your media device from your computer. You can synchronize your device manually when you connect it, or Windows Media Player 11 can automatically start synchronization when it detects the device has been connected.

To set up synchronization:

1. Click the Sync button, and then select your device name on the menu (see Figure 14-7).

2. Click Set Up Sync.

14

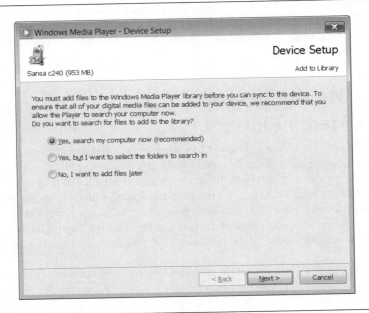

FIGURE 14-5 Adding files to the Media Library

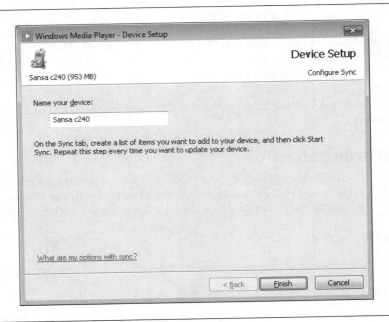

FIGURE 14-6 Provide a name for your media device.

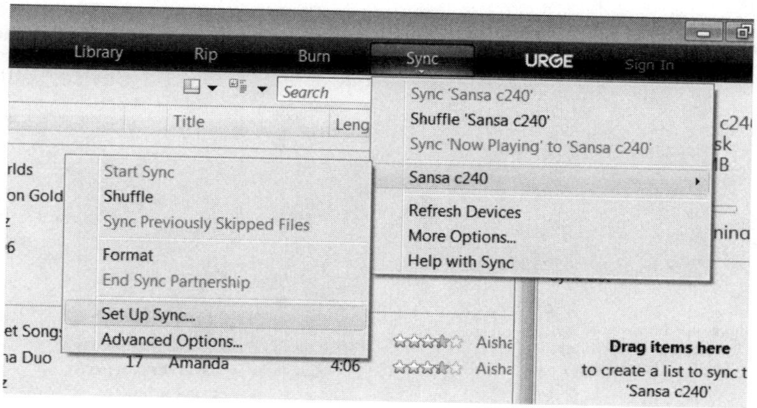

FIGURE 14-7   Sync menu

3. Windows Media Player can synchronize your own playlists, custom auto-playlists, or a set of built-in auto-playlists that comes with Media Player. First, select Sync This Device Automatically (see Figure 14-8). On the left side of the window is a list of all of your personal playlists. On the right side of the window is a list of all of the playlists Windows Media Player 11 will synchronize to the device when you connect it. By default, Windows Media Player 11 adds several playlists, such as "TV recorded in the last week," "Pictures rated at 4 or 5 stars," and more. Remove the playlists that you do not want to synchronize to your device by selecting them and clicking Remove. If you have a music device that cannot show pictures or videos, make sure you remove the picture and video playlists.

4. Remember that the priority of the playlist is governed by the order in which they appear in the list on the right side of the window. Move the playlists that you want to be considered higher priority by selecting them one at a time and then clicking the up arrow in the lower-right corner of the window.

5. If you want to shuffle the playlist, click Shuffle What Syncs, and then click Finish.

Advanced Synchronization Options

Windows Media Player 11 makes synchronizing media devices easy. Just by connecting your media device to your computer, Windows Media Player 11 recognizes it and lets you synchronize videos, pictures, television shows, and music to the device. If you're a more

14

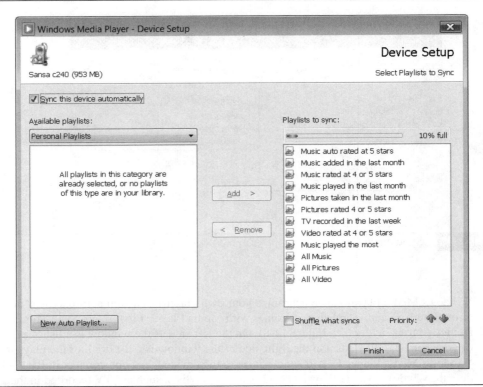

FIGURE 14-8   Synchronization setup

advanced user, however, and you want more control over what gets copied to your media device during synchronization, you can use the advanced options in Media Player to personalize synchronization even further.

To access advanced options:

1. Click the Sync button, and then select your device's name.

2. Click Advanced Options (see Figure 14-9).

There are two tabs in the Advanced Options dialog box: Sync and Quality.

The Sync Tab

On the Sync tab, you can rename your media device by typing a new name into the Device Name text box (see Figure 14-10). You can also disable automatic device synchronization by clearing the Start Sync When Device Connects option.

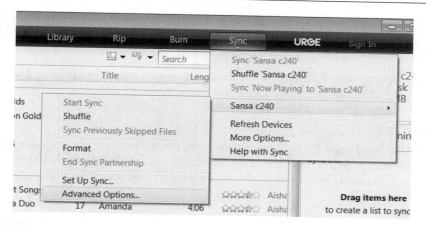

FIGURE 14-9   Accessing the Advanced Options menu

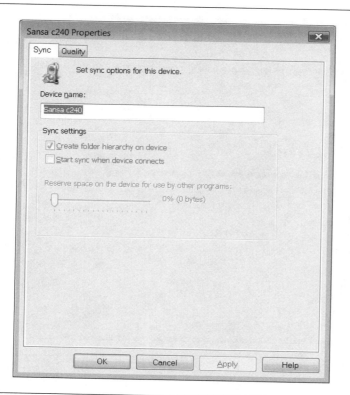

FIGURE 14-10   The Sync tab

14

If you use your media device to store other information, such as documents or applications, you may want to set aside some storage space so that you have room to copy this information to the media device for storage. This is easy to do from the Advanced Options menu: Just use the slider under the Reserve Space On The Device For Use By Other Programs option.

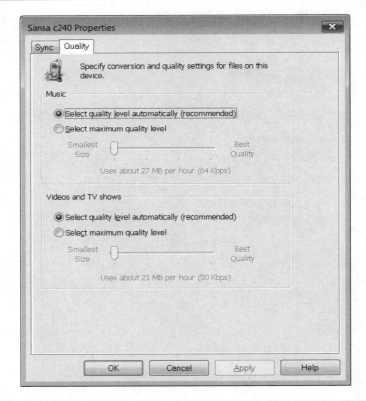

NOTE   *If your device doesn't support storing extra information outside of Windows Media Player 11, the reserved space slider will be disabled.*

The Quality Tab

On the Quality tab (see Figure 14-11), you can adjust the quality level for music files as well as videos and TV shows. Select between setting the quality level automatically and manually setting the maximum quality level. You can fit more data if you use the maximum-quality level

FIGURE 14-11   The Quality tab

option and set the maximum quality level lower, but this will result in lower-quality media files. For example, you may notice that music on your media device doesn't sound nearly as good as it does when you listen to it at your computer. This option follows the same concept that was discussed earlier for burning media to media discs.

Configure Privacy Settings in Media Center

Media Center integrates directly with the Internet so that you can experience additional enhancements, such as the Guide and information about sports, movies, and more. Media Center also integrates with Windows Media Player 11—another application that uses the Internet extensively to retrieve additional information about DVDs, artists, and albums.

To access the privacy settings in Media Center, follow these steps:

1. Open Media Center from the Windows Vista Start menu.
2. Scroll down to Tasks, and then scroll left to Settings.
3. Select General.
4. Scroll down, and select Privacy.

Privacy Policy

Like many Web sites, even Media Center has a privacy policy. This policy describes all of the features in Media Center that may affect your privacy on the Internet. These features include:

- The Electronic Program Guide (EPG)
- Digital tuner with CableCARD
- Enhanced playback and Internet services
- Non-Microsoft Web sites and applications
- Cookies
- Playback of protected digital content
- Enhanced playback of CDs and DVDs
- Usage history within Windows Media Center
- Customer experience

If you are concerned about your privacy and would like to know more about how all of these features affect you, click Online Windows Media Center Privacy Statement.

Privacy Settings

Windows Media Center has two settings that you can change to adjust the protection of your privacy. To access these options, select Privacy Settings.

14

The two privacy settings are:

- **Use The Guide And Send Anonymous Information To Microsoft To Improve The Quality And Accuracy Of The Service**   Media Center will occasionally transmit information to Microsoft about how you use the Guide. This information is entirely anonymous and is not linked to you in any way. It is only used to improve the service.

- **Turn Off The Most Viewed Filter In The Guide**   The Guide may display additional information about programs that you view the most. This may make some people feel uncomfortable. If you are not comfortable with the idea of having your most viewed programs available through the Guide, then select this option.

Customer Experience Improvement Program

The Customer Experience Improvement Program is completely optional. If you join, information will be sent to Microsoft regarding how you use Media Player. No personally identifiable information is ever sent. The Customer Experience Improvement Program only gathers anonymous data so that Microsoft can improve the product in future editions. If you have an Internet connection, you should join the program so that Microsoft can improve future editions of the product. To join:

1. Open Media Center from the Windows Vista Start menu.

2. Scroll down to Tasks, and then scroll left to Settings.

3. Select General, scroll down, and select Privacy.

4. Select Customer Experience Settings, and then select Send Anonymous Usage And Reliability Information To Microsoft.

5. Select Save.

Configure Privacy Options in Media Player 11

Windows Media Player 11 extensively uses the Internet to look for more information about any songs that you play. It also looks for chapter information for DVDs. Media Player does this so that your information can be organized efficiently and accurately so that you, in turn, can find artists, albums, and songs quickly using the Media Library's Search feature. If you've made your own music or DVDs, you might not want Windows Media Player 11 to connect to the Internet and look up more information about your personal music and videos.

If you use an Internet music service such as URGE or Napster, some files may need to be refreshed with the music store, or digital rights information may need to be downloaded to see if you have permission to access the file. Sometimes, you may not want Media Player to do this. In this section, we'll review related privacy options in Windows Media Player 11 and how they affect how you use the program.

To access the privacy options:

1. Click the Now Playing button on the toolbar.

2. Click More Options (see Figure 14-12).

3. Click the Privacy tab (see Figure 14-13).

There are four sections on this tab: Enhanced Playback And Device Experience, Enhanced Content Provider Services, Windows Media Player Customer Experience Improvement Program, and History. We'll review each of these sections next.

Enhanced Playback and Device Experience

Windows Media Player goes beyond playing music and video files. If you have a connection to the Internet, Media Player downloads the latest information about your files in your library. With Enhanced Playback and Device Experience features you can control all of the little details about how Media Player uses the Internet to enhance your media library.

- **Display Media Information From The Internet**   This option controls whether or not Windows Media Player connects to the Internet to find additional information about audio CDs and DVDs you play. Media Player sends a unique identifier for the song or DVD to a Web site. The Web site looks up this unique identifier and sends back any information about the audio CD or DVD. This may be an online music store or a Microsoft-operated music and DVD database, if Windows Media Player 11 can't connect with an online music store. Select or clear this option as desired.

- **Update Music Files By Retrieving Media Info From The Internet**   Sometimes, a music file may be missing important information, such as the artist, album title, or album art. When this happens, Windows Media Player 11 connects to a Microsoft-operated

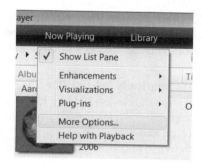

FIGURE 14-12   Selecting More Options

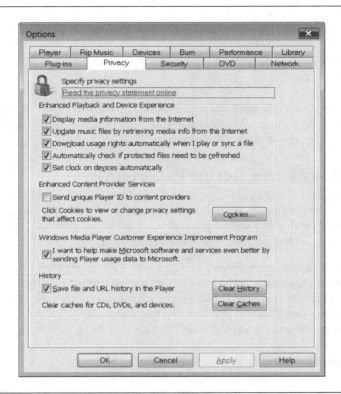

FIGURE 14-13 The Privacy tab

database to search for the information. If the information is found, Media Player may automatically save it to the file. This means that your files are better organized and contain complete data about the artist and album. If you do not want Windows Media Player to search the Microsoft database for more information, clear this option. It is selected by default.

■ **Download Usage Rights Automatically When I Play Or Sync A File** If you purchase music from an online music store in Windows Media Player 11, it is likely protected in a rights management technology that prevents the file from being played or copied without permission. When you purchase and download a song, information is stored about what rights you have with regards to it. This information is only valid for a certain period of time, and then it expires. When it expires, Media Player must check with a server to see if you still have permission for the song. When you play or sync a file, Windows Media

Player 11 sends a unique identifier for the song or video file, a unique identifier for your computer, information about the digital rights management files on your computer, and the action that you're attempting, such as burning the file or playing the file. If this option is not selected, then Media Player will prompt you every time you play a song file that uses rights management technology. This option is selected by default.

- **Automatically Check If Protected Files Need To Be Refreshed**   When you buy rights-protected music or video files, information is stored in the file about how long you have particular rights. This information is only valid for a certain amount of time before Windows Media Player 11 has to contact the online store and see if you still have permission to access it. For example, if you rent a movie from an online store, you may only have permission for three days to play or burn the movie. With this option selected, Windows Media Player 11 automatically scans your library for protected music or video files. When it finds one, it checks with the online store to see if you still have rights for it. When it does this, it sends a unique identifier for the song or video file, a unique identifier for your computer, and information about the digital rights management files on your computer. This option automatically checks to see if you have rights so that you'll be warned when your rights are about to expire. This option is selected by default.

- **Set Clock On Devices Automatically**   Portable devices, like music players and video players, that can play protected music and video files must have a secure clock that keeps track of the current date and time. Windows Media Player 11 sets the current date and time on your portable device to a date and time obtained from a secure Microsoft server. If Media Player can't obtain the current date and time from the secure Microsoft server, then it will not copy files to the portable device. This option is selected by default.

Most of these options had to do with digital rights management. The rest of the privacy options pertain more to your personal use of Media Player, even if you don't use an online store.

Enhanced Content Provider Services

When Windows Media Player communicates with online services to enhance your media library, sometimes additional information about your identity is sent and received. You can control how much information about your identity is sent over the Internet by altering these settings:

- **Send Unique Player ID To Content Providers**   Your computer has a unique identifier so that Web servers can tell when repeated requests are coming from the same computer. There is no way for the Web server to tell any more information about your computer from the unique identifier, other than what it knows from previous connections with the same unique identifier. This information may be used by Internet content providers to gather statistics like how many other videos your computer has watched or how often you use the Web site. It does not provide any other personally identifiable information. If you want to find definite information about how a content provider uses this unique ID, read their privacy policy. This option is not selected by default.

■ **Cookies** This option refers to the cookies-related settings in Internet Explorer. Windows Media Player 11 uses Internet Explorer to communicate with many Internet services. Cookies may be used to provide personalized information on Web sites from content providers. To change this option, click the Cookies button. Remember that this changes settings in Internet Explorer, not in Media Player.

The next section only deals with one setting: the Customer Experience Improvement Program in Windows Media Player 11. You may recognize this program from other Microsoft applications, like Windows Live Messenger and Microsoft Office 2007. This option isn't anything to worry about, and we'll cover it in the next section.

Windows Media Player Customer Experience Improvement Program

Selecting **I Want To Help Make Microsoft Software And Services Even Better By Sending Player Usage Data To Microsoft** option sends anonymous information to Microsoft about how you use Windows Media Player 11 and also information about your computer hardware. This information helps Microsoft identify trends in how people use Media Player, such as options or dialog boxes that may confuse people. No personal information is collected, and no one will ever contact you about this information. It is recommended that you join the Customer Experience Improvement Program; otherwise, Microsoft can never know about how people use Windows Media Player 11 or how to improve it.

History

Some of the options are discussed below.

■ **Save File And URL History In The Player** When you watch a video or movie or play a music file with Media Player, the address to the video, movie, or music file is saved on the File menu for the most recently accessed files. It is also shown in the Open and Open URL dialog boxes. Anyone who uses Windows Media Player 11 can see this information. To stop collecting this information, clear the check box. It is selected by default.

■ **Clear History** When you click this button, all information is deleted regarding the video, movie, and music files that have recently been accessed. This means that no information will appear on the File menu, in the Open dialog box, or in the Open URL dialog box.

■ **Clear Caches** When you click this button, all information is deleted about CDs you have played, DVDs you have watched, and portable devices you have connected to your computer. This also includes information about any watched folders in the Media Library and synchronization relationships with portable devices. If you play a DVD or audio CD, Windows Media Player 11 will have to re-download album art or chapter information. If you want to clear information about a portable device, make sure that you disconnect it first, and then click this button to clear the information pertaining to it.

Part IV

Customize, Create, and Manage Personal Pictures and Home Videos

Chapter 15

Create a Personal Photo and Video Library

How to...

- Navigate Media Center's Pictures + Videos menu
- Import existing photos and video
- View a sample photo and sample video
- Edit your Picture Library
- Configure pictures and video options
- Perform additional video-related tasks

Aside from using Media Center to watch live TV, you have a wealth of options for viewing your personal pictures and home videos. Media Center scans your designated picture and video folders to bring you the latest additions. That's why in this chapter, you'll learn how to work with Windows Photo Gallery as well as photo and video options within Media Center. We'll even go so far as to look at importing and editing options for both pictures and video.

Navigate Media Center's Pictures + Videos Menu

Media Center's Pictures + Videos menu provides one location to view all of your picture and video files. You can view everything you've imported using Windows Photo Gallery, from photos you took using your digital camera to clip art images you've downloaded from the Internet and everything in between—all directly within the Pictures + Videos menu.

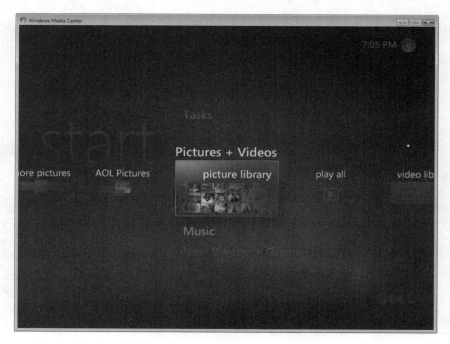

Media Center has four photo and video options (all of which we're going to cover in more detail in this chapter), including:

- Picture Library
- Play All
- Video Library
- More Pictures

Picture Library

Inside the Picture Library, you'll enjoy instant access to all of the images available on your computer. The pictures Media Center offers initially include anything stored in the Sample Music folder. However, once you begin to add your own personal images, the Picture Library expands. To access Media Center's Picture Library, simply click the Picture Library icon under Pictures + Videos from the Media Center main screen. By default, the Picture Library displays as shown in Figure 15-1, with available images displayed by folder.

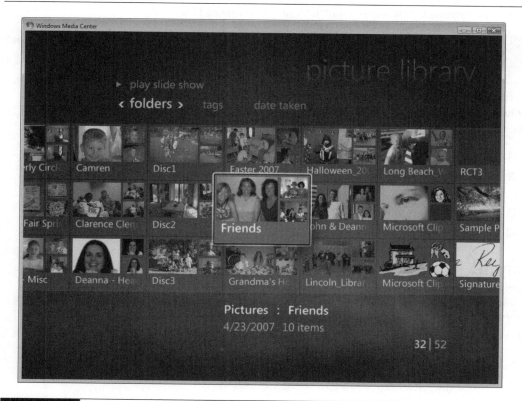

FIGURE 15-1 The Picture Library

15

However, the Folders view shown in Figure 15-1 is just one of many. Inside the Picture Library, using the category options across the top of the window, you can view your images according to the following categories:

- **Folders**   As mentioned, the Folders view displays each folder that contains pictures. By default, the Picture Library watches both default pictures folders: your personal Pictures folder and the Public Pictures folder. If you don't have any subfolders inside either default picture folder, you'll simply see individual images in this view.

- **Tags**   The Tags view displays images grouped by tags you define using Windows Photo Gallery. Tags provide a unique way of categorizing your images beyond folders.

- **Date Taken**   The Date Taken view displays your images grouped by the month and year the image was created.

NOTE   *Once you begin using the Picture Library's views to display your available images, each time you open Media Center, you'll be presented with the most recent view you used instead of the default Folders view.*

If you click any folder in the Picture Library, you will open a new screen that displays only the images contained in the chosen folder, as shown in Figure 15-2.

TIP   *When viewing the thumbnails, you can right-click any to display a shortcut list with several options. Among those options are typically two different views: Large and Small. Use these views to customize the way thumbnails are displayed.*

Each image is represented by a thumbnail; it grows slightly when you rest your mouse over it. Once you see an image thumbnail (in any view), click the image to view the picture in full-screen view. To view a picture in the Picture Library, follow these steps:

1. Click Picture Library, located under Pictures + Videos on the Media Center main screen.

2. Use the navigation criteria at the top of the window to display your images by folders, tags or date taken.

3. Click the folder that contains the image you want to view.

4. Click the image you want to view.

Play All

For those times when you want to view all of the images shown under Pictures + Videos, the Play All option is the one to choose.

Clicking Play All immediately navigates you to a slideshow view, playing all of the images accessible by Media Center in random order (as the default state is Shuffle).

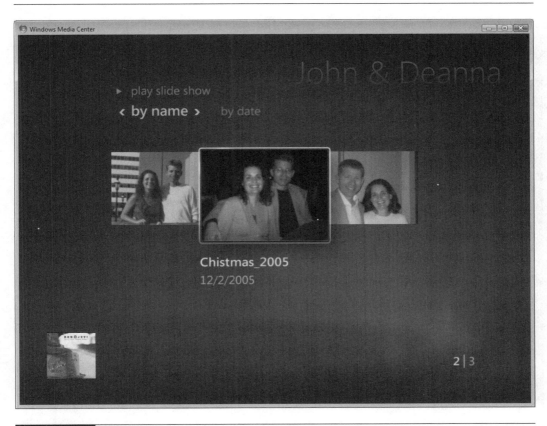

FIGURE 15-2   Each folder displays a set of related thumbnails.

One of the coolest things about this picture slideshow is the way each image slowly zooms in and out, making you feel as though you're watching a movie of your favorite pictures.

Video Library

Inside the Video Library, you'll enjoy instant access to all of the videos available on your computer. The videos Media Center offers initially include anything stored in the Sample Videos folder. However, once you begin to add your own personal videos, the Video Library expands.

To access Media Center's Video Library, simply click the Video Library icon under Pictures + Videos from the Media Center main screen. By default, the Video Library displays as shown in Figure 15-3, with available images displayed by folder.

15

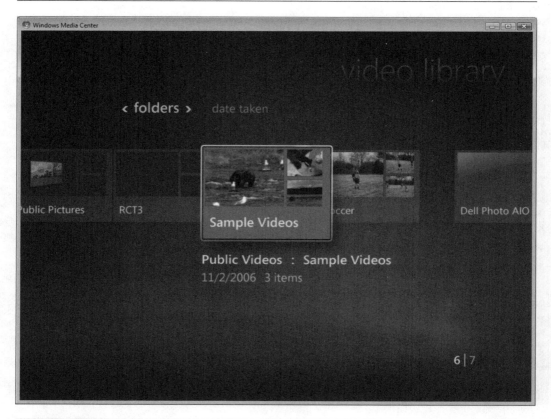

FIGURE 15-3   The Video Library

However, the Folders view shown in Figure 15-3 is just one of many. Inside the Video Library, using the category options across the top of the window, you can view your images according to the following categories:

- **Folders**   As mentioned, the Folders view displays each folder that contains videos. By default, the Video Library watches both default videos folders: your personal Videos folder and the Public Videos folder. If you don't have any subfolders inside either default videos folder, you'll simply see individual images in this view.

- **Date Taken**   The Date Taken view displays your videos grouped by the month and year the video was created.

As with working with the Picture Library, once you begin using the Video Library's views to display your available videos, each time you open Media Center, you'll be presented with the most recent view you used instead of the default Folders view.

If you click any folder in the Video Library, you will open a new screen that displays only the videos contained in the chosen folder, as shown in Figure 15-4.

Each video is represented by a thumbnail; it grows slightly when you rest your mouse over it. Once you see a video thumbnail (in any view), click it to view the video in full-screen view. To watch a sample video, follow these steps:

TIP   *As with working with the Picture Library, when viewing the thumbnails, you can right-click any to display a shortcut list with several options. Among those options are typically two different views: Large and Small. Use these views to customize the way the thumbnails are displayed.*

1. Click Video Library, located under Pictures + Videos on the Media Center main screen.

2. Use the navigation criteria at the top of the window to display your videos by folders or date taken.

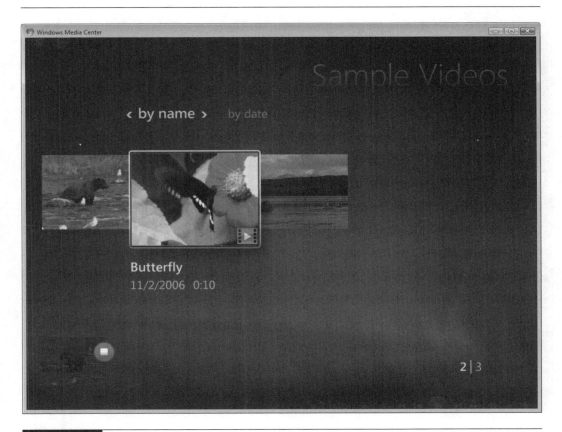

FIGURE 15-4   Each folder displays a set of related thumbnails.

15

3. Click the folder that contains the video you want to view.

4. Click the video you want to watch.

More Pictures

In addition to the pictures available on your computer, you can access more image choices from the More Pictures window, shown in Figure 15-5.

Clicking More Pictures actually opens the same window you see when you click Explore under Online Media. The Explore window offers a navigation bar across the top with the following categories:

- Showcase
- TV + Movies

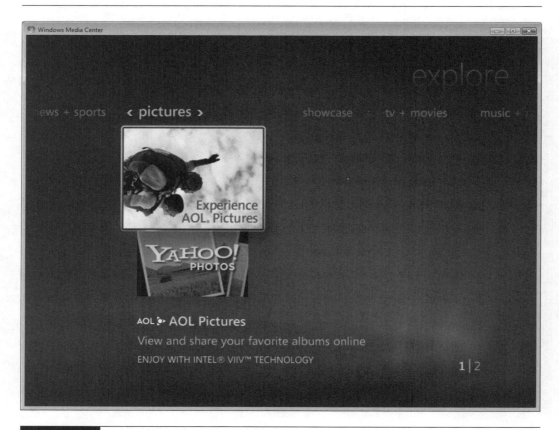

FIGURE 15-5　The Explore Online Media window

- Music + Radio
- News + Sports
- Pictures

Clicking any of the thumbnails shown in the Explore window typically opens a Web site outside of Media Center, but that site is displayed within the Media Center window. Each thumbnail is actually a link to a specific Web site. As such, it's difficult to predict what you'll see when you click each thumbnail. The best way to find out is to click the thumbnails that interest you. From any of the windows, you'll always have access to the Windows button located in the upper-left corner that will direct you safely back to the Media Center main screen.

For example, you can choose Yahoo! Photos to be directed to a Web site that allows you to upload your digital images for printing and creating photo albums you can share with others.

Import Existing Photos and Video

In order to use Media Center to its fullest, you'll want to import all of your media files (images and videos) from all of their different storage locations. If you're like most people, you probably have your media files stored all over the place, including:

- In another computer
- On a digital camera
- Saved on CDs and/or DVDs
- Stored on camcorders
- Located online

Don't worry—you're not alone. However, remember that since Media Center only displays media files you already have stored in other locations, you'll actually need to use a program like Windows Photo Gallery or Windows Media Player to import all of your randomly stored media files. Then, once they're locally stored on your computer or network, Media Center can pick them up.

> NOTE   Importing *simply means copying files stored in other locations to your current computer.*

15

If you're unsure if your media files will work with Media Center, check out the list of importable file extensions in Table 15-1.

Using Windows Photo Gallery

With Windows Photo Gallery, not only can you import your images, you can also use Vista's integrated search features and extreme photo organization capabilities through metadata and captions.

Video	Audio	Picture	Video	Audio	Picture
.asf	.aif	.bmp	.mpe	.mp3	.jpeg
.avi	.aifc	.dib	.mpeg	.mpa	.jpg
dvr-ms	.aiff	.emf	.mpg	.snd	.png
.m1v	.asf	.gif	.mpv2	.wav	.tif
.mp2	.au	.jfif	.wm	.wma	.tiff
.mp2v	.mp2	.jpe	.wmv		.wmf

TABLE 15-1   Importable File Extensions

Much like Media Center, you can use Windows Photo Gallery to view slideshows and burn pictures to a CD. However, you can also use Photo Gallery to import and print pictures.

Using Windows Media Player

When you think of Windows Media Player, you might think it's just for playing music and video. On the contrary, Media Player can also be used to view pictures and live TV.

Although you'll probably prefer Media Center's smooth interface and ease-of-use, you want to use Media Player to upload and view many different types of media.

Media from Another Computer

When moving (or copying) your existing photos and videos from one computer to another, you have a couple of different options. The choice you make will ultimately depend on the materials you have on hand and the level of control you want to maintain. For example, do you want to copy only specific images or everything in a particular folder?

Sneakernet

Offering the most flexibility and control over which files you copy from one computer to another is the old-fashioned "sneakernet." This is when you copy your files to a portable medium (like a CD or DVD) and then walk (with your sneakers) to the next computer.

This method may sound slightly antiquated, but it's actually quite efficient and, best of all, easy. For more information on saving media to a CD or DVD, refer to Chapter 16.

This technique works best when you're copying only a few folders or files. With CDs and DVDs, you're limited slightly to copying as much data as the individual medium can hold.

Windows Easy Transfer

For those times when you have a large amount of files to transfer, using a program such as Windows Easy Transfer may be the choice for you. Windows Easy Transfer comes with Windows Vista, so there's no special setup or installation required. In fact, Easy Transfer is by far the most intuitive file-transfer utility Windows has produced.

Easy Transfer was designed to help you transfer all of your important files, including user accounts and program data files. This wizard can also help you transfer photos, music, and video—everything you need for Media Center.

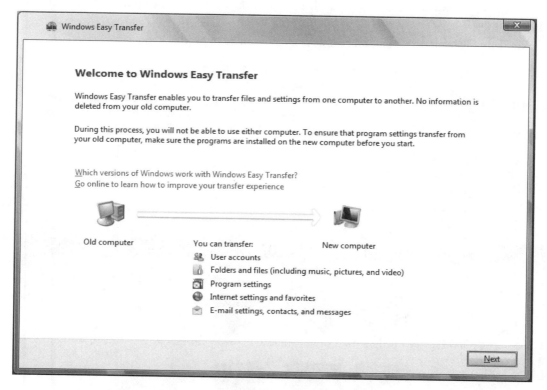

Although you can use Windows Easy Transfer to copy data across a home or small business network to a removable hard disk and to CDs or DVDs, the easiest method is through an Easy Transfer Cable that physically connects two computers for a brief period while the data is transferred.

Windows Easy Transfer is so simple that all you have to do is connect the two computers through an Easy Transfer Cable, and the wizard launches automatically. You will need to purchase an Easy Transfer Cable, but they are readily available from most computer manufacturers and retailers. With an Easy Transfer Cable, you'll receive specific instructions for connecting the two computers.

Media from a Digital Camera

Typically, all you need to do to prepare your computer for your digital camera is to plug the camera in and turn it on. Most of the time, this technique works seamlessly, and Vista locates the

15

appropriate driver information that allows it to recognize your camera each time it's plugged into your computer. To install your camera automatically, follow these steps:

1. Connect your camera using the cable provided when you purchased it to the Universal Serial Bus (USB) or appropriate port.

2. Turn the camera on, and, if necessary, set the camera to playback mode.

Windows Vista should automatically install the latest compatible device driver, either from its preexisting library or from a recent Windows update.

Once the camera driver has been installed, you're ready to import your images from your digital camera to your computer. The easiest place to accomplish this task is by using the Windows Photo Gallery, shown in Figure 15-6. To import images using Windows Photo Gallery, follow these steps:

NOTE *A link for the Windows Photo Gallery can be found on the Start menu. If you don't see it there, type **Photo Gallery** in the Start menu Search box.*

FIGURE 15-6   Windows Photo Gallery

1. Open Windows Photo Gallery.

2. Choose File: Import From Camera Or Scanner.

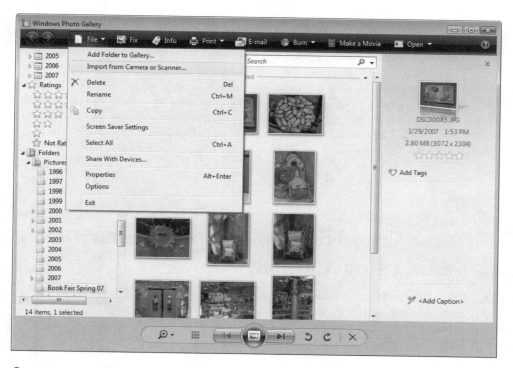

3. Select your camera from the list, and then click Import.

4. Type one or more words to add to the description of each of the imported images. While this step is optional, it can make images easier to find after they've been imported.

5. Whether you choose to enter tags or not, click Import.

TIP *When the Tag dialog box appears, you can choose to add words that best describe your images. However, any words you enter in this box will be added as tags to all imported images. For multiple tags, separate them with semicolons (;).*

Each time you import a new set of images, Windows Photo Gallery places them in your default folder and adds them to the Recently Added list. This makes new images incredibly easy to locate.

NOTE *You can't choose which images on your camera you want to import. Windows Vista will automatically import any file it hasn't seen before. It's always a good idea to check the Recently Added folder to make sure you want to keep every image you've just imported. With the new large thumbnails, Windows Photo Gallery makes it easy to see each image and make the determination as to whether or not you want to keep it.*

How to ... ## Copy Files from a Digital Camera Using AutoPlay

Instead of automatic installation, you may see the AutoPlay dialog box. Typically, this dialog box only offers one option: Open Folder To View Files. If you see this dialog box, click the option to open the folder. Then follow these steps:

1. Choose Organize, and then click Select All. This highlights all of the images stored on the camera.

2. Choose Edit, and then click Copy. This copies each image to the Windows Clipboard, allowing you to choose a different location to copy the images to.

3. Open your personal Pictures folder (or another folder of your choice).

4. Create a new folder in which to store your copied images (this is optional).

5. Right-click the folder you are copying the images to, and then click Paste. Your pictures are copied to the designated folder.

NOTE *By default, imported images are copied to your personal Pictures folder. However, you can change this setting from within Windows Photo Gallery by choosing File and then selecting Options. Once the Options dialog box appears, click the Import tab. Now, all you need to do is click Browse next to Import To, and choose a new folder.*

Media from CDs and DVDs

Images and video stored on CDs and DVDs can easily be imported just by inserting the disc into the computer's CD/DVD drive. Inserting a disc launches the AutoPlay dialog box, shown in Figure 15-7. From the AutoPlay dialog box, under Pictures Options, click Import Pictures. To import media from CDs or DVDs, follow these steps:

NOTE   *As when importing from a digital camera, you'll be given the option of adding tags to the images. Remember that any words you enter in the Tag dialog box will be added to all imported images.*

If the AutoPlay dialog box doesn't appear, or if you just want more control over which files you import, you can import your files using the Copy and Paste commands.

1. Insert the CD or DVD into your CD/DVD drive.

2. On the Start menu, click Computer. The Computer window opens.

3. Double-click the drive associated with the CD/DVD you just inserted. This displays all of the available files on the disc, including images and videos.

4. Select the files you want. To select all files, choose Organize, and then click Select All.

FIGURE 15-7   DVD/CD AutoPlay dialog box

15

5. Choose Organize, and then click Copy. This copies all selected files to the Windows Clipboard.

6. Navigate to the folder you are copying the files to.

7. Choose Organize, and then click Paste.

Media from Camcorders and Video Players

Importing images and video from a camcorder or other video player is a lot like importing media files from a digital camera. Both techniques require the use of a specific transfer cable. Often, the cable you need is included when you purchase your camera.

Whereas a digital camera connects to your computer—most often through a USB port—a digital video camera typically connects through an IEEE 1394 connection. This type of connection provides a high-quality import from camcorder to computer, and for newer devices is definitely the way to go. Many computers have a corresponding IEEE 1394 connection on the front of the computer. This connection is smaller than a USB connection and rectangular in shape.

However, if you have a computer than supports streaming over a USB port, you can connect your device using this method. When in doubt, check your device manufacturer's Website for the connection cable you'll need to use.

Typically, all you need to do to prepare your computer for your camcorder is to plug the camcorder in and turn it on. Most of the time, this technique works seamlessly, and Vista locates the appropriate driver information that allows it to recognize your camera each time it's plugged into your computer. To install your camcorder (or other device) automatically, follow these steps:

1. Connect your camcorder using the appropriate cable to the IEEE 1394 (or appropriate) port.

2. Turn the camcorder on, and set it to playback mode.

Windows Vista should automatically install the latest compatible device driver, either from its preexisting library or from a recent Windows update.

Once the device driver has been installed, you're ready to import your media to your computer. The easiest place to accomplish this task is by using the Windows Photo Gallery.

About Video Formats

One of the choices you'll need to make when importing video is the format. This doesn't have to be a random guess. The video format, quite simply, determines the video file type. Among the choices are:

■ **Windows Media Video (WMV)**   Windows Media Video is Microsoft's proprietary compression format for video. This file type uses Windows Media Player for media delivery.

■ **Audio Interleaved (AVI)**   Audio Interleaved files are typically larger than WMV files. This file type uses the default player specified by the local computer for media delivery. Generally, the AVI file type is the one that is created when clips are imported from a digital camcorder to a computer.

How to ... Import Video Using Windows Photo Gallery

1. Open Windows Photo Gallery.
2. Choose File: Import From Camera Or Scanner.
3. Select your camcorder from the list, and then click Import.

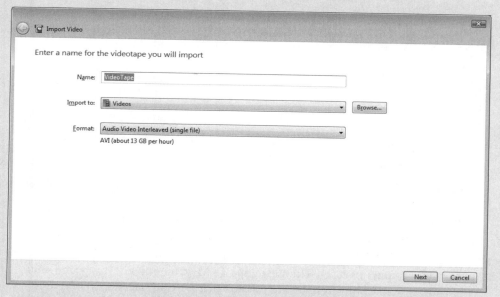

4. Enter a name for the imported video.
5. Select a folder location for the imported video.
6. Choose a video format, and then click Next.

(Continued)

15

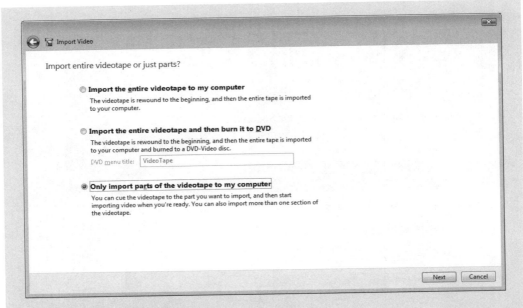

7. Choose one of the following options:

■ **Import The Entire Videotape To My Computer**   This option imports the contents of the entire videotape.

■ **Import The Entire Videotape And Then Burn It To DVD**   This option imports the contents of the entire videotape and burns it to a DVD disc with a DVD title of your choice.

■ **Only Import Parts Of The Videotape To My Computer**   This option offers the most flexibility by allowing you to watch the video and import only sections of the recorded media.

8. Click Next to begin the import process.

9. Follow the on-screen instructions. These instructions are specific to what you want to import and whether or not you are burning the import to a DVD immediately.

NOTE   *You can also import video using Windows Movie Maker by choosing File and then choosing Import From Digital Video Camera in the Windows Movie Maker program.*

Media from Online Sources

The number of online sources for video and other media entertainment is constantly increasing. Several online options are available through Windows Media Player and Media Center.

FIGURE 15-8   The TV + Movies screen in the Explore Online Media window

To see the options available in Media Center, click Explore under Online Media on the main screen. This opens the Explore window shown in Figure 15-8.

Each online option takes you to a different screen based on the thumbnail you click. These options are often as individual as the company each thumbnail represents. However, at a minimum, you have access to a whole host of television clips and movies you can purchase and download.

View a Sample Photo and Sample Video

Media Center comes preloaded with several sample photos and videos. For each category—photos and videos—Media Center offers a few samples to help get you started working with images and video. These are great files to practice with when you're first learning to work with your photos and videos in Media Center.

15

Navigate to Sample Media

Sample photos are stored in your personal Pictures folder under Sample Pictures, while sample videos are stored in your personal Videos folder under Sample Videos.

To view the 12 sample photos, follow these steps:

1. On the Media Center main screen, under the Pictures + Videos category, click Picture Library.

2. Click the Sample Pictures thumbnail. This displays the available sample pictures shown in Figure 15-9.

3. To view any image full-screen, click its thumbnail. To return to the sample picture thumbnails, click the Back arrow in the upper-left corner. To return to the Media Center main screen, click the Windows button in the upper-left corner.

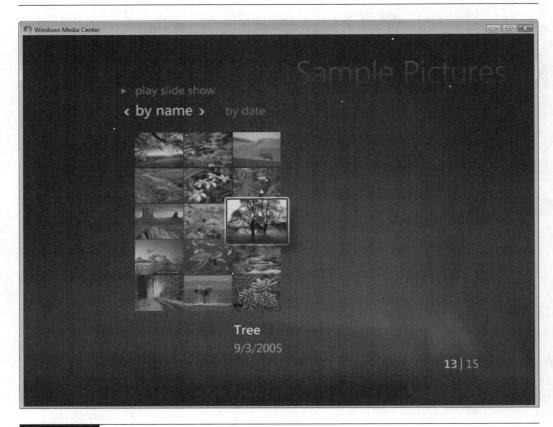

FIGURE 15-9   Sample pictures in Media Center

To view the three sample videos, follow these steps:

1. On the Media Center main screen, under the Pictures + Videos category, click Video Library.

2. Click the Sample Videos thumbnail. This displays the available sample videos shown in Figure 15-10.

3. To view any video full-screen, click its thumbnail. To return to the sample video thumbnails, click the Back arrow in the upper-left corner. To return to the Media Center main screen, click the Windows button in the upper-left corner.

NOTE *You can also view the sample pictures and videos using Windows Media Player or opening the folder each one is stored in. Pictures are easy to find because there's a link on the Start menu to the Pictures folder. However, videos are a little trickier to locate. To open the Videos folder, type **Videos** in the Start menu Search box. This displays the Videos folder in the Start menu temporarily for easier access.*

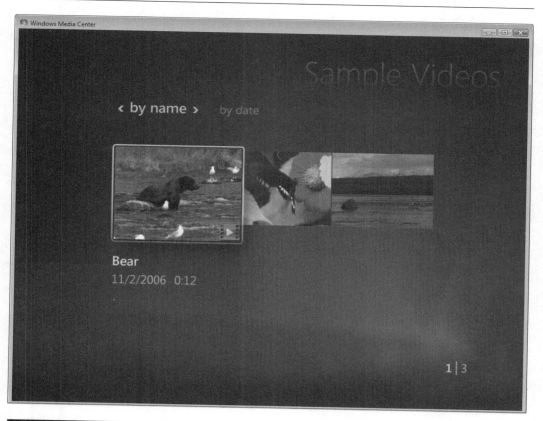

FIGURE 15-10   Sample videos in Media Center

15

Play a Slideshow

A slideshow is a presentation of a series of pictures of your choice, which are most often grouped together by one of the sorting options listed in the Picture Library (folder, date taken, or tag).

To view all pictures in your Picture Library, open the Picture Library, and then click Play (located at the top of the window). Your pictures are displayed in the order they appear in the Picture Library. While you can use the slideshow toolbar buttons (shown at the bottom of the window) to pause or move back and forward between slides, you can also use your UP ARROW and DOWN ARROW keys on the keyboard. To play a slideshow for specific pictures, follow these steps:

TIP *When viewing a slideshow, if you don't see the toolbar in the lower-right corner of the screen, just move your mouse slightly. This movement will display the navigation toolbar.*

For those times when you only want to view specific images, it's best to have those images stored in their own folder. This way, you can view a slideshow comprised of only the images that are grouped together.

1. On the Media Center main screen, under Pictures + Videos, click Picture Library.
2. Using the grouping options at the top, display your photos.
3. Click a collection of pictures. Depending on how Windows Media Center has grouped your content, pictures are sorted by folders, date taken, or tags.
4. Click Play Slide Show.

Configure Slideshow Settings

At any point during a slideshow, you can right-click the window to display a shortcut menu. From the shortcut menu, choose Settings to access the main Settings window.

TIP *You can also open the main Settings window from the Media Center main screen by clicking Settings, which is located under Tasks.*

From the main Settings window, click Pictures to modify how pictures are displayed during a slideshow. The Pictures Settings window is shown in Figure 15-11.

For your slideshows, you can specify the following options:

■ **Picture Order**   Selecting the Show Pictures In Random Order check box will display the pictures in a slideshow using a different random order each time the slideshow is played.

■ **Show Pictures In Subfolders**   Selecting Show Pictures In Subfolders shows any photos saved in subfolders inside the main slideshow folder that was chosen.

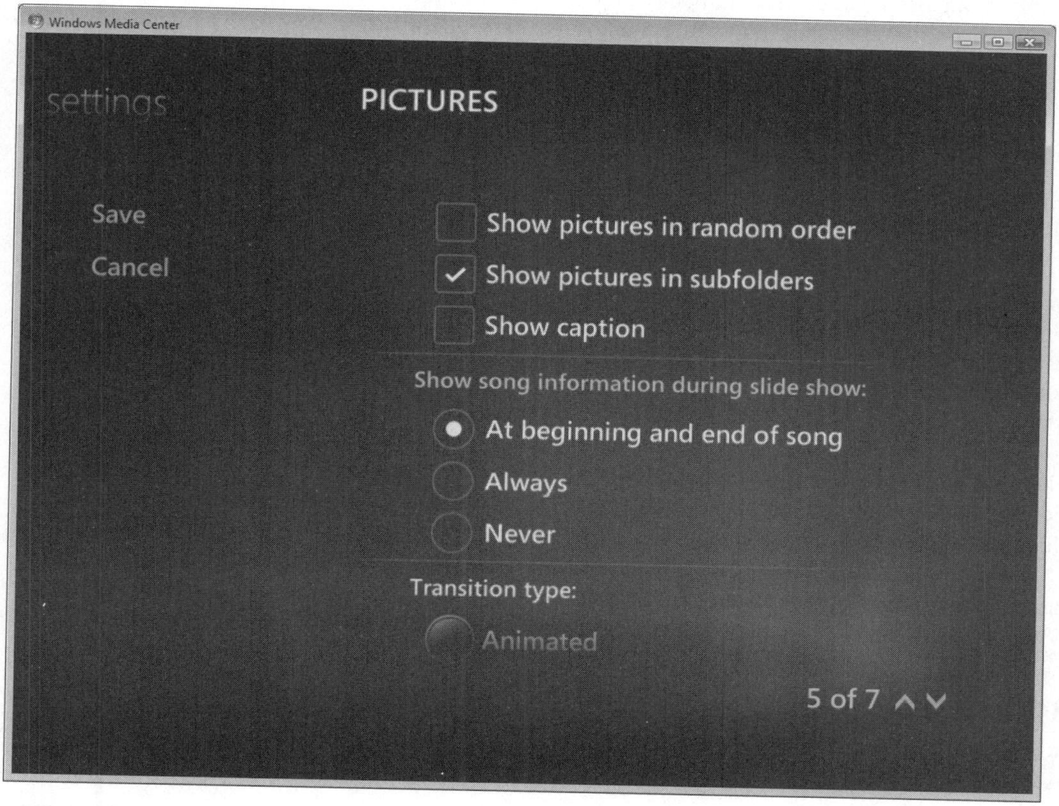

FIGURE 15-11   Picture settings in Media Center

■ **Caption**   Selecting Show Caption will display any custom captions that have been added to the images, along with the images in the slideshow.

■ **Song Information**   If music is playing in the background while the slideshow is running, you can choose when (if ever) you see the song information.

■ **Transition Type**   Choose the type of transition you want. You can choose between Animated, Cross Fade, and None.

15

- ■ **Transition Time**   The number entered in the Transition Time box determines the length of time between transitions. Essentially, this number defines how long each individual image is displayed by setting the amount of time that elapses from one transition to the next.
- ■ **Background Color**   The Background Color option sets the color of the area behind the displayed images to white, 50% gray, or black.

After you have specified your slideshow settings, click Save. The settings will be applied to all future slideshows.

Edit Your Photo Library

Printed photos can quickly become scattered unless you neatly organize them into photo albums. Your digital photos are no different. Organizing digital photos is as necessary as putting printed photos into albums—that is, if you want to be able to easily locate them again.

Furthermore, how many times have you looked through a stack of photos only to forget when it was taken—or worse—who is in the photo? So you flip it over only to discover you didn't make any notes on the back. Believe it or not, it's just as difficult to recognize people in old photos stored on your computer. That's where metadata comes in.

Storing information about your images and grouping similar images together in a folder are easily done using Windows Photo Gallery. In addition, any organization levels you create in Windows Photo Gallery automatically translate to how you view your images in Media Center.

Add Metadata

In a nutshell, the term "metadata" refers to "data about data." In terms of your digital pictures, examples of metadata include *date taken, subjects, photographer, file size, title, rating, comments, tags.*

When you upload your digital photos, they typically have some preexisting metadata, such as date taken and file size. In Windows Photo Gallery, you can customize much of the metadata, including tags, captions, and rating.

Tags

Using descriptive file names is a great way to organize your pictures, but it doesn't make images particularly easy to locate. However, all of that changes with tags.

Tags are metadata you can add to your images. It's like putting one picture in several photo albums. For example, if you have a picture of two children, you can only give it one file name, but you can assign multiple tags. This means that you can add a tag for each child and still maintain only one photo. To add tags to your digital pictures to make them easier to locate, follow these steps:

1. Open Windows Photo Gallery.

2. Double-click the picture you want to tag. This opens the image in a larger view with the Info pane on the right, as shown in the following illustration.

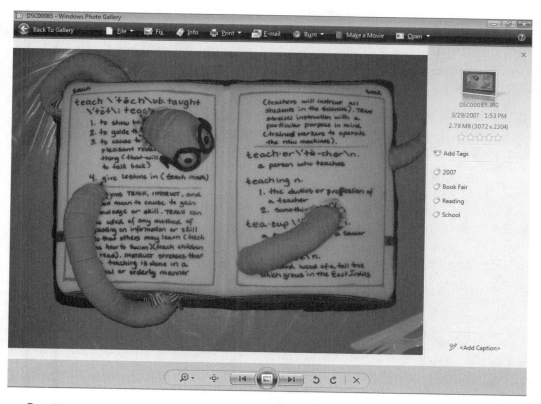

3. Click Add Tag in the Info pane on the right side of the window.
4. Type the word or phrase for tag, and then press ENTER.
5. To add additional tags, click Add Tag, and repeat steps 1–4.
6. When you've finished adding tags, click Back To Gallery in the toolbar.

15

TIP *To add the same tag to several images, select the images you want to tag in the Gallery by holding down CTRL as you click each one. Right-click one of the images, click Add Tag, and follow the steps in the procedure.*

In the Info pane, you can also add a caption and rate the picture. You can rate pictures from to one to five stars.

The number of tags you can add to any one image is virtually limitless. And with each new tag, a new method of organization is added to the Windows Photo Gallery, as the new tag is displayed in the navigation pane, shown in Figure 15-12.

TIP *To add an image to an existing tag (without typing), try dragging. That's right! In the Windows Photo Gallery, you can drag an image displayed in the main pane on top of the chosen tag in the navigation pane to add that tag to the selected image.*

Not only do tags allow you to easily navigate to specific photos using the navigation pane, but they also provide a quick search term. To find an image with a specific tag or other metadata,

FIGURE 15-12   Windows Photo Gallery navigation pane

such as captions, just type the tag name in the Search box (located in the upper-right portion of the Photo Gallery window, just below the toolbar).

Captions

Remember all those notes you typically write (or, at the very least, intend to write) on the back of hard-copy photos? The digital equivalent is captions. With captions, you can make notes about individual images. This way, when you look at the pictures years from now, you'll remember what the photo was about and, maybe more importantly, who is in the photo. To add a caption to a picture, follow these steps:

1. Open Windows Photo Gallery.
2. Double-click the picture you want to add a comment to. This opens the image in a larger view.
3. Click Add Caption on the bottom of the Info pane.
4. Type a caption, and then press ENTER.

Ratings

Just like tags and captions, ratings are another form of metadata that you can customize. With ratings, there are five levels of stars. As with many ratings systems, the more stars, the better the image.

You can rate your own images by clicking the appropriate number of stars in the Info pane (either in full-image view or in Gallery view), as shown in Figure 15-13.

Once you've assigned ratings to your images, you can use the navigation pane shown in Figure 15-14 to view your photos based on your ratings.

FIGURE 15-13   Click the star that best represents your rating for the selected picture.

15

FIGURE 15-14   Click a ratings level to display images assigned to it.

Group Similar Photos

There are several ways in Windows Photo Gallery to group your photos. You've already learned about assigning tags, captions, and ratings. But let's take this a step further and look at other ways you can group similar photos.

One way is to create nested groups of tags. You may find that once you start creating tags, it soon feels as though you have as many tags as you have pictures. For example, consider the following possible tags:

- Apples
- Bananas
- Oranges
- Pears

These are all specific. But they all could feasibly be placed in a larger tag named Fruit. This allows individual tags to be specific, with a slightly more generic main tag.

Creating nested groups of tags is extremely helpful, as it allows you to collapse and expand the top-level tag as if it were a folder with subfolders. This way, you can hide the tags you don't need and narrow your focus, as shown in Figure 15-15. To create nested groups of tags, follow these steps:

1. Create the tags as normal.

2. Using the navigation pane, drag each tag you want to be nested on top of the tag you want to make the top-level tag.

3. Repeat for each nested tag.

FIGURE 15-15   Nesting tags makes finding photos assigned to specific categories easier.

How to ...   Rename Multiple Pictures at One Time

Beyond tags, you can globally rename a group of images. This is particularly useful for imported images. If you have a digital camera, you've probably noticed the camera doesn't give very descriptive file names, choosing instead to apply names like DSC001.jpg and P000123.jpg. While renaming each photo would be the most organized method, it's often far too time-consuming.

However, you can eliminate the virtually meaningless file names in favor of ones that are more descriptive. For example, a group of newly uploaded photos from a soccer game could take on names like April_Soccer (1).jpg and April_Soccer (2).jpg. If you provide the file name, Windows Photo Gallery will add consecutive numbers to the end. How great is that?

And the steps are:

1.   Open Windows Photo Gallery.

2.   Select all of the pictures you want to rename.

3.   Right-click one of the selected pictures, and choose Rename from the shortcut menu.

4.   In the Info pane, type a new name (without the numbers), and then press ENTER.

15

TIP *You can create a nested tag at the same time you create and assign a tag to a picture by adding a slash (/) between the top-level tag and the nested tag. For example, type **Fruit/ Apple** to add the Apple tag nested under Fruit.*

Configure Pictures and Video Options

Using Media Center to view your pictures and videos creates a memorable slideshow presentation that looks like a professional spent many hours creating. But, really, it's all in the options that you define in the Settings window, shown in Figure 15-16.

From the Settings window, you can change everything from picture transition type and time between pictures to the default background color and more.

Show Pictures in Random Order

By default, when you view a slideshow, the order the pictures are displayed on the screen is based on their order in the folder in which they are saved, which is typically alphabetically by file name.

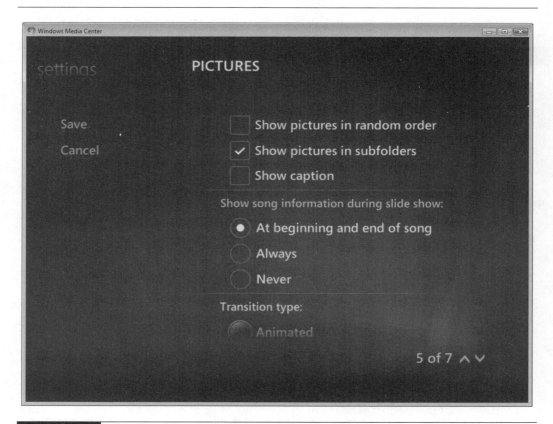

FIGURE 15-16 Customize Media Center's Picture Settings

But to see your pictures in a different order each time you play the slideshow, you can choose to view your images in random order. This is done from the Settings window, as shown in Figure 15-16. To display your pictures in random order, follow these steps:

1. On the Media Center main screen, under Tasks, click Settings. The Settings window opens.

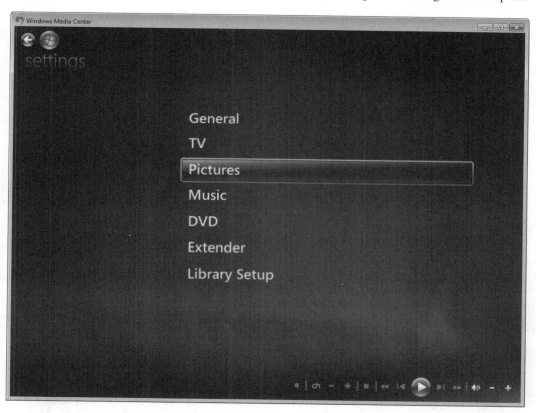

2. Click Pictures. This displays the options for displaying pictures and slideshow settings. Choose whether pictures display during a slideshow in normal or random order.

3. Select the Show Pictures In Random Order check box. This causes the picture to be displayed randomly.

4. Click Save. This saves your changes and returns you to the Settings window.

5. Click the Windows button in the upper-left corner to return to the Media Center main screen.

TIP   *At any point during a slideshow, you can right-click the window to display a shortcut menu. From the shortcut menu, choose Settings to access the main Settings window.*

Show Song Information

If music is playing in the background while the slideshow is running, you can choose when (if ever) you see the song information.

As you can see in Figure 15-17, when the song information is displayed, it appears in the lower-left corner of the slideshow window.

FIGURE 15-17   Choose when song information displays during a slideshow.

There are three options for when song information is displayed:

- **At The Beginning And End Of Song**   The song information caption displays only at the beginning and end of each song.
- **Always**   The song information caption is always visible on the slideshow screen.
- **Never**   The song information caption is never visible on the slideshow screen.

To change when song information displays, follow these steps:

1. On the Media Center main screen, under Tasks, click Settings. The Settings window opens.
2. Click Pictures. This reveals the options for displaying pictures and slideshow settings.
3. Choose when song information displays during a slideshow, as shown in the following illustration.

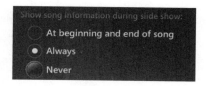

4. Choose At The Beginning And End Of Song, Always or Never.
5. Click Save. This saves your changes and returns you to the Settings window.

Select Transition Type and Time

Two settings related to how the pictures are displayed in the slideshow are transition type and transition time. The effect you see when one picture leaves the slideshow and another appears is the transition; while the length of time between transitions is known as the transition time.

There are three options for transition settings:

- Animated
- Cross Fade
- None

To change the picture transition type or time, follow these steps:

1. On the Media Center main screen, under Tasks, click Settings. The Settings window opens.
2. Click Pictures. This reveals the options for displaying pictures and slideshow settings.
3. Choose the transition type—Animated, Cross Fade, or None—as shown in the following illustration. If you don't see the Transition Type area, use the arrows in the lower-right corner of your screen to scroll up or down as needed.

4. Click Save. This saves your changes and returns you to the Settings window.

15

Along with transition type, you can change the transition time. The number entered in the Transition Time box determines the length of time between transitions. That is, this number defines how long each individual image is displayed. To change the picture transition time, follow these steps:

1. On the Media Center main screen, under Tasks, click Settings. The Settings window opens.

2. Click Pictures. This reveals the options for displaying pictures and slideshow settings.

3. Choose the transition time. Use the plus sign (+) and minus sign (–) buttons to increase or decrease the transition time.

4. Click Save. This saves your changes and returns you to the Settings window.

Configure Background Color

The final slideshow setting you can modify is the background color. There are three background colors to choose from:

- White
- 50% gray
- Black

To change the background color, follow these steps:

1. On the Media Center main screen, under Tasks, click Settings. The Settings window opens.

2. Click Pictures. This reveals the options for displaying pictures and slideshow settings.

3. Choose the background color. Use the plus sign (+) and minus sign (–) buttons to choose White, 50% Gray, or Black.

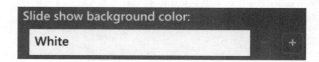

4. Click Save. This saves your changes and returns you to the Settings window.

Additional Video Tasks

Slideshows provide a way to create motion on still images. However, when you work with videos, you obviously have a few additional options. Videos are actual moving images, and the controls are similar to those used when operating a CD or DVD player.

However, beyond working the controls to play a video, it's helpful to know how to locate videos and sort them for easy access.

Find a Video

Once you've been using Media Center for any amount of time to store and watch your videos, you may find it becomes increasingly difficult to locate a specific video. That's where the Search feature comes in handy. However, unlike the Music category, the Pictures + Videos category doesn't have its own Search option. So to search for videos, you'll need to do a small amount of digging.

The most obvious place to locate videos is in the Videos folders. But since Vista doesn't provide a quick shortcut to this folder from the Start menu, you'll first have to search for the Videos folder. Luckily, there's the handy Search box on the Start menu. To locate the Videos folder, follow these steps:

1. Click the Start button, and then type **Videos** in the Search box.

2. Click Videos at the top of the Start menu. This opens the Videos folder.

15

You may have individual videos displayed here or videos saved in subfolders. Double-click any video to open Windows Media Player and watch it.

How to ... Use Windows Media Player to Find Videos

If you have videos saved in places other than the Videos folders, you can use Windows Media Player to locate them. Just follow these steps:

1. Open Windows Media Player.
2. Click the Library tab, and from the menu, choose Video.

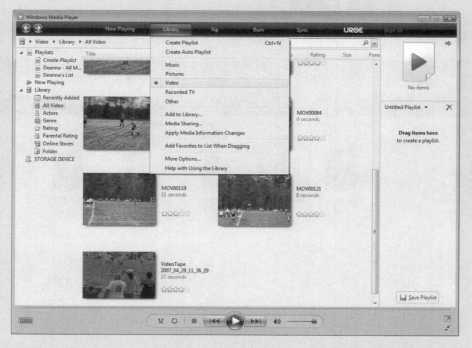

The available videos are shown as thumbnails. Double-clicking any of them plays the video from the beginning.

If you know you have videos that you don't see in Media Center, it could be that Media Center doesn't know to look in the folder in which they are stored. By default, Media Center looks in:

- Picture (Users and Public)
- Videos
- Recorded TV

However, if you're storing your media in a different location, you'll need to tell Media Center about these additional folders.

To set up Media Center to search additional folders for media (including videos and pictures), follow these steps:

1. On the Media Center main screen, under Tasks, click Settings.

2. Click Library Setup. This displays the Library Setup screen.

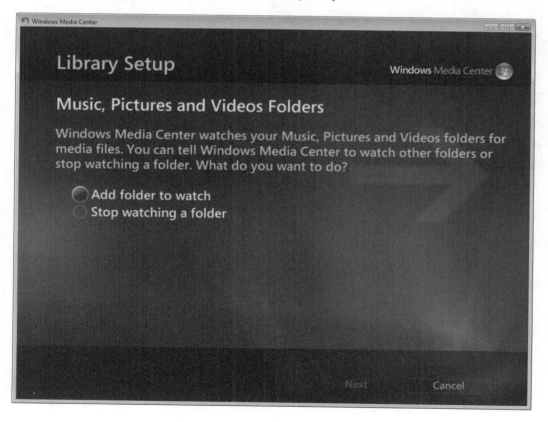

3. Click Add Folder To Watch, and then click Next.

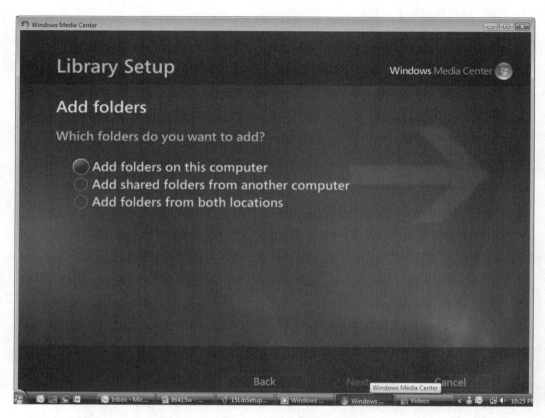

4. Choose one of the following options, and then click Next:

- Add Folders On This Computer
- Add Shared Folders From Another Computer
- Add Folders From Both Locations

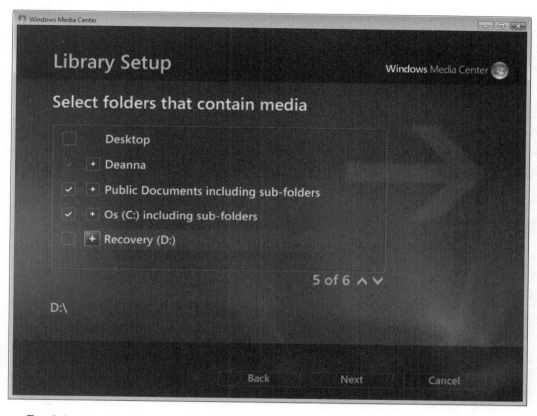

5. Select the check box next to any folder you want Media Center to "watch." When you've selected all necessary folders, click Next.

15

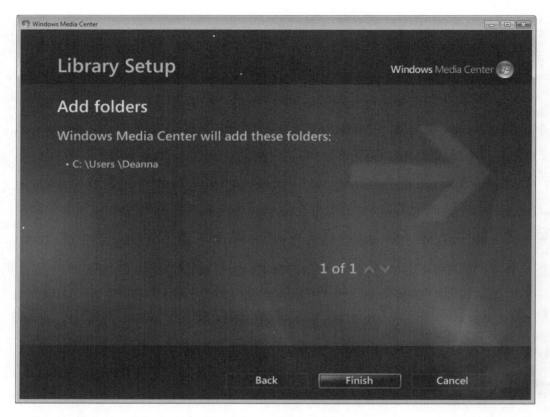

6. Click Finish. Depending on the strength of your network connections and the number of folders you choose to watch, it may take several seconds to several minutes for the new files to appear in the Music Library. Click OK if you wish to continue using Media Center while the media is added.

Sort Videos

When you click Video Library (located under Pictures + Videos on the Media Center main screen), you see a list of available videos stored on your computer. Typically, these videos are arranged in alphabetical order by folder name, as shown in Figure 15-18.

However, the Folders view shown in Figure 15-18 is only one of two viewing options. Inside the Music Library, using the category options across the top of the window, you can view your music by:

- ■ **Folders**   As previously mentioned, the Folders view displays each folder (or video) as a thumbnail, and when highlighted with the mouse, shows the folder storage location, date, and the number of videos in the highlighted folder.

- ■ **Date Taken**   The Date Taken view, shown in Figure 15-19, organizes the video folders by month and year.

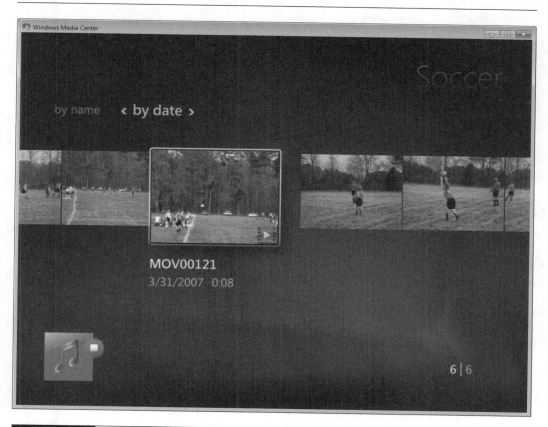

FIGURE 15-18   The Folder view in the Video Library is one of two available views in Media Center.

15

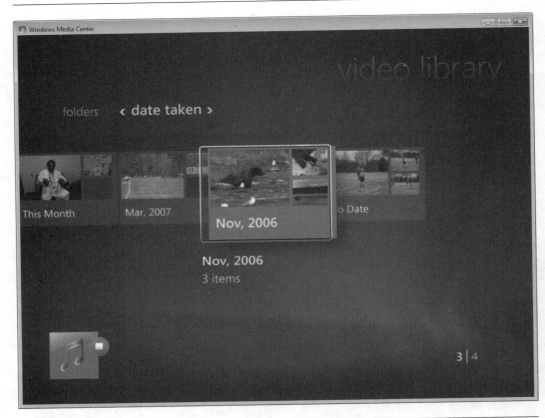

FIGURE 15-19   The Date Taken view in the Video Library is one of two available views in Media Center.

Play a Video

Finding a video is the hard part. Once you've located the video you want to watch in Media Center, playing it is easy. All you have to do is click the video thumbnail, and the video clip immediately launches. Or, if you're a keyboard fan, you can also highlight the video thumbnail using the arrow keys on the keyboard, and then press CTRL-SHIFT-P to play the highlighted video. Once your video has finished playing, you can view it again by clicking Restart as shown in Figure 15-20.

Actually, when the video reaches the end, you have three options:

- ■ **Done**   Returns you to the previous screen and displays the available videos.
- ■ **Restart**   Plays the video again from the beginning.
- ■ **Delete**   Deletes the video from Media Center and your computer.

FIGURE 15-20 When a video reaches the end, you can view it again by clicking Restart.

Control Playback

Once the video begins playing, a whole row of navigation elements is shown across the lower-right edge of the window. This navigation row is similar to the Play and Pause buttons you'll see when you watch TV inside Media Center. Luckily, the buttons in each case (watching TV and watching a video) perform the same functions.

15

The first few buttons (Record and Channel Down and Channel Up) are grayed out and unavailable when watching a video. However, the remaining buttons work fine and are (in order from left to right):

- Stop
- Rewind
- Go To The Beginning
- Play/Pause
- Go To The End
- Fast-Forward
- Mute
- Decrease Volume
- Increase Volume

Sometimes, working with these playback settings is easier using the keyboard. Table 15-2 lists some handy keyboard shortcuts for watching your videos in Media Center.

A common point of confusion lies in figuring out the difference between the Stop button and the Play/Pause button. After all, both of these, when clicked, stop playing the video. While that's true, there is a distinct difference.

The Play/Pause button simply pauses the movie at the current location without offering additional options. When clicked, the Play/Pause button changes so that when it's clicked again the video resumes playing. The Play/Pause button is more of a toggle option, whereas the Stop button is an option button, offering several choices when clicked (see Figure 15-21), including:

- **Done**   Stops the video and returns you to the previous screen.
- **Resume**   Plays the video from its current position.
- **Restart**   Plays the video from the beginning.
- **Delete**   Deletes the video from Media Center and your computer.

To	Press	To	Press
Stop	CTRL-SHIFT-+S	Mute	F8
Skip	CTRL-F	Volume down	F9
Pause	CTRL-P	Volume up	F10

TABLE 15-2   Video Playback Keyboard Shortcuts

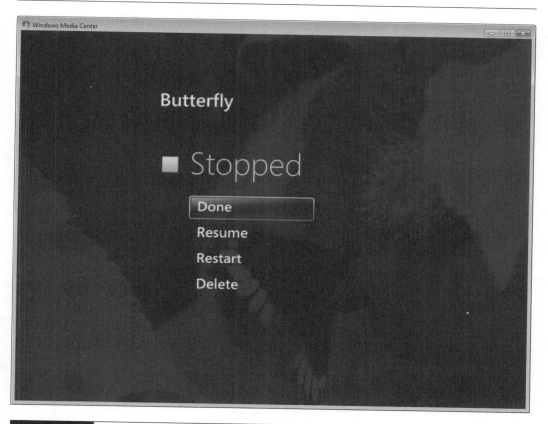

FIGURE 15-21   The Stop button offers several choices.

15

Chapter 16

Share Your Photos and Videos

How to...

- Edit pictures
- E-mail your pictures
- Burn pictures to a CD
- Create a DVD of pictures to play on your DVD player
- Get photos printed online
- Search the Photo Library
- Create and save search folders

Sharing your photos can be just as important as organizing them. However, occasionally, you may wish to make some minor changes to your images, such as reducing the appearance of red eye and adjusting the image contrast, before sending them on to others. You can make such edits using Media Center.

Once the edits have been made, you have a few different options for sharing your images, including e-mail, CDs, DVDs and online print options. You'll learn about all of these in this chapter.

Edit Pictures

Media Center offers a few options for editing your images, including the popular red-eye reduction. From within Media Center, you can:

- **Rotate** Rotating allows you to display all of your images at the proper angle. For instance, some images appear to be lying on their side. With these images, you can use the Rotate command to flip an image so that it displays in an upright position.

- **Print** Printing from within Media Center allows you to print a full-page image based on the selected picture.

- **Touch Up** With this option, you'll access several additional editing options, including:

  - **Contrast** Based on the original image, the contrast option applies an automatic lightening or darkening to the selected image.

  - **Fix Red Eye** This option locates instances of red eye in your digital photos and works to correct the problem.

  - **Crop** To remove external portions (or people) from your pictures, you can use the Crop feature.

Each of these options is image-specific. This means that you can edit each image individually for maximum results. Many of these edits can be accomplished by using the Picture Details window, a portion of which is shown in Figure 16-1.

| FIGURE 16-1 | Many picture-editing options can be accessed from the left side of Picture Details window. |

Rotate

Rotating allows you to display all of your images at the proper angle. For instance, some images appear to be lying on their side. This is typically due to the position of the camera at the time the photo was taken. With these images, you can use the Rotate command to flip an image so that it displays in an upright position. To rotate an image in Media Center, follow these steps:

1. On the Media Center main screen, under Pictures + Videos, click Picture Library.

2. Right-click any picture you want to rotate, and then choose Picture Details from the shortcut menu.

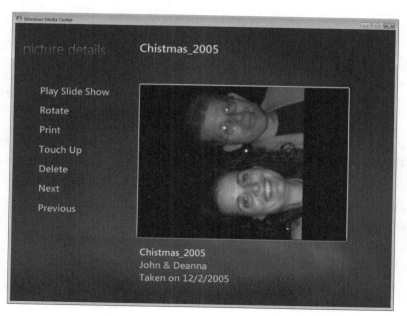

16

3. Click the Rotate option (located to the left of the image) one time for each 90-degree rotation.

4. Click Save.

5. If prompted, click Yes to confirm that you want to save the changes. This saves your rotation changes and returns you to the previous menu.

> **TIP**
>
> *In Media Center, you can only rotate an image one direction: 90 degrees to the right. This means that if you need to rotate an image 90 degrees to the left, you'll need to click the Rotate command three times.*

Contrast

The contrast of an image refers to the difference in tone between its light and dark areas. The Contrast command applies an automatic lightening or darkening to the selected image, based on the original image. Because this is an automatic process, the guesswork has been taken out of applying the right contrast level. To adjust the contrast of an image, follow these steps:

1. On the Media Center main screen, under Pictures + Videos, click Picture Library.

2. Right-click any picture you want modify, and then choose Picture Details from the shortcut menu.

3. Click Touch Up. This displays the Touch Up window, shown in Figure 16-2.

4. Click Contrast. This applies the automatic contrast formatting to the selected image.

5. Click Save.

> **NOTE**
>
> *To undo any edits to an image, you can always click Cancel to return to the previous window without saving your changes.*

Fix Red Eye

Red eye is one of the most common occurrences in photography. When you have a printed photo with red eye, you can use a special red-eye marker to color in the red of the pupils to black. However, on digital images, a special red-eye marker won't do you any good. That's why many image-editing programs now have red-eye reduction features built-in.

The Red Eye option in Media Center locates instances of red eye in your digital photos and works to correct the problem. To correct red eye, follow these steps:

1. On the Media Center main screen, under Pictures + Videos, click Picture Library.

2. Right-click any picture you want modify, and then choose Picture Details from the shortcut menu.

3. Click Touch Up. This displays the Touch Up window, shown in Figure 16-2.

4. Click Red Eye. This reduces any red eye that exists in the selected image.

5. Click Save.

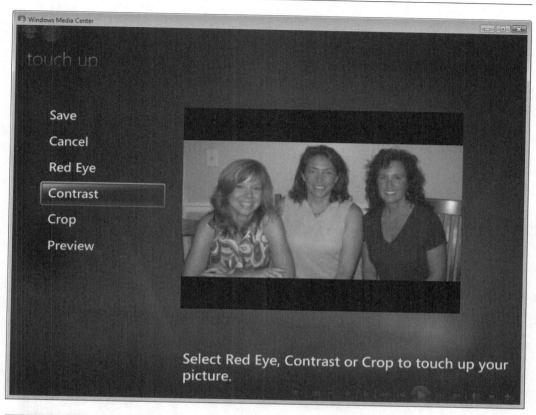

FIGURE 16-2 The Touch Up window displays options for adjusting red eye and contrast as well as providing access to the Crop feature.

Crop

Another particularly helpful tool is the Crop feature. Cropping simply means "to remove." This is useful when you need to remove external portions (or people) from your pictures.

Cropping uses lines that are parallel to the outside images of the pictures. Typically, the Crop feature works with a resizable rectangular box that you can move and make smaller or larger. Any area of the image that is positioned inside this box will become the new image after you apply the Crop command. The area positioned outside of this box will be removed. To crop a picture, follow these steps:

1. On the Media Center main screen, under Pictures + Videos, click Picture Library.

2. Right-click any picture you want modify, and then choose Picture Details from the shortcut menu.

16

3. Click Touch Up. This displays the Touch Up window, shown in Figure 16-2.

4. Click Crop. This displays the cropping rectangle on the image, as shown in Figure 16-3.

5. Click the last button on the right on the Crop toolbar to switch between a portrait or landscape cropping rectangle.

6. Use the Zoom In and Zoom Out buttons to increase or decrease the area of the rectangle.

7. Click the arrow keys on the interface to reposition the cropping rectangle.

8. Once the rectangle encompasses the portion of the image you want to retain, click Save.

9. Click Yes to confirm the action and return to the previous window.

FIGURE 16-3   Use the Crop feature to remove extraneous bits from your photos.

E-mail Your Pictures

One way to share your pictures with others is through e-mail. Unfortunately, you can't e-mail directly from Media Center, but you can use several other methods:

- Using your e-mail program, you can include any image on your computer as an attachment to a new message.
- From a file window (such as Computer or Pictures), you can right-click an image and choose Send To: Mail Recipient from the shortcut menu.
- Use Windows Photo Gallery.

TIP

From an open e-mail message, you can use the drag-and-drop method to attach an image by simply dragging an image thumbnail to the open e-mail. However, using this method removes the option of choosing the picture size.

How to ...   Use Windows Photo Gallery to E-mail a Picture

Windows Photo Gallery is often used in conjunction with Windows Media Center as a means of working with your photos. One of the options offered by Windows Photo Gallery is the ability to email your photos directly from within the Photo Gallery program.

To use the Photo Gallery to email a picture, follow these steps:

1. Open Windows Photo Gallery.

2. Navigate to the picture you want to e-mail. If you prefer, you can select several images to e-mail by holding down CTRL while you click each one.

3. Click E-mail on the menu bar. This opens the Attach Files dialog box.

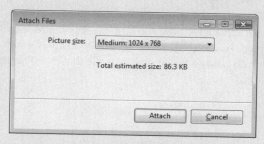

4. Click Attach. A new e-mail message opens using your preferred e-mail program with the image(s) attached.

5. Using your e-mail program's specific commands, address and send the e-mail.

E-mail Limitations

Although you may be tempted to send an image at the largest size possible (1280 × 1024), doing so often increases the size of the file significantly. While it may seem like a good idea at first, you should know that some e-mail servers limit the individual message size. There isn't one message size standard, but it typically falls between 1 and 10 megabytes (MB). Plus, smaller file sizes have a faster download rate.

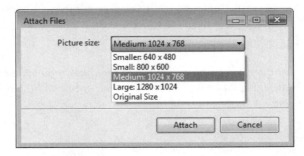

Optimizing your images by choosing a smaller image size, such as 800 × 600, reduces the overall file size of the image and thus the file size of the e-mail. Optimizing your images in this way does not affect the quality of the original image on your computer, but it does resize the image that you send.

TIP
When sending pictures via e-mail, a safe photo size is Smaller: 640 × 480. This reduces the file size of the attachment, allowing the e-mail and associated attachment to download faster on the recipient's computer.

NOTE
From Windows Photo Gallery, you can e-mail selected videos by clicking the same e-mail command; however, you can't resize a video. Since video files are often quite large, you should always try to e-mail videos only to users with a high-speed Internet connection.

Resizing

If you try to send an e-mail message whose file size exceeds the recipient's server size limit, your message will most likely get bounced by the server and marked as undeliverable. Typical causes of bounced messages include either a video or image file that is too large or an e-mail message that contains several pictures.

If the latter is true (too many pictures), you can send a few different messages with fewer attachments in each. However, if the overall file size is too large, you can reduce the size of the image in the Attach Files dialog box. To resize an image before e-mailing, follow these steps:

1. Open Windows Photo Gallery.

2. Navigate to the picture you want to e-mail. If you prefer, you can select several images by holding down CTRL while you click each one.

3. Click E-mail on the menu bar. This opens the Attach Files dialog box.

4. Click the Picture Size down arrow, and choose one of the following:

    - Smaller: 640 × 840
    - Small: 800 × 600
    - Medium: 1024 × 768
    - Large: 1280 × 1024
    - Original Size

5. Click Attach. A new e-mail message opens using your preferred e-mail program with the image(s) attached.

6. Using your e-mail program's specific commands, address and send the e-mail.

Compressing

If you've used the smallest picture size setting and the image is still too large to send via e-mail, you can try compressing—or zipping—the image file. On the whole, compressed files take up less storage space than files in their native state. As such, compressed files can often be e-mailed to others more quickly.

As a bonus, if you have several files to send, you can include all of them in one compressed file, making it even easier to attach a group of images to an e-mail because you only need to attach one file instead of multiple files.

1. Navigate to the file (or files) you want to compress using a file window (such as Computer or Pictures).

2. Right-click the selected file(s). This opens a shortcut menu.

3. Choose Send To: Compressed (Zipped) Folder.

4. Type a file name for the compressed file, and then press ENTER.

5. Right-click the compressed file, and then choose Send To: Mail Recipient.

6. Using your e-mail program's specific commands, address and send the e-mail.

TIP *To add files to an existing compressed folder, for those times when you have a pre-existing compressed (or zipped) folder and you need to include additional files, drag the files you want to add to the compressed folder.*

Burn Pictures to a CD

If you have a large amount of photos that you want to share with others, burning them to a CD is a great alternative to e-mail, especially if you want to share those images with someone who has a dial-up connection to the Internet.

Beyond sharing, CDs also serve as an awesome backup strategy, and if you haven't yet backed up your pictures, now is a good time to do that.

Before you can create a CD of your pictures, however, you'll need a few supplies:

- **Writeable CD**   Be sure to choose writable CDs that are compatible with your CD burner. If you're unsure, check with the CD burner or computer manufacturer.

- **CD burner**   These days, many new computers come with a standard CD burner. But, as with the writeable CDs, if you are unsure, you'll want to check with your computer or CD burner manufacturer to verify that you have the appropriate equipment.

Once you've verified that you have the necessary equipment to burn your pictures on a CD, you're ready to begin the process using Windows Media Center.

1. Insert a writeable CD into your CD burner.
2. On the Media Center main screen, under Pictures + Video, click Picture Library.
3. Right-click the folder you want to burn to the CD, and choose Burn from the shortcut menu.

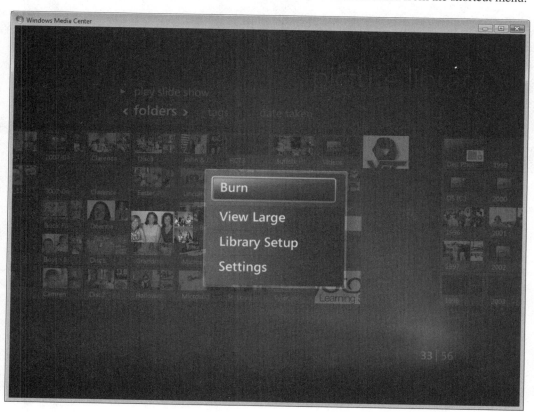

4. Select Data CD, and click Next.

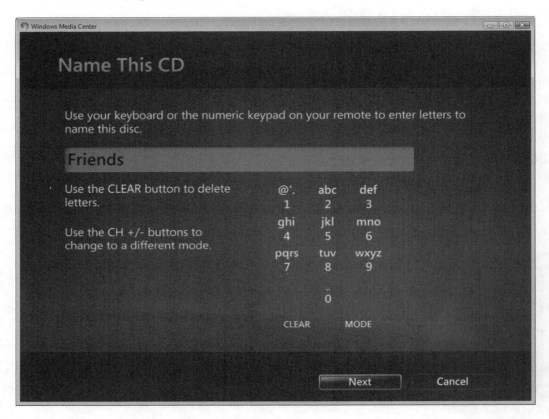

5. Enter a name for the CD, and click Next.

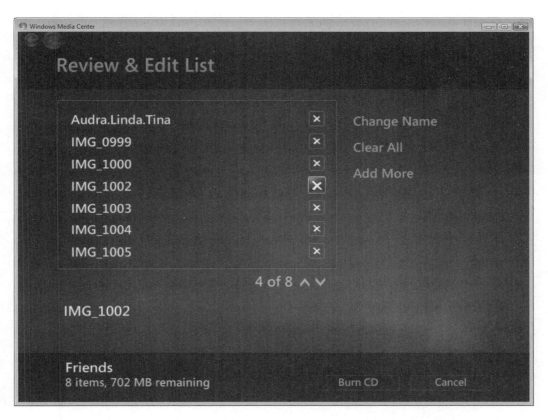

6. Click the X next to any image that you don't want to burn to the CD to remove the X, thereby leaving the images you do want to burn untouched.

7. To include pictures that are not stored in the folder you initially selected, click Add More, and follow the on-screen prompts.

8. When finished, click Burn CD.

9. Click Yes to confirm the burn procedure.

10. You can watch the status bar as the burn is in progress, or click OK to work on another task while Media Center completes the task. You'll be notified when the CD is finished.

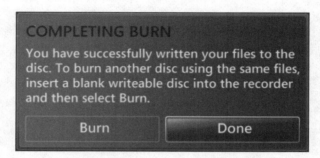

You can also use Windows Photo Gallery to burn a similar data CD.

1. Open Windows Photo Gallery.

2. Select the images you want to copy. If you want to copy entire folders, use CTRL to select multiple folders in the left pane. Then press CTRL-A to select all of the displayed images.

3. Choose Burn, and then choose Data Disc.

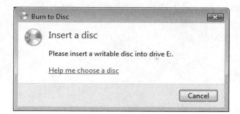

4. When prompted, insert a writeable disc.

5. Add a meaningful disc title, and then click Next.

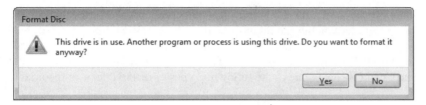

6. If prompted to format the disc, click Yes.

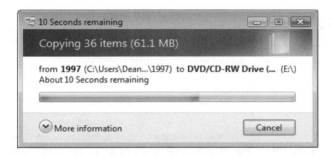

7. Eject the disc when the burn process is complete. You may see a balloon message near the system tray indicating that the disc is preparing to eject.

Data CDs are intended to be viewed on a computer, not on other electronic devices, such as standalone CD players and DVD players.

Create a DVD of Pictures to Play on a DVD Player

You can choose to archive digital media files, such as music, pictures, and video, to a CD or DVD in Windows Media Center. This lets you burn the selected files to a CD or DVD to play back on another computer. When burning this type of disc—called a data DVD or data CD—the files are not converted to another file format before they are burned. Therefore, the files that you choose are simply copied to the CD or DVD in their original format that the computer recognizes. This lets you archive, or back up, digital media files in the same format as the files that are stored on your computer.

The type of recordable DVD disc that you use depends on your DVD burner. Certain DVD burners can only burn to certain types of recordable DVDs. For example, with some DVD burners, you can only record to a DVD+R or DVD+RW or to a DVD-R or DVD-RW. However, other DVD burners will let you burn to all of these recordable DVD types. To determine what types of DVDs your DVD burner supports, consult the manual.

As long as your DVD burner supports burning to these types of discs, you can burn a DVD in Windows Media Center by using one of the following types of recordable or re-recordable DVDs:

- DVD+R
- DVD+RW
- DVD-R
- DVD-RW

To create a DVD of pictures for a DVD player, follow these steps:

1. Insert a recordable DVD into your DVD burner.

2. On the Media Center main screen, under Tasks, click the Burn A CD/DVD notification.

3. Select Video DVD, and then click Next.

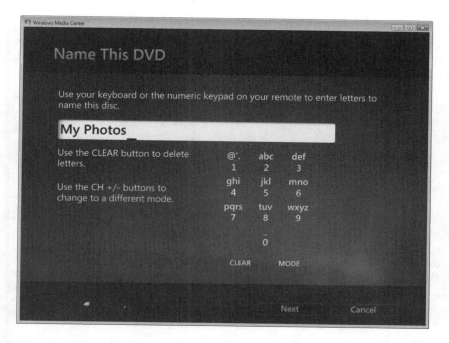

4. Enter a name for the DVD, and then click Next.

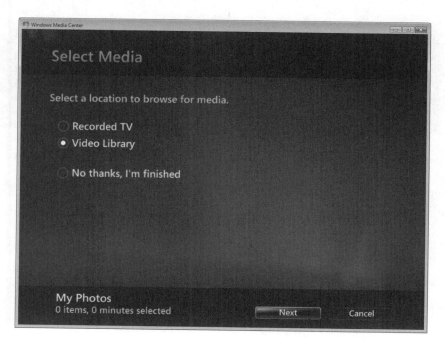

5. Choose Video Library, and then click Next.

6. Click the videos or pictures you want to add to your DVD. You'll know you've selected a file when you see a check mark in the lower-right corner of the selected thumbnail. When you've finished, click Next.

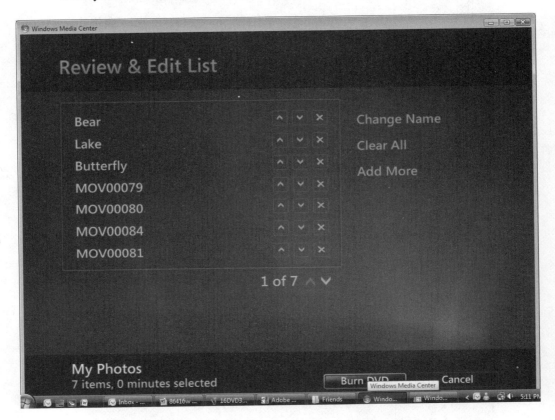

7. Click the X next to any image or video you don't want to burn to the DVD to remove the X, thereby leaving any file you do want to burn untouched.

8. To include images or video that is not already listed, click Add More, and follow the on-screen prompts.

9. When finished, click Burn DVD.

INITIATING COPY

Would you like to burn a disc with these files?

Yes   No

10. When prompted, click Yes to continue.

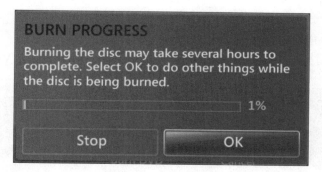

BURN PROGRESS

Burning the disc may take several hours to complete. Select OK to do other things while the disc is being burned.

1%

Stop   OK

11. You can watch the status bar as the burn is in progress, or click OK to work on another task while Media Center completes the task. You'll be notified when the DVD is finished.

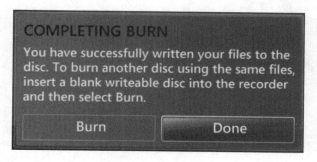

COMPLETING BURN

You have successfully written your files to the disc. To burn another disc using the same files, insert a blank writeable disc into the recorder and then select Burn.

Burn   Done

12. When the disc is completed, click Done.

Create a Slideshow and Add Music

You've already seen Media Center's slick slideshow feature in action. Now you're going to learn how to combine the slideshow feature with your Media Center music into one cool DVD that you can share with others.

The process is easy. All you need to do is select the images for your slideshow, select the music, and then combine those two things onto one DVD. The images and music are encoded on the DVD in such a way that the music and the pictures play at the same time, leading to a professional-looking slideshow.

Even better, the DVD you create can be played on any computer using Media Center or any standard DVD player. To create a slideshow with music on a DVD, follow these steps:

1. Insert a recordable DVD into your DVD burner.

2. On the Media Center main screen, under Tasks, click the Burn A CD/DVD notification.

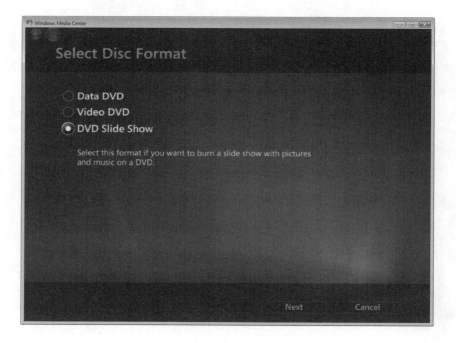

3. Select DVD Slide Show, and then click Next.

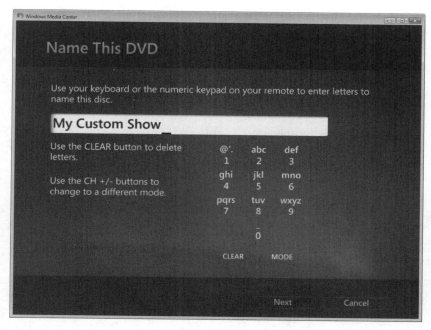

4. Enter a name for the DVD, and then click Next.

5. Choose Picture Library, and then click Next.

6. Click the pictures you want to add to your DVD. You'll know you've selected a file when you see a check mark in the lower-right corner of the selected thumbnail. When you've finished, click Next.

7. To include music, click Add More.

8. Choose Music Library, and then click Next.

9. Click the music you want to add to your DVD. As with photos, you'll know you've selected a file when you see a check mark in the lower-right corner of the selected thumbnail. When you've finished, click Next.

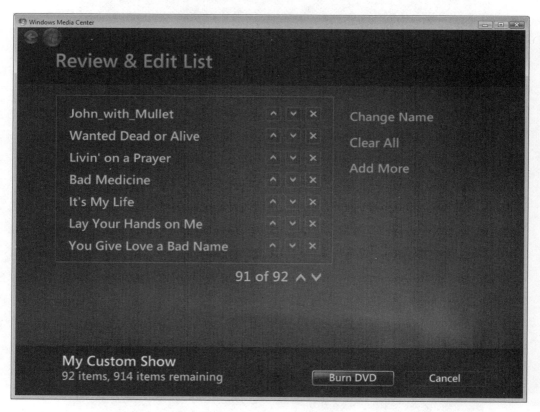

10. Click the X next to any image or music you don't want to burn to the DVD to remove the X, thereby leaving any file you do want to burn untouched.

11. To include images or music that is not already listed, click Add More, and follow the on-screen prompts.

12. When you have added all the items you want, click Burn DVD.

13. When prompted, click Yes to continue.

14. You can watch the status bar as the burn is in progress, or click OK to work on another task while Media Center completes the task. You'll be notified when the DVD is finished.

15. When the disc is completed, click Done.

Get Photos Printed Online

For all of the advances in technology, there will still be times when nothing beats a printed picture. With Windows Vista, a couple of different companies are readily available to assist you in your image-printing needs.

But the printing company is not the only thing you'll choose. You'll also be asked for the:

■ Picture size
■ Picture style
■ Picture quality

And the best part? Your printed images are delivered directly to your own mailing address (or another address of your choosing).

16

At the time this book was written, the photo-printing companies you could choose from were AOL Pictures and Yahoo! Photos. To access either of these printing companies, follow these steps:

1. On the Media Center main screen, under Online Media, click Explore.

2. Choose <Pictures> at the top.

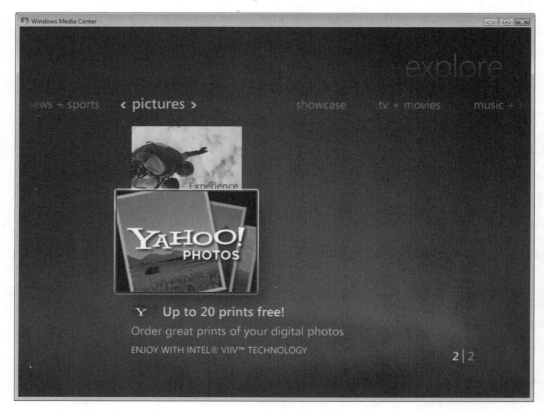

3. Choose the image-printing company of your choice. Each company will have a different set of steps to follow, so be sure to follow the on-screen instructions that are specific to your chosen company.

Search the Photo Library

Unlike the Music Library, there is no search feature built-in to the Picture Library in Media Center. However, you can use Windows Photo Gallery to categorize your media items and search through your folders. To search for items using Photo Gallery, follow these steps:

1. Open Windows Photo Gallery.

2. In the Search box (shown here), located in the upper-right portion of the window, type the text you want to find. Note that wildcard characters, such as * and ?, do not work in this Search box.

3. As you type, the search feature works, narrowing down your search results. To search based on a different term, click the Clear Search button located at the end of the Search box, and type a new term.

How to ...   Order Prints Through Windows Photo Gallery

One of the options for ordering prints from an online service can be found using the Windows Photo Gallery program. Although each online printing company many have a different set of specific instructions to follow, those directions are almost always shown on-screen. To order prints of your photos through Photo Gallery, follow these steps:

1. Open Windows Photo Gallery.

2. Select the picture(s) you want to print.

3. Click Print, and then click Order Prints from the Photo Gallery toolbar.

4. Select a photo-printing company, and then click Send Pictures. This sends your picture(s) to the directly to the company.

5. As mentioned, each company will have a different set of steps to follow, so be sure to follow the on-screen instructions that are specific to your chosen company.

16

TIP
Using tags and other metadata ensures that your files will be easier to locate later. Tags are covered in more detail in Chapter 15.

NOTE
A similar search function is also present in Windows Media Player.

Create and Save Search Folders

You can use Windows Vista Search folders from the Start menu by clicking Search to locate and then categorize photos. Once categorized and in folders, you can easily access those photos in Media Center.

The Search window is a little different from the rest of the windows you'll encounter in Windows Vista. To open a new Search window, choose Start, and then click Search. The Search option is located on the right side of the Start menu and is separate from the Start menu Search feature located on the lower-left of the Start button. A new Search window is shown in Figure 16-4.

After typing your search criteria, you can further modify your results using the options on the menu bar. To limit your search results to only images, you can click Picture. For example, Figure 16-5 shows a search for all pictures related to the search term "Tyler."

Even better is the option to save your searches. This way, you can create a search based on a particular word or phrase and category, and each time you open the search criteria, the results are updated automatically. To create a saved search folder for your pictures, follow these steps:

1. From the Start menu, click Search. This opens the Search window.

2. Select Picture on the menu bar.

3. Enter your search word or phrase in the Search box.

4. Verify that the results are what you expected. If not, refine your search before going further.

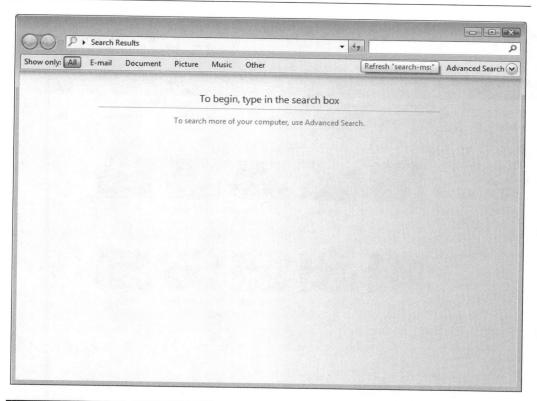

FIGURE 16-4 The Search window

5. Click Save Search. This opens the Save Search dialog box, shown in the following illustration.

6. Type a name for the Search folder.
7. Click Save.

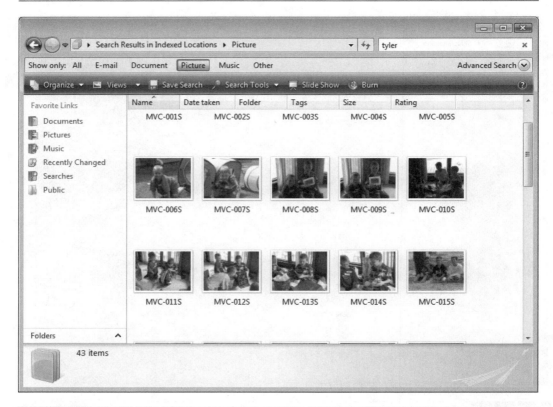

FIGURE 16-5   You can see how the results of the search match the term "Tyler" as the computer searches both metadata and the Picture category

Once you've created a Search folder, you can open it anytime to view the most up-to-date search results. The Search window, shown in Figure 16-6, will open again and navigate to the same folder in which the Search folder was saved.

When the folder view is displayed, simply double-click the Search folder you want to view.

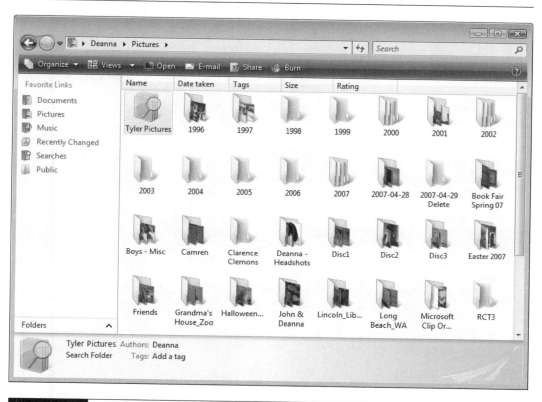

FIGURE 16-6 A saved search

Part V

Add Hardware to Get More from Media Center

Chapter 17

Access Your Media from an Xbox 360 or Other Windows Vista PCs

How to...

- Select the appropriate type of home network
- Connect an Xbox 360 to your home network
- Add an Xbox 360 extender to Media Center
- Access your Media Library from an Xbox 360 or another Windows Vista PC

You're not always going to want to head to the home office or a gathering area in the home to watch a movie or listen to a music album with Media Center. You don't have to anymore. With a media extender, like an Xbox 360, you can access all of your media from another room in your home, or even show a movie in a home theater. With an Xbox 360, you can connect to your Windows Vista PC from anywhere in your home through a wired or wireless network connection, and use the Xbox 360 to "extend" it.

In case you're not sure what an Xbox 360 is: This is a device capable of displaying (referred to as "extending") Media Center from a Windows Vista PC, over a network, to your home theater display, living room, or any display that you can connect an Xbox 360 to. You can even directly access your Windows Media Player Library without having to open Media Center on the Xbox 360 and play entire albums directly in certain video game titles, replacing the game's soundtrack with your own.

In this chapter, you'll learn how to connect an Xbox 360 to your Windows Vista PC so that you can access Media Center and your Media Library.

NOTE   *Although accessing Media Center from an Xbox 360 requires a high-performance network, accessing your media in Windows Media Player 11 (through Media Sharing) from an Xbox 360 does not. An Xbox 360 can also access Zune media on your computer, though we will not discuss how to use an Xbox 360 with Zune software in this chapter.*

Select a Type of Home Network

An Xbox 360 can be used to access media stored on your Windows Vista PC. The media will look and feel just the way it does when you're sitting at your PC when you view it with an Xbox 360. When you access Media Center on an Xbox 360, you can access all the same media, including high-definition television.

Media Sharing is a way to directly access media in your Windows Media Player 11 media library, too. Think of it as accessing the media files directly over your network. Accessing shared media does not require as fast a network as accessing Media Center does. As a result, you can use a slightly lower-performance network. If you're concerned about whether your current home network is suitable, check to see if it is certified for Windows Vista. For a list of certified Windows Vista home networking devices, visit www.microsoft.com/windows/products/windowsvista/buyorupgrade/logo.mspx.

In this section, we'll discuss what type of network connection is appropriate for how you share media or access Media Center. If you're not familiar with how to configure network settings for your computer or Xbox 360, you may want to consult Windows Vista Help, or the Xbox 360 Web site. Let's take a closer look at what kinds of networks are appropriate for Media Sharing and Media Center.

> NOTE
>
> *In this section, we'll assume that you already have a wired or wireless home network set up, most likely with a home router device, such as a Linksys product. If you do not already have a home network, or if your computer is connected directly to your Internet connection and you are wondering how to connect your Xbox 360 to your computer, visit www.xbox.com/en-US/support/connecttolive/xbox360/homenetworking/basics.htm for more information.*

Select a Wired Network

Accessing Media Center over a wired network from an Xbox 360 requires a high-performance network. Ordinary wired networks are great for browsing the Web or checking e-mail, but in order to access Media Center, you'll want to make sure that your network has a speed of at least 100 megabits per second (Mbps). Table 17-1 spells this all out.

Media Sharing is very different from accessing Media Center on an Xbox 360. When you access Media Center on an Xbox 360, all of the same rich high-fidelity effects are possible on the Xbox 360 (for example, the glowing shifting background on the Media Center Start page). This requires a high-performance network. However, when you access your media through Media Sharing, you are simply accessing the media files directly. This doesn't require a high-performance network, and as a result, a 10-Mbps network will suffice for accessing most shared media, although a faster network is recommended if multiple computers will be accessing the network or if multiple Xbox 360s are using the network. You may also want to consider a quicker network if you are accessing high-definition video.

A wired high-performance network is best for accessing Media Center from an Xbox 360. It provides minimal interference, maximum speed, and is more reliable than a wireless network.

Select a Wireless Network

If you are not able to run a wired connection to your Xbox 360, a wireless connection may be the next best option. It's important to keep in mind that not all wireless networks provide the best experience when used with an Xbox 360 for Media Center access. In fact, wireless networks may

Type of Access	Speed
Media Center	100 Mbps or faster
Media Sharing (Windows Media Connect)	10 Mbps or faster

TABLE 17-1   Recommended Wired Networks for Media Center and Media Sharing

17

Type of Access	Speed
Media Center	802.11a, 802.11n
Media Sharing (Windows Media Connect)	802.11b, 802.11g, 802.11a, 802.11n

TABLE 17-2 Recommended Wireless Networks for Media Center and Media Sharing

cause the most trouble. Other devices in homes, such as cordless phones and microwave ovens, can interfere with wireless signals and cause connections to become unreliable or data transfer speed to degrade. This is why wired connections are highly recommended. In general, 802.11b wireless networks are not recommended for use with Media Center on an Xbox 360 due to the slow speed. Typically, 802.11a is highly recommended, because it is faster than 802.11b and operates on a separate frequency from 802.11b and the other devices mentioned that may interfere. While 802.11g is suitable, it may suffer from the same interference problems. See Table 17-2 for more information.

If you want to purchase a wireless router that has been certified to work with Windows Vista and Media Center, visit www.microsoft.com/windows/products/windowsvista/buyorupgrade/logo.mspx for a list of Windows Vista–certified products.

Add an Xbox 360 Extender to Media Center

A device that displays Media Center over a network is called a Media Center extender. An Xbox 360 can act as an extender and, as of this writing, is the only Windows Vista Media Center extender device available. You'll want to make sure that you have a high-performance network that is capable of transferring data quick enough to display your media without delay (sometimes referred to as latency). Later in this chapter, we'll take a look at how to test the performance of your network and improve connectivity.

To begin, connect your Xbox 360 to your home network. If you are connecting to a wired network, it should be as easy as just plugging in the Ethernet cable. Follow the instructions included with the Xbox 360 or at www.xbox.com if you aren't sure or if the Xbox is new. If you are connecting to a wireless network, you may need to configure wireless security and other settings on the Xbox 360 first.

On the Xbox 360

After the Xbox 360 has been connected to the home network, turn it on. Then follow these steps on the Xbox 360:

1. From the Media tab, select Media Center.

2. When prompted to connect the Xbox 360 to a Media Center PC on your network, as shown in Figure 17-1, press A (Select) to continue.

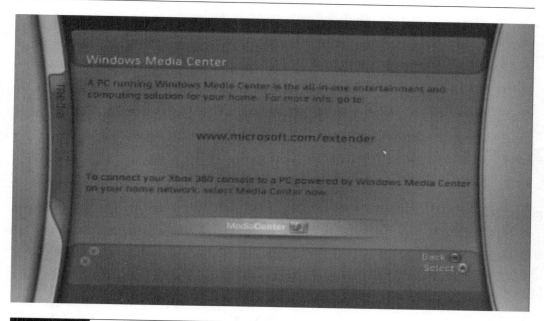

FIGURE 17-1   Media Center extender introduction screen

CAUTION   *If the Xbox 360 is connected via an 802.11b or 802.11g wireless network, you might be warned that poor performance may result. You should switch to a higher-performance wireless network (such as 802.11a) if your wireless router supports it. Be careful, however, as other devices on your network may not support 802.11a.*

3. If the Xbox 360 can locate your Windows Vista PC on the connected network, a Media Center setup key is displayed on the screen, as shown in Figure 17-2. This code is used to ensure that the Xbox 360 connects only with your Windows Vista PC and not any others on the network. Write this code down on a piece of paper, and go to your Windows Vista PC.

4. If the Xbox 360 cannot locate your Windows Vista PC, verify that your PC and Xbox 360 are connected to the same network. If any firewall software other than the Windows Firewall included with Windows Vista is installed, you'll have to make sure that this software isn't blocking the Xbox 360 from communicating with your Windows Vista PC. Windows Firewall automatically allows Media Center extender communication with an Xbox 360. For information about how to configure a firewall with Media Center, see www.microsoft.com/windowsxp/mediacenter/extender/setup/firewall/config.mspx.

17

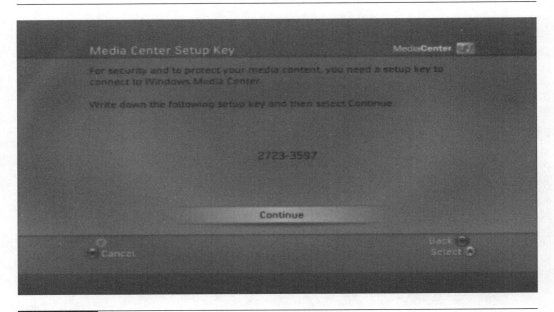

FIGURE 17-2 Media Center setup key on the Xbox 360

On the Windows Vista PC

Now it's time to work with the Windows Vista PC:

1. Click Start, and then click Media Center.

2. Scroll down to Tasks, and then scroll right to Add Extender. You may also be notified that a Media Center extender has been found on the network (see Figure 17-3). If you are notified, select Yes; otherwise, select Add Extender from the Tasks list.

3. Click Next to continue.

4. Enter the eight-digit setup key displayed by the Xbox 360, as shown in Figure 17-4.

5. Click Next to continue.

Media Center will configure setup so that the Xbox 360 only communicates with your Windows Vista PC and no other hardware. When this process is complete, you'll have a chance to configure options for your Windows Vista PC and Xbox 360.

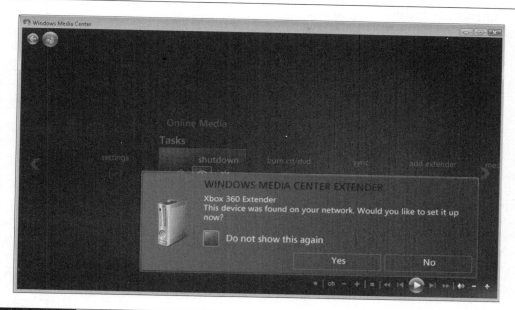

FIGURE 17-3   A message appears when a Media Center extender is found on the network

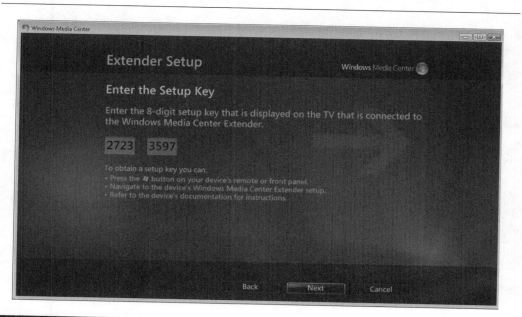

FIGURE 17-4   Enter the setup key from the Xbox 360

17

Configuration Options

To complete the setup process, you'll need to configure how you want Media Center to work with your Xbox 360. There are two options to consider.

First, you can turn Away mode on or off. Away mode is a special power mode for your computer. When the computer becomes inactive, all audio is muted, video is turned off, and input devices such as the mouse and keyboard are turned off. (This is so that your computer isn't activated by children bumping the keyboard or pets walking across it). At the same time, the computer still listens on the network for Media Center requests. If a Media Center extender attempts to connect, the computer "wakes up" to accept the connection. This saves energy while making sure your computer is still available for the Xbox 360 to connect to it, in case you decide to use Media Center on the Xbox 360 while your Windows Vista PC is idle.

Second, you need decide whether the Xbox 360 can access the same media you see on your computer, as shown in Figure 17-5. This is recommended if you have video and pictures in your personal folders that you may want to display from the Xbox 360. When you click Next, Media Center finalizes your settings and configures the Xbox 360 to connect to Media Center on your Windows Vista PC, as shown in Figure 17-6. Next, you'll see the Xbox 360 display a Connecting screen (Figure 17-7) while Media Center finalizes your settings.

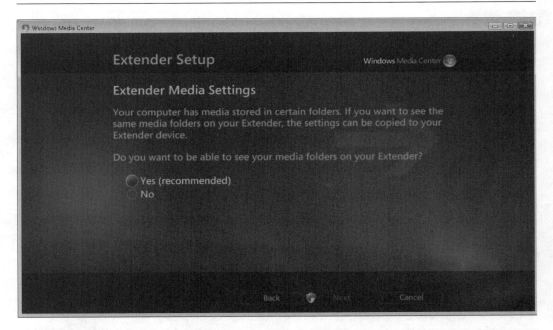

FIGURE 17-5   Additional Media Center extender configuration options

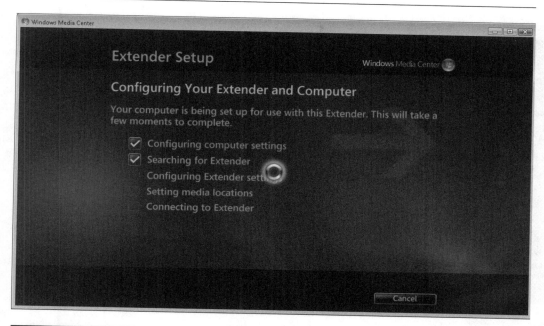

FIGURE 17-6   Extender settings are finalized.

If the Xbox 360 is connected through a wireless connection, the configuration process is not over yet. Next, you'll have a chance to fine-tune your network connection so that you get the best possible video out of your Windows Vista PC over your home network. This is an important step, and you shouldn't skip it.

Test Network Connectivity

Media Center extenders need a high-performance network in order to provide the best experience for viewing high-definition movies, music, photos, and more. Windows Vista includes a tool for testing your network and optimizing the signal of wireless Media Center extenders. You need to test your network to see how it stacks up.

To test your network:

1. Open Media Center, click Tasks, click Settings, and then click Extender.

2. Select the Media Center extender, and then select Tune Network. If you just added the extender, you may also be asked to tune the network, as shown in Figure 17-8.

17

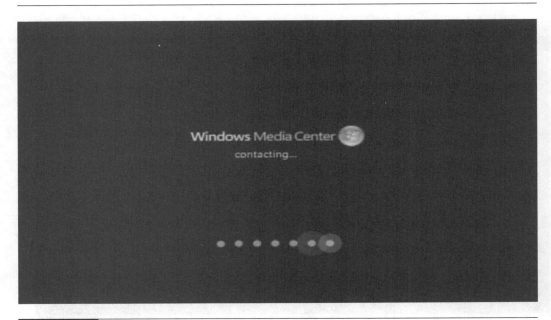

FIGURE 17-7   Xbox 360 connects to a Media Center PC.

3. Click Next to begin the network performance test. If you are using an 802.11b or 802.11g network, you may receive a notification message about marginal network performance, as shown in Figure 17-9. In this case, you may not be able to watch high-definition TV or video without making additional adjustments to the position of your wireless router's antenna or to the Media Center extender's antenna or location.

4. Select how you'd like to view the current quality of signal between your Windows Vista PC and Media Center extender, as shown in Figure 17-10. The bar view shows the quality of the signal as it changes, while the graph view shows a plot of the signal over time. Both views indicate what the current quality signal can be used for: standard television or high-definition television.

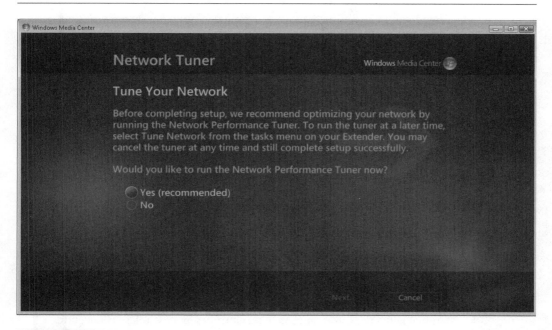

FIGURE 17-8   After a wireless Media Center extender is added, you should tune the network.

5. Adjust the antennas and position of your Windows Vista PC and Media Center extender until the signal is as good as it can get (see the Tip).

> TIP
>
> *Imagine a straight line between the two antennas. The more obstacles there are between the two points, the more your signal may decrease in quality. You may not be able to obtain a high-quality connection over an 802.11b or 802.11g network. Currently, 802.11a networks are the best in speed and quality for Media Center extenders. If all else fails and you are unable to achieve a good connection, use a wired connection. The speed is much better than wireless and so is the quality!*

6. Finish tuning the network.

17

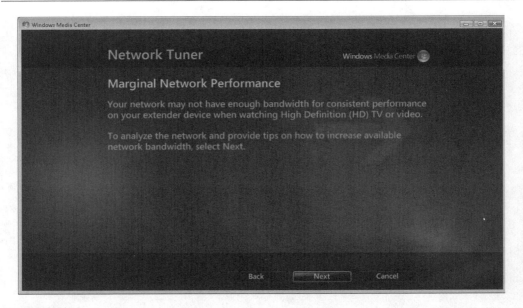

FIGURE 17-9 Marginal network performance may result from a poor wireless connection.

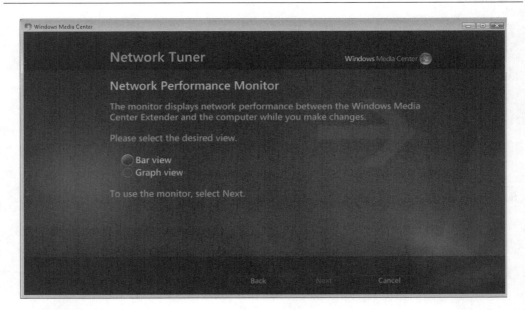

FIGURE 17-10 Bar view shows instant changes in signal while Graph view shows changes over time.

Media Sharing

Among many new features in Windows Media Player 11 is Media Sharing. With Media Sharing you can access your media library from anywhere on your home network. With Windows Media Player 11 you can stream media from your Windows Vista PC to devices such as an Xbox 360 or even older Windows Media Connect devices (like a Roku SoundBridge). In fact, there is a whole ecosystem of devices that integrate with home theater and stereo systems so that you can access media from anywhere in the home. Just look for any Windows Media Connect–compatible devices when you're shopping.

Media Sharing is a part of Windows Media Player 11 that shares your library across your home network. Only media in your Media Player library is accessible to other devices on your network. If you're worried about how to control access to your media so that you don't share all of it, don't be! Media Sharing in Windows Media Player 11 is flexible, and you can share media by star rating, parental rating, and media type. First, you'll want to check your network security before you configure Media Sharing.

In this section, we'll take a look at how to access your media from another Windows Vista computer and how to access your media from an Xbox 360 by using the Media Sharing feature in Windows Media Player 11.

Check Your Network Security

When you connect to a new network, Windows Vista asks if the network is a home, work, or public connection (see Chapter 3 for more information). If the connection is a home or work connection, Windows Vista assumes it is a private connection and lets more applications communicate with your computer on the network. With a private connection, Windows assumes that you are not directly connected to the Internet; therefore, it is safe to allow more applications to communicate with your computer.

If the network is public, Windows Vista locks down your computer and increases security on Windows Firewall so that fewer applications can communicate with your computer. Windows assumes that a public Internet connection is connected directly to the Internet. Tables 17-3 and 17-4 detail these security settings.

If your computer is connected to a public network, Media Sharing is disabled. It is enabled, however, on a public network. To see what type of network you are connected to, click the arrow under the Library button in Windows Media Player 11, and then click Media Sharing. Windows displays the current status of media sharing at the bottom of the Media Sharing window.

Connection	Network Type
Home	Private (lower security)
Work	Private (lower security)
Public	Public (increased security)

TABLE 17-3   Network Connections by Type

Network Type	Security
Private	Windows Firewall is turned on, Media Sharing is turned on, and other computers can find your computer and your computer can find other computers.
Public	Windows Firewall is turned on, and there is limited discoverability and restricted network access.

TABLE 17-4   Security for Each Network Location

Since Windows Vista automatically adjusts your network security settings based on the type of network that you are connected to, Media Sharing only works if you are connected to a private network. Before you continue, check to see what type of network your Windows Vista PC is currently connected to. If it is not a private network, you'll need to change the network type.

To determine what type of network you are connected to and change the network type:

1. Click Start, click Control Panel, and under Network And Internet, click View Network Status And Tasks (see Figure 17-11).

2. In the Network And Sharing Center, verify that your network is a private network, as shown in Figure 17-12.

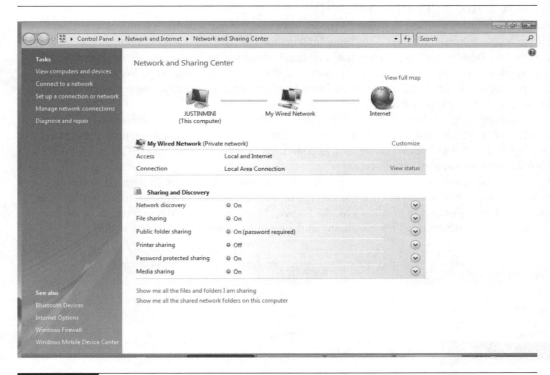

FIGURE 17-11   Locate View Network Status And Tasks

FIGURE 17-12   The Network And Sharing Center displaying a private network

3. To change the network type, click Customize.

4. Select Private.

5. Click Next, and then click Close.

Configure Media Sharing

With Windows Media Player 11, you can use Media Sharing to share your Media Library with other computers and devices. For example, if you have a laptop computer and you are lying in bed and want to listen to music located on your desktop computer in another room, you can use Media Sharing on your laptop to access this album.

Another situation in which you might use Media Sharing is on an Xbox 360. Many games on the Xbox 360 let you play your own soundtrack in place of the one included with the game. Using Media Sharing in Windows Media Player 11, you can access a playlist or album on your Windows Vista PC from the Xbox 360 and play it on your home theater system, complete with visualizations or just as background to a game. Let's take a closer look at how to configure a Windows Vista PC and Xbox 360 so that the Xbox 360 can access the Media Library on the PC.

17

Configure Media Sharing on the Windows Vista PC

To configure Media Sharing on the Windows Vista PC:

1. Click Start, point to All Programs, and select Windows Media Player.

2. Click the arrow under the Library button, and then click Media Sharing. This is shown in Figure 17-13. Windows Media Player 11 lists all devices that have been allowed or denied access to your Media Library.

NOTE   *Because you must explicitly grant any device access to your media library, when a new device is discovered on the network, it is automatically added to the Media Sharing dialog box with a yellow and black exclamation point, as noted in Figure 17-14. The exclamation point means that you haven't allowed or denied the device access to your Media Library. As a result, it does not have access to any of your media. If you own an Xbox 360 that has been turned on and is on the same network, it is listed in the Media Sharing dialog box as "Xbox 360" and has a yellow and black exclamation point.*

3. To access your Windows Vista PC's media library from an Xbox 360, connect the Xbox 360 to the same network as the Windows Vista PC, and turn it on. Windows Vista will detect the Xbox 360 after several minutes, and the Xbox 360 will appear in the Media Sharing dialog box with a yellow and black exclamation mark. Select the Xbox 360, and then click Allow. Make sure you click Apply and then click OK to close the Media Sharing window. If you don't do this, the settings will not take effect and you will receive a connection error on the Xbox 360 later on.

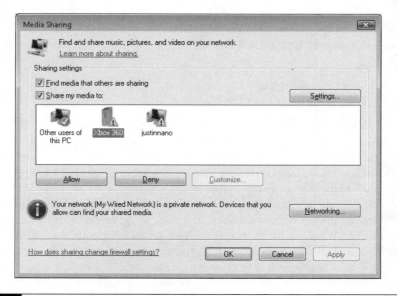

FIGURE 17-13   Access the Media Sharing feature

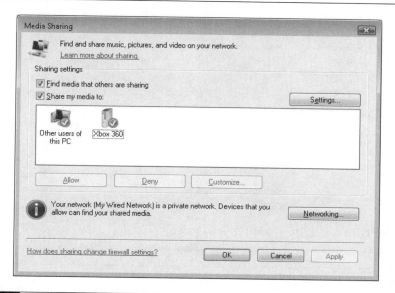

FIGURE 17-14   New devices appear with a yellow and black exclamation point

Once shared, Media Sharing is quite configurable. You can control what type of media is available to each Windows Media Connect device based on star rating and parental rating (such as explicit music content, TV-PG video, etc.). To see how this works:

1. In the Media Sharing dialog box, click the device, and then click Customize, as shown in Figure 17-15. (You can only click Customize if you've already allowed the device access to your Media Library. The Customize button will be disabled and will appear dim if the device has been denied access to your Media Library.)

2. Clear the default settings to customize media types, star ratings, and parental ratings (see Figure 17-15).

3. Click OK to close the Media Sharing dialog box.

Configure Media Sharing on the Xbox 360

Before you can access a computer's media library from the Xbox 360, you must first connect to it. Fortunately, connecting is easy. On the Xbox 360, go to the Media tab, and then select Music, Pictures, Or Video. Select Computer, and then press A (Select). Select the Windows Vista PC from the list of computers on the network, as shown in Figure 17-16, and press A (Select). That's it! Now you can access music, pictures, or videos from your Xbox 360.

17

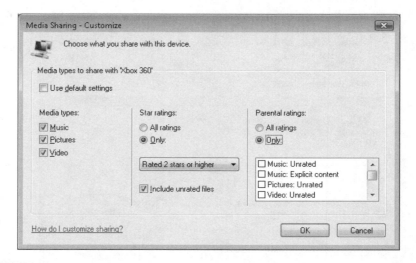

FIGURE 17-15   Customization options for the extender

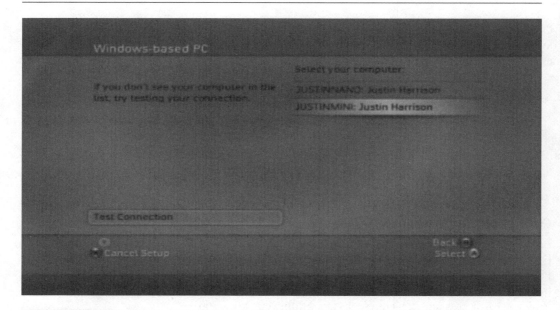

FIGURE 17-16   Choose your Vista PC from the list.

Chapter 18

Purchase and Install a DVD, HD DVD, or Blu-ray Disc Drive for Your Computer or Xbox 360

How to...

- Distinguish among DVD, HD DVD, and Blu-ray drives
- Select a drive that's right for you
- Find a drive for a video game console
- Install a DVD, HD DVD, or Blu-ray drive

An optical disc drive is included in nearly every Windows Vista PC. Most optical disc drives are DVD drives, but newer Windows Vista PCs may include high-definition (HD) DVD or Blu-ray disc optical drives. If your PC doesn't have what you want, you're not out of luck! Finding a DVD, HD DVD, or Blu-ray disc drive is not too difficult. Before you look around for a drive to purchase, however, there are a few things that you should know.

In this chapter, we'll take a look at the different kinds of DVD media. We'll also examine the two competing HD DVD and Blu-ray disc standards, and see how next-generation video game consoles support them. Finally, you'll learn how to install an optical disc drive in your computer.

DVD Media Options

DVD, also known as Digital Versatile Disc, is a current-generation optical disc format for storing data and high-definition video—in fact, it is the dominant format. DVD was designed by several companies collectively known as the DVD Forum. Windows Vista includes built-in support for watching DVDs in Windows Media Player and Media Center. No other software is necessary to watch DVDs in Windows Vista, which is different from Windows XP, which required additional software to watch DVDs.

DVD Disc Readers and Writers

There are standalone DVD disc readers and writers that connect to televisions, and there are DVD disc readers and writers that connect to computers. It's important to keep in mind that there are many different kinds of DVD discs available, depending on what you want to accomplish. Let's look first at the options for DVD readers and writers.

Disc Readers

If you are watching a DVD on your DVD player or on your computer, the DVD disc is a DVD-video disc. If you are listening to music on your computer from a DVD, the DVD disc is a DVD-audio disc. DVD-video and DVD-audio discs are both called DVD-ROM discs. This isn't too important to know—just remember that any DVD disc you purchase from a store and put in your DVD player or computer is likely to be a DVD-ROM.

Disc Writers

The situation is different for writable DVD discs. There are two types: DVD RW and DVD R.

DVD RW stands for DVD Rewritable. A DVD RW can be written to, erased, and rewritten to again many times. DVD R stands for DVD Recordable. A DVD R can be written to only one time. After the disc is written to, it may never be erased or rewritten to again.

If you are familiar with DVD discs, you'll notice that the aforementioned DVD RW discs and DVD R discs are both missing the plus or minus sign that usually separates "DVD" from "R" and "RW" (for example, DVD-R). This is because there is difference between DVD-R, DVD-RW, DVD+R, and DVD+RW. DVD+ discs are different from DVD- discs. The DVD- format is developed by the DVD Forum. The DVD+ format is developed by a collection of corporations known as the DVD+RW Alliance. The DVD Forum does not recognize the DVD+ format as being an official DVD format, but it is regarded by many as being a superior format to DVD-. DVD+ stores slightly less data than DVD-, but the difference is not really noticeable. DVD- and DVD+ both store 4.7 gigabyte (GB) of data. If you're getting lost, don't worry—all of this information is summarized later in Table 18-1.

Dual Layer Discs

There is another type of DVD disc besides DVD R and DVD RW. This one is referred to as DVD DL, or DVD double layer. DVD DL can store twice as much data as a normal DVD ROM, DVD R, or DVD RW disc. There are plus and minus versions of DVD DL, just as with DVD R and DVD RW. A DVD DL disc stores 8.5 GB of data. DVD DL can apply to DVD R and DVD RW discs—that means there can be DVD R DL and DVD RW DL discs.

DVD Discs: A Summary

When purchasing a DVD drive for your computer, you need to check what type of DVD discs the drive reads and writes. Most DVD drives can read and write both plus and minus DVD formats. Make sure that that type of writable DVD disc you are purchasing corresponds to the DVD disc format that your DVD drive reads or writes. Most modern DVD drives read and write all of the aforementioned DVD disc formats, but computers purchased before 2005 may only read plus or minus DVD disc formats. This is stated on the front of the disc tray that ejects from the DVD drive. Look for DVD+RW or DVD-RW.

HD DVD Options

HD DVD, also known as High Definition Digital Versatile Disc, is a next-generation optical disc format for storing data and high-definition video. It is one of two next-generation optical disc

DVD Disc Type	Capacity
DVD-ROM	4.7 GB
DVD RW, DVD R	4.7 GB
DVD RW DL, DVD R DL	8.5 GB

TABLE 18-1   Different Types of DVD Discs

18

formats fighting to supplant DVDs as the primary optical disc format used by millions of people. HD DVDs store up to three times as much data as DVDs—up to 15 GB. HD DVD is designed by Toshiba and NEC. A double-layer HD DVD disc can hold up to six times as much data as an ordinary DVD—30 GB.

There are both standalone HD DVD disc readers that connect to televisions and HD DVD drives for computers available on the market. As of this writing, no HD DVD disc writer computer drives are available, however.

Blu-ray Options

Blu-ray disc, sometimes referred to as BD, is a next-generation optical disc format for storing data and high-definition video. It competes directly with HD DVD. A single Blu-ray disc can hold up to five times as much data as an ordinary DVD, and a double-layer Blu-ray disc can hold up to ten times as much data. Blu-ray discs are named for the blue-violet laser used to read and write to them.

Both standalone Blu-ray disc readers that connect to televisions and Blu-ray disc reader and writer drives for computers are available on the market.

Make the Purchase

Before you search for a DVD, HD DVD, or Blu-ray disc drive, take a look at your Windows Vista PC and evaluate whether your computer has the capacity for an additional internal optical disc drive. Optical disc drives use a 5.25-inch-wide drive bay, usually located in the front of your computer. Most computers include one or two 5.25-inch-wide drive bays. If your computer does not have the necessary space for an additional optical drive, consider an external DVD, HD DVD, or Blu-ray disc drive. Optical disc drives typically connect via Universal Serial Bus (USB) or FireWire ports and may require an external power source, such as a power adapter that plugs in to the wall.

You'll also want to check whether your computer has the necessary internal connection to support an additional optical disc drive. Optical disc drives connect via an Integrated Drive Electronics (IDE) or Serial Advanced Technology Attachment (SATA) ribbon connection. Look at the existing optical disc drive connection to see what this connector looks like. IDE connectors are wide, and SATA connectors are much smaller. Check to see if your computer has a spare ribbon connection available. If not, you may want to consider purchasing an external optical disc drive.

Once you know what you're looking for, finding the right DVD, HD DVD, or Blu-ray disc drive for your Windows Vista PC isn't hard.

1. Open up your Internet browser, and head to www.windowsmarketplace.com.

2. At the top of the Windows Marketplace home page, click Hardware.

3. Under Browse Hardware, click Storage.

4. Under By Category, click Removable Media Drives.

5. Scroll down to browse through the list of Windows Vista–compatible removable media drives. Click the product names to find out more information about a particular drive. Remember to search other retailers' Web sites to compare prices and find more information. Some optical drives may be available at a local retailer, but the best price is likely to be found online.

Find an HD DVD or Blu-ray Drive for a Video Game Console

There are two next-generation video game consoles. The Xbox 360 by Microsoft supports high-definition video and digital surround sound. The PlayStation 3 from Sony uses Bluetooth technology for its controllers, has built-in wireless networking capabilities, and even comes with a Blu-ray disc drive in its basic and premium configurations.

Xbox 360

The Xbox 360 is available in three different packages (see Table 18-2):

- Xbox 360 Arcade includes a wired controller, a memory card, five free Xbox Live Arcade game, and a High Definition Multimedia Interface (HDMI) connector for high-definition video.

- Xbox 360 includes a 20-GB hard drive, a headset, and one wireless controller.

- Xbox 360 Elite includes a 120-GB hard drive and a HDMI connector.

	Controller	Video Connector	Hard Drive	Headset	Color	Optical Drive	Wireless Internet
Xbox 360 Arcade	One wired controller	Supports Composite and component, HDMI (Video Graphics Array [VGA] available)	None	None	White	DVD (HD DVD available)	Wi-Fi add-on available
Xbox 360	One wireless controller	Supports Composite and component (VGA available)	20-GB hard drive	One wired headset	White	DVD (HD DVD available)	Wi-Fi add-on available
Xbox 360 Elite		Supports Composite, component, HDMI (VGA available)	120-GB hard drive	One wired headset	Black	DVD (HD DVD available)	Wi-Fi add-on available

TABLE 18-2   The Three Models of Xbox 360

18

	Controller	Video Connector	Hard Drive	Headset	Color	Optical Drive	Wireless Internet
PlayStation 3 Basic	Available	Composite video cable included, HDMI and component available	20 GB	Available	Black	DVD/ Blu-ray	Built-in
PlayStation 3 Premium	One wireless controller	Composite video cable included, HDMI and component available	60 GB	Available	Black	DVD/ Blu-ray	Built-in

TABLE 18-3   The Two Models of PlayStation 3

As mentioned in the table, Microsoft sells an HD DVD add-on for the Xbox 360. This is an external, separately connected optical disc drive that plays HD DVDs. It works in conjunction with the built-in DVD drive on the Xbox 360 so that you can watch DVDs or play games that are in the DVD drive in addition to HD DVDs that are in the HD DVD drive. None of the aforementioned Xbox 360 models include an HD DVD—you must purchase this separately. For more information about the HD DVD drive add-on for the Xbox 360, see www.xbox.com.

PlayStation 3

The PlayStation 3 is a next-generation video game console from Sony. It offers Bluetooth technology for its controllers, has built-in wireless networking capabilities, and even comes with a Blu-ray disc drive in its basic and premium configurations (see Table 18-3 for more details). Currently, a PlayStation 3 is one of the more inexpensive ways to acquire a Blu-ray drive. Standalone Blu-ray players and computer drives are rather expensive as of this writing.

Install a DVD, HD DVD, or Blu-ray Drive

Finding the right DVD, HD DVD, or Blu-ray disc drive was the hard part. Once you've purchased an optical drive, installing it in your Windows Vista PC is easy. Before you begin, open the packaging the optical drive comes in, and remove the manual. Thoroughly read the manual, as some of the instructions may differ from the ones included here. Always follow the instructions in the manual, especially if they are different from the ones here. The instructions given in the following procedure should work for most computers, but some important specific details may only be given in your optical disc drive's manual. Also consult the manual that comes with your Windows Vista PC.

To install your DVD, HD DVD, or Blu-ray drive:

1. Turn off your computer, and disconnect all peripherals (keyboard, mouse, speakers, etc.). Don't forget to check how all of your peripherals are connected so that you remember how to reconnect them later. It might be helpful to draw a diagram so that you remember.

2. Remove the cover or side panel on your computer. This will require unscrewing several screws located on the rear of your system. For some systems, this may be a little more difficult. Consult the manual that came with your computer for more information about how to access the inside.

3. Before you touch anything in your computer, be sure to discharge any static electricity from yourself. Static electricity can damage components inside of your computer. Discharge static electricity by touching another separate metal item around you, such as a desk or file cabinet.

4. If the optical disc drive connects via an IDE ribbon connection (40 pins, wide connector) and is the only drive on the ribbon, it must be set to a master setting. Consult the manual for more information on how to do this. If the optical disc drive connects to an IDE ribbon connection and is an additional drive on the ribbon, it must be set to a slave setting. Consult the manual for more information on how to do this. Make sure to set the drive to a master or slave setting before continuing, as this will be harder to do once the drive is in the system. SATA optical drives do not need to be configured for master or slave settings.

5. Find the 5.25-inch bay in your computer where you have decided to install the disc drive. Read your Windows Vista PC manual. Most computer cases have a slot cover in unused 5.25-inch bays. Remove the slot cover from the optical drive bay. Consult your system's manual for more information. Some bay covers snap off, while others screw off.

6. This step is only suitable for some systems. If your case has a built-in button for the optical disc drive and does not expose the optical disc drive button directly through the case, you may need to carefully adjust the disc drive until it is a suitable distance away from the built-in button trigger. To test this, screw the optical disc drive in, connect the power plug to it, plug the system in, and turn it on. Press the button for the optical disc drive. Press it again to close the disc tray. If the button is working properly, your optical disc drive is installed successfully.

7. Connect the IDE or SATA connection and power connection to the optical disc drive. Make sure that the connections are fully pushed in to the disc drive and are not loose. If they are loose, the drive may not receive power or the computer may not recognize it.

8. Put the case cover or side panel back on the computer, and screw or snap it back in. Reconnect all peripherals and wires, and turn the computer on. As the system boots, you may see it list the new optical drive as being recognized. If not, allow the computer to fully boot to Windows Vista to check. If the drive is not listed, it may not be connected correctly or powered correctly. Check the manual for the optical drive and for your computer for more steps on how to troubleshoot this.

No drivers should be required to install an optical drive to Windows Vista, but if drivers are necessary or included with the optical drive, be sure to install them.

18

Chapter 19

Install and Configure
a Second TV Tuner

How to...

- Know what a second TV tuner offers
- Find a second TV tuner to purchase
- Install and configure a second TV tuner

A television tuner is a device that translates a television signal to a format that a computer can understand and display or store. Most Windows Vista PCs that are built for Media Center include a single TV tuner. A TV tuner can only understand and translate one television signal at a time. A Windows Vista Media Center PC with one TV tuner is great for watching or recording one channel at a time. However, a problem arises if you want to watch one channel while recording something on another channel at the same time, or if you want to watch a television channel on your Windows Vista PC while a Media Center extender, such as an Xbox 360, displays another television channel at the same time in the living room.

For these situations, you'll need more than one TV tuner. Fortunately, there are many options for adding a second tuner to your Windows Vista PC. Read on to understand your options and what you need to keep in mind while looking for a second TV tuner.

Understand Your Options

If you want to watch more than one television channel at once or record one television channel while watching another television channel at the same time, you'll need two TV tuners. Before you shop for a second tuner, you'll need to gather some information about your current television signal and TV tuner. Table 19-1 details these two options.

Identify Your Television Signal Type

First, you must identify the kind of television signal your Windows Vista PC currently receives. This may be an analog signal from a set-top box, direct cable connection, or from an antenna. It may also be a high-definition digital connection from a direct cable connection or an antenna. If your Windows Vista PC receives its television signal from a set-top box (a cable box), it is receiving an analog signal. Take a look around to identify your signal type, and if you can't identify it yourself, call your cable company.

Option	Description
One TV tuner	Watch one television show at a time or record one television show and watch that show at the same time.
Two TV tuners	Watch one television show while recording a television show on a different channel, or watch two television shows at once: one from a Windows Vista PC and another from a Media Center Extender. Or, add a complementary digital high-definition television signal or analog television signal to your Windows Vista PC.

TABLE 19-1   Television Options with One and Two TV Tuners

Know What Type of TV Tuner to Purchase

The TV tuner you purchase will need to be able to receive the same type of television signal as the one your Windows Vista PC already receives. For example, if your Windows Vista PC currently receives an analog television signal, you'll need to purchase an analog television tuner. If your Windows Vista PC currently receives a digital high-definition television signal, you'll need to purchase a digital high-definition television tuner. Both TV tuners must receive the same television signal and channel lineup in order for Media Center to work correctly.

Make Changes to Your TV Setup

If you want to add a new type of television signal to your Windows Vista PC—for example, if you want to add a digital high-definition television signal to a Windows Vista PC that currently receives an analog television signal, you'd need to purchase a digital high-definition TV tuner. You can't view a high-definition signal without a high-definition tuner!

NOTE   *Media Center can receive two analog television signals that are the same or an analog television signal and a digital high-definition signal that are different. Media Center cannot receive two different analog television signals that have different channel lineups, nor can it receive two different digital high-definition television signals that have different channel lineups. However, Media Center can receive two different analog and digital high-definition television signals that have different channel lineups. Media Center only supports up to two TV tuners at the same time, but some advanced enthusiasts have figured out how to make any number of TV tuners work with Media Center. Making more than two TV tuners work with Media Center at the same time is a complicated task, but if you're up for a challenge, visit http://blogs.msdn.com/ peterrosser/archive/2006/04/03/MCE_TechTalk_1.aspx or search Google for the phrase Media Center N Tuners.*

If you add a second TV tuner to your Windows Vista PC for the purposes of being able to record one television channel while watching another or to be able to watch two different television channels at once, both TV tuners must receive the exact same signal and have the same channel lineup. Media Center requires that both sources be exactly the same. For example, if one TV tuner receives the television signal from a set-top box, you must obtain a second set-top box for the second TV tuner so that it receives the exact same signal and channel lineup. Media Center only supports one Electronic Program Guide (the on-screen channel guide) analog source at a time. Table 19-2 shows this information. Note that your cable or satellite provider

If Using	You'll Need
Two analog signals	Two analog TV tuners that receive the same television signal and channel lineup
One analog signal, one digital signal	One analog TV tuner that receives an analog television signal from a set-top box, satellite receiver, antenna, or direct cable. One digital TV tuner that receives a digital high-definition television signal from an antenna or direct cable source

TABLE 19-2   Required hardware

19

may charge more for a second set-top box or satellite receiver. It's OK if the two set-top boxes are different models as long as they both receive the same television signal and channel lineup. You'll also need to attach an IR control cable to your second set-top box so that Media Center can change the channel. For more information about IR control cables, see Chapter 3.

Once you've figured out what you want to accomplish by adding a second TV tuner and what type of tuner you need to purchase, it's time to find the right TV tuner for you.

Purchase a TV Tuner

At this point, you should know what you want to accomplish by adding a second TV tuner, whether it's to add a new television signal type to your Windows Vista PC or gain the ability to watch one television channel while recording another one. You should also know what type of television signal your Windows Vista PC currently receives. If you want to watch one television channel while recording another, you'll need to buy a TV tuner that receives the same television signal type. Keep this in mind, as you'll need to keep a shopper's eye open for compatible TV tuners later on.

Know Your TV Tuner Type

Some computers include internal TV tuners. Other computers include external TV tuners that connect through Universal Serial Bus (USB). Internal TV tuners are preferred because they are more reliable and the television signal is often of higher quality. This is at the expense of ease of installation, however. An external TV tuner can be as simple to install as just connecting the USB cable to your computer. An internal tuner requires opening your computer case, which may void your warranty. External television tuners work best if they are connected directly to your computer and not to a USB hub. See Table 19-3 for a summary of this information.

Inspect your computer closely. If you are able to install your own hardware, you are not concerned about potentially voiding your Windows Vista PC's warranty, and your computer has an extra slot available, consider an internal TV tuner. However, if you're concerned about opening your computer case to install a TV tuner, or if your computer does not have a free slot available, consider an external USB tuner.

Type of Tuner	Pros and Cons
Internal TV tuner	Pros: Higher-quality signal, more reliable
	Cons: Harder installation, requires a free slot in your computer
External TV tuner (USB)	Pros: Easy installation, does not require you to open up the computer case
	Cons: Lower-quality signal, lower reliability, requires a dedicated USB 2.0 port

TABLE 19-3   A Comparison of Internal and External TV Tuners

Make Sure Your TV Tuner Is Vista-Compatible

You'll want to make sure that the TV tuner you purchase is compatible with Windows Vista. Any tuner that has the Certified for Windows Vista logo on it works great with Media Center and your Windows Vista PC. Windows Marketplace maintains a list of all Vista-compatible TV tuners.

First, open your Internet browser, and head to www.windowsmarketplace.com. Then look for a link to the Hardware Compatibility List (HCL). As of this writing, it is located at the bottom of the Windows Marketplace home page (see Figure 19-1). It's hard to see, but it's at the very bottom of the page.

Choose Certified For Windows Vista Devices, and then select your processor type. Under Select A Category, select TV Tuner Cards, and then click Start (see Figure 19-2).

TIP *If you're not sure if your processor is 32-bit or 64-bit, click Start, then right-click Computer, and click Properties. Under the System heading, look for System type. If your system is 32-bit, it says 32-bit Operating System.*

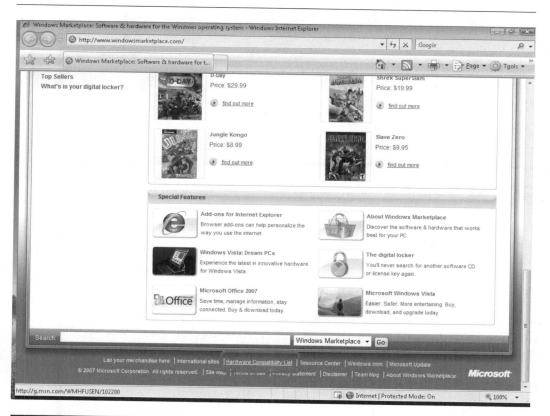

FIGURE 19-1 Check the Windows Marketplace Hardware Compatibility List to make sure your TV tuner is compatible with your PC.

19

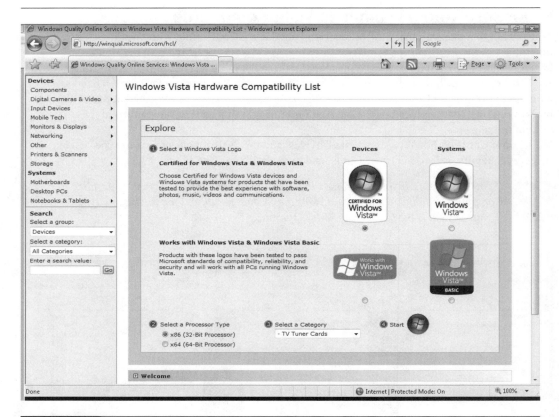

FIGURE 19-2   Search the Hardware Compatibility List for your tuner.

All of the TV tuner cards that are listed are compatible with Windows Vista and Media Center. Browse the list, and to see more information, click the product name (see Figure 19-3). You can use Web sites like www.newegg.com and www.buy.com to find more information about each product or to purchase the product. Remember to make sure that the TV tuner is an analog or digital high-definition tuner, depending on what you're trying to accomplish by adding a second TV tuner. If you are adding a second analog TV tuner and you use a set-top box for the first analog TV tuner, you'll need to purchase another IR control cable if your Windows Vista PC did not include two.

Once you've purchased and received your new TV tuner, continue to the next section to learn how to make it work with Media Center.

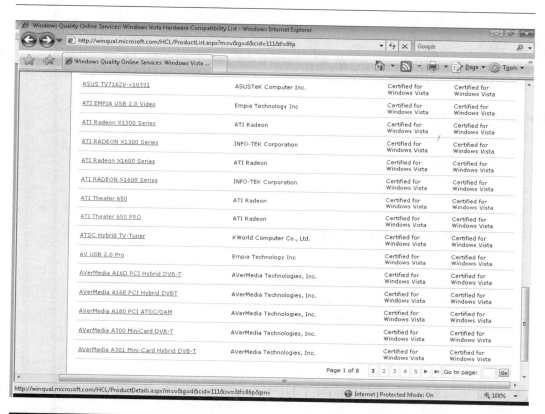

FIGURE 19-3   List of "Certified for Windows Vista" TV Tuner cards

Install a Second TV Tuner

Once you're sure that you've purchased the correct TV tuner to suit your needs, you're ready to install it. Installation and configuration differ, depending on the type of tuner you purchase.

Install an External TV Tuner

To install a second TV tuner that is an external USB 2.0 TV tuner, follow the instructions that are included with it. For the most part, you'll need to install the tuner's driver software, which is included on a disk that comes with it. The installation procedure is generally as simple as inserting the disk and working through the wizard(s) provided.

19

After that, you'll connect the TV tuner to a USB 2.0 port on the computer. You'll need to connect the TV tuner to an unused USB 2.0 port directly on your computer, not on a USB hub or any other device, such as a keyboard.

Finally, you'll plug the tuner into an electrical outlet and connect it to the TV signal. This can be a cable connection, satellite, or even rabbit ears. Once installed, the tuner should be ready to use.

Install an Internal TV Tuner

If you need to install an internal TV tuner, turn off your computer and disconnect all peripherals (keyboard, mouse, speakers, etc.). Follow the instructions that are included with the tuner. For the most part, installing an internal tuner will consist of the following steps:

1. Open the computer case, and set aside all screws or other hardware.

2. Ground yourself so as not to "shock" the motherboard by touching a metal part of the case.

3. Insert the TV tuner into the appropriate slot on the motherboard. You may have to remove a back slot to insert the tuner. This is detailed clearly in the instructions that come with the tuner.

4. Make any additional connections. Usually, there isn't anything to do except insert the tuner into the slot, but it never hurts to check the instructions one more time.

5. Close the case and reattach it using the screws.

6. Turn on your Windows Vista PC. Windows Vista may automatically detect and install driver software for your new TV tuner. If Windows Vista asks for the disc, insert it. Otherwise, use the drivers Windows Vista offers.

7. Follow the instructions that are included with your new TV tuner. You may need to install additional software to make it function correctly.

Install Additional Hardware

If you use a set-top box for your analog television signal, you'll need to obtain a second box for your second TV tuner. You'll also need a second IR control cable. To install the second IR control cable:

1. Plug one end of the IR control cable in to the rear of your infrared remote receiver. This receiver must have two ports in order to support two set-top boxes. If it does not, you must purchase a new infrared remote receiver.

2. Attach the other end of the IR control cable to the set-top box over the infrared receiver window, as was done similarly on your first set-top box.

After this final task is complete, you're ready to configure Media Center for your second TV tuner!

Configure the TV Tuner

Once the TV tuner is properly installed, start Media Center by pressing the green button on your Media Center remote control. You can also click Start, type **Media Center,** and press ENTER on your keyboard. As soon as Media Center starts, it should detect your new TV tuner (see Figure 19-4). If it does, click Setup to configure the new tuner. Follow the steps outlined in the Once the Tuner is Connected section. If Media Center does not automatically detect it, work though the troubleshooting section next.

If the Tuner Is Not Detected

If Media Center does not detect your new TV tuner, make sure that the driver software is correctly installed, and follow any troubleshooting steps provided by your tuner's manufacturer. If you installed an internal TV tuner, you should open the computer case and check the connections as well. The tuner needs to be firmly seated in the appropriate slot. Finally, make sure that all connections to set-top boxes, cable outlets, and electrical outlets are properly made by re-reading the directions that came with the TV tuner.

If you are sure that the TV tuner is installed properly but you still don't see the New Tuner Found screen shown in Figure 19-4, you'll need to manually start the Media Center configuration by clicking Tasks, then clicking Settings, then clicking TV, and finally selecting Set Up TV Signal.

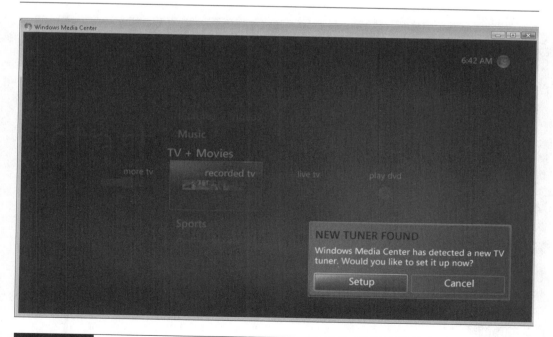

FIGURE 19-4   Media Center often automatically detects new TV tuners.

Once the Tuner Is Connected

Once you've clicked Setup, shown in Figure 19-4:

1. Media Center warns you that setting up the new TV tuner interrupts any current TV recording or TV/radio viewing on a Media Center extender, as shown in Figure 19-5. Select Yes to continue.

2. Media Center will confirm your region settings. If your region is correct, select Next to continue; otherwise, change it to the correct one.

3. Select Automatic TV Signal Setup or Manual TV Signal Setup, as shown in Figure 19-6. For now, use the recommended setting, Configure My TV Signal Automatically. If you select the automatic option, Media Center checks all TV tuners to configure your TV signal. If you select the manual option, you will need to select which TV tuners to configure along with your television signal source (antenna, satellite, or cable). In this case, we've configured two analog television tuners for a cable television signal.

4. If the automatic TV signal setup finds two TV tuners that do not have matching signals (see Figure 19-7), Media Center will configure one of the TV tuners but leave the other one unused. You'll have a chance to try to reconfigure both TV tuners later.

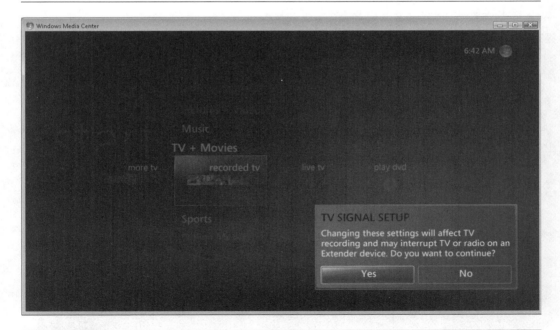

FIGURE 19-5   Media Center warns you that setting up a new TV tuner interrupts any current television viewing or recording.

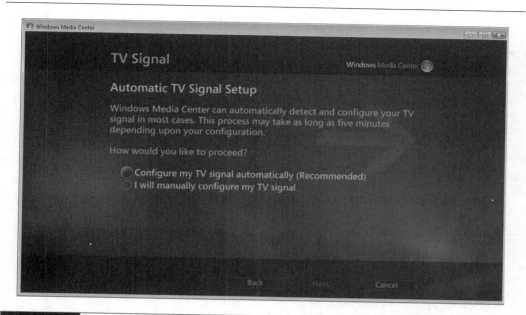

FIGURE 19-6   Media Center can automatically configure a new TV tuner or you can do it yourself.

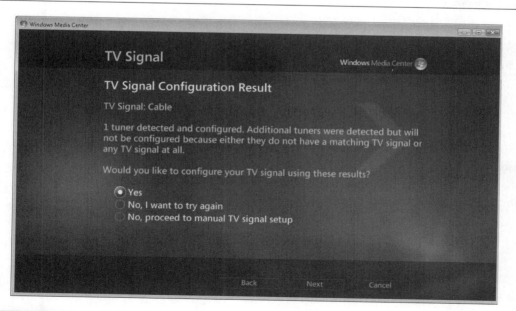

FIGURE 19-7   If two television signals do not match, Media Center enables only one of the tuners and allows you to try again later.

19

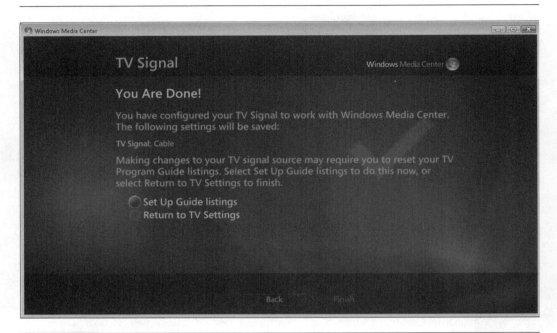

Media Center has configured the TV tuners for use, and TV signal setup is complete.

5. After the TV signal is configured, Media Center is ready to use both of your TV tuners! If you are just adding a second analog TV tuner, there is no need to set up Guide listings if you've already done it (see Figure 19-8). If you are adding a new digital high-definition or analog tuner, you'll have to set up Guide listings for the new tuner. At the end of the TV signal setup process, select Set Up Guide Listings, and then select Next. Otherwise, select Return To TV Settings, and then select Finish.

Your TV tuners should now be all ready to go! Now you can watch two television channels at the same time, record one television channel while watching another television channel, or enjoy digital high-definition television shows in addition to analog television shows.

Chapter 20

Install and Configure a Preferred Display

How to...

- Choose a secondary display technology
- Choose a secondary display type
- Physically connect the new hardware
- Configure the new display in Windows Vista
- Use the preferred display with Media Center

As you learned in Chapter 3, there are lots of technologies and hardware types to choose from when selecting a display for Media Center. These hardware options can be used to add a second display for Windows Vista and/or a "preferred" display for Windows Media Center. A *preferred display* is the TV or monitor you want to use Media Center with when watching and working with media, and is often a large TV in the family room or a high-end computer monitor. The display you add may not be the same display you work with when e-mailing or working with spreadsheets, however, as the monitor may be too big for such tasks! Thus, you can have two monitors: one for watching media in Media Center and one for working with Windows Vista.

If you've yet to choose a secondary display, you should review the technologies available first. After making the physical connections, you can then configure the second display for use with Windows Vista and also as the preferred display for Windows Media Center.

Review Display Connections

If you skipped Chapter 3 and have not purchased a new display, you should return there and read the entire chapter before continuing. If you read the chapter a while back and need a quick refresher, this section offers a quick review.

First, there are two types of connections: analog and digital. *Analog connections* are less precise than digital connections and provide lower-quality pictures. *Digital connections* offer exact pixel-to-pixel image reproduction on digital displays.

Digital video interface (DVI) is an up-to-24-pin digital video connection designed for connecting to digital displays and is suitable for high-definition video. DVI is one of the only connection standards that can carry analog as well as digital data.

High-Definition Multimedia Interface (HDMI) is a 19-pin digital video and audio connection similar to DVI, but with two exceptions. An HDMI connection carries both digital audio and video in an uncompressed high-quality format. It is also compatible with the high-bandwidth digital content protection (HDCP) standard. HDCP prevents unauthorized copying of protected copyrighted content. This is an up and rising connection type that can be found on newer video game consoles and high-definition televisions.

Separate Video (S-Video) is a 4-to-7-pin analog video connection that is popular on computer video cards. S-Video connections do not provide high-bandwidth connections and, therefore, are not used for high-definition video connections.

Composite connections use an RCA-type connector and carry analog video. Often, it is paired with two other RCA-type connectors for the left and right channels of sound. The video connector is yellow, and the sound connectors are red and white. On consumer electronics where S-Video is offered, you will almost always find plugs for composite connections as well. Composite connections are usually used to connect consumer electronics (VCRs, game consoles, DVD players, etc.) to televisions, although they are quickly being phased out for component video connections.

Component video is an analog video connection that consists of three RCA-type plugs: one colored red (Yr), another colored blue (Pb), and the last colored green (Y). It is similar to S-Video, but offers better high quality because data is transmitted on three distinct wires, rather than all on one wire. Component video connections are suitable for high-definition video as a result. They can be found on newer video game consoles, DVD players, and high-definition televisions.

Video graphics array (VGA) connections, sometimes referred to as an RGB or D-Sub connection, are analog video 15-pin connections. Each pin on a VGA connector carries different information, such as red, green, or blue color information. It is similar to component video and is usually used to connect computers to analog displays.

A *coaxial* connection carries analog audio and video. It is similar in quality to composite and S-Video, and has traditionally been used to connect devices such as video game consoles and cable boxes to older televisions.

For the most part, you can look at the back of your computer to see what types of displays you can connect. Just count the pins or decide on available technologies by colored inputs.

Review Display Types

As with display connections, if you skipped Chapter 3 and have not chosen a display type, you should return there and read the entire chapter before continuing. If you read the chapter a while back and need a quick refresher, this section offers a quick review.

Traditionally, most displays have been *cathode ray tube* displays (sometimes referred to as CRT displays). These monitors often produce the best picture quality of all display technologies. The only downside to CRT monitors is that they are large and usually quite heavy.

Liquid crystal displays (LCDs) are the opposite of CRTs. LCDs are usually flat—you can hang them on your wall quite easily. On the downside, the light on the screen is provided by a fluorescent front or back light mounted inside of the display case just by the LCD panel. As a result, the display is very bright, but sometimes too bright to accurately reproduce sensitive colors such as black.

Plasma displays are similar to LCDs—they're flat and offer as good, or sometimes better, color reproduction. On the downside, they can be quite heavy and consume a lot of electricity. Plasma displays usually offer DVI and component connections.

Finally, there are *digital light processing*, or DLP, projectors. DLP projectors offer great image quality and color reproduction—almost on par with CRT monitors. In fact, as of this writing, DLP projectors offer the best way to show a large picture without image degradation. The only downside is that some DLP projectors are rather loud because of the fans required to cool them. Projectors usually offer RGB, DVI, and component connections.

Connect the Display

Connecting a new display *should* be as simple as plugging the display's electrical cord into the wall socket and connecting the computer to the new monitor using the appropriate cable. However, not all computers come with the required components. For instance, your computer may have DVI but no HDMI, while your monitor has HDMI and no DVI. If you find that's the case, you'll need to purchase the appropriate adapter to make the connection. In this case, you'd purchase a DVI-to-HDMI adapter. The same is true of VGA. If your newer computer only comes with DVI connections and you need to connect an older VGA monitor, you'll need a DVI-to-VGA adapter to achieve this.

In addition, you'll want to connect your monitor and computer using the best technology your hardware offers. For instance, if you have a computer and display that support both a DVI connection and a VGA connection, by all means use DVI. You'll get a better picture by using the newer technology.

Once you've decided how to connect your PC to your new monitor, do so. If you need more assistance, read the information that came with the monitor and computer, and reread Chapter 3 for more detail about display types and technologies.

View the Second Display in Vista

Windows Vista sees your primary display as the default monitor to show applications, the logon screen, your e-mail, Web browser, the Start menu, the taskbar, etc. If you connect more than one display to Windows Vista, you will be asked whether you want to clone your display output or extend your desktop to both displays. If you clone your display, you'll see the exact same thing on both displays. If you extend your displays, you'll be able to drag applications from one display to another. In the following procedure, we connected a VGA monitor to a Windows Vista PC, rebooted, and then added a second monitor using an additional DVI connection. You can do the same.

After connecting your display, follow these directions to configure it in Windows Vista:

1. Right-click the desktop, click Personalize, and then click Display Settings.

2. By default, your first monitor is the primary monitor and is displayed with a 1 on it; your second monitor is the one displayed with a 2 on it. The dialog box is shown in Figure 20-1. If desired, change the resolution before continuing.

3. To use the secondary monitor in Windows Vista for applications and Vista-related tasks, click the secondary monitor, and then select the Extend The Desktop Onto This Monitor check box. Set the resolution as desired.

4. Click Identify Monitors, and verify that the monitors are verified and numbered correctly (see Figure 20-2).

5. Click OK.

6. If the second monitor does not work correctly, restart the computer. This usually resolves any problems.

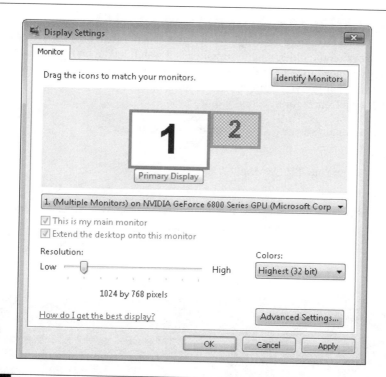

FIGURE 20-1   Your monitors will be labeled as primary and secondary.

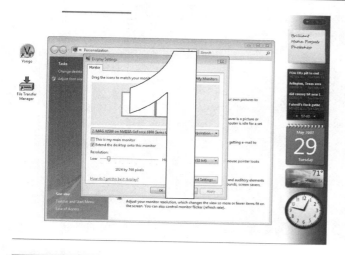

FIGURE 20-2   Identify monitors and verify they are numbered correctly

Use the Second Display with Media Center

In most instances, you'll be adding a second monitor that's better than the primary one. You'll likely continue to work on the older, smaller monitor and watch media on the newer, larger one. Whatever the case, you need to tell Media Center that you've installed a second monitor and would like to use it as your preferred monitor from now on.

To configure Media Center for a second monitor:

1. Open Media Center, select Tasks, and then select Settings.

2. Select TV.

3. Select Configure Your TV Or Monitor.

4. Click Next to start the wizard.

5. On the Display page, where it says Is Your Preferred Display Connected?, make the appropriate choice. Either you see the wizard on your preferred display or you do not. Click Next after selecting an option (see Figure 20-3).

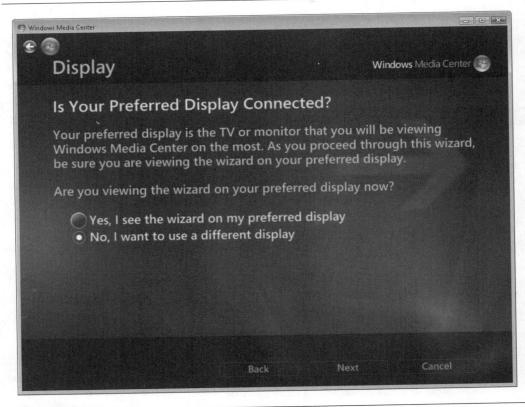

FIGURE 20-3   Select the appropriate option for your preferred display.

6. Hover your mouse over the display type options to see which one describes your monitor best, then select your display type, and click Next:

   ■ Monitor

   ■ Built-In Display

   ■ Flat Panel

   ■ Television

   ■ Projector

7. Select the connection type, and click Next. Figure 20-4 shows the DVI, VGS, Or HDMI option selected.

8. Select your display width, and click Next:

   ■ Standard (4:3)

   ■ Widescreen (16:9)

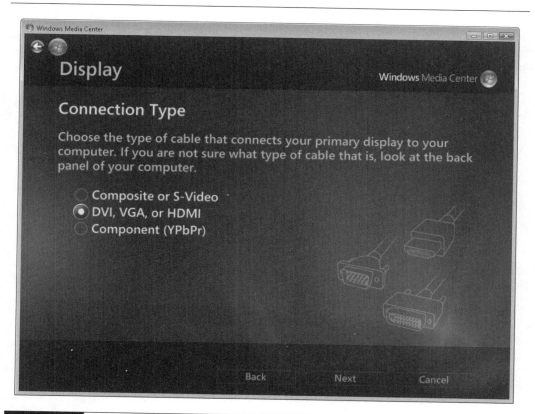

FIGURE 20-4 Select your connection type.

9. Select to keep your current display resolution or configure a different one. If you choose to configure a new display resolution, you'll need to work through an additional wizard page to do this. Click Next.

10. Select Adjust Display Controls. Click Next.

11. Click Next to configure the display's calibration.

12. Select each display characteristic, and make the appropriate changes. The wizard pages will change, depending on what you choose and how and if you make changes to the default settings:

   ■ Onscreen Centering And Sizing

   ■ Aspect Ratio (Shape)

   ■ Brightness (Black And Shadow)

   ■ Contrast (White)

   ■ RGB Color Balance

13. Click Finish.

At this point, you might want to spend some time configuring your new TV's audio. Audio settings are configured from the Tasks menu (click Settings, click TV, and then select Audio). For more information about setting up audio, refer to Chapters 3 and 4.

Chapter 21

Install and Configure a Cable Card

How to...

■ Understand the different types of cable card hardware

■ Install the cable card

■ Configure the newly installed cable card

Installing new computer hardware can be a time-consuming and slightly intimidating process. After all, you don't want to install one piece of hardware only to break another. That seems to be the most common concern. But with a little patience and a good set of instructions, you can stop worrying. In this chapter, you'll start by looking at your hardware options when it comes to cable cards. Then you'll walk through the installation process and configure your newly installed cable card.

Hardware Options

Typically, cable cards are placed inside the computer, although some cards allow you to connect externally through a Universal Serial Bus (USB) port. However, internal cards are typically less expensive when compared to external cards. And, as if cost wasn't enough of a reason, internal cards often offer a greater range of features.

Before you can begin the installation process, it's helpful to understand a few basic computer components and terms:

■ **Cable card** The cable card is the piece of hardware you purchased and need to install. This card has been designed to receive television signals through a cable connection for which you've paid. After installed, it acts like a "cable jack" right on your computer.

■ **Coaxial cable** The coaxial cable is the cable you use to connect the cable card to the cable box. This type of cable is capable of carrying a signal from the cable connection to your computer.

■ **PCI slot** The Peripheral Component Interconnect (PCI) slot is typically where you'll find internal modems, sound cards, and video cards, among other peripherals. In fact, if you look at the back of your computer (before you open it), you'll probably find one to two PCI slots already occupied with your modem and video card. Above these occupied slots, there are typically a few unoccupied slots. It's in these unoccupied spaces that your new cable card will reside.

About Cable Cards

There are two types of cable cards: SCards and MCards. SCards offer single-stream support and allow you to watch one channel at a time. They are commonly referred to as CableCARD 1.0. On the other hand, MCards offer multiple-stream support and allow you to watch up to six channels at the same time. They are commonly referred to as CableCARD 2.0.

Internal or External?

The type of cable card you use may depend on a few factors:

- **Do you have an open PCI slot?**   An open PCI slot is necessary for installing an internal cable card. If the answer is no, then external is the card for you.

- **Did your cable company give you a cable card?**   If you received a card from your cable company, there's no need to go out and buy one. You can simply use the one you were given.

- **How much do you want to spend?**   Believe it or not, internal cable cards are typically less expensive than external ones. So if you're looking to spend less money, internal is the card for you.

Physical Installation

If breaking open your computer case and installing a piece of hardware feels above your current skill level, relax. Installing hardware doesn't have to be difficult. The key, really, is just to follow the steps one at a time. Don't try to skip ahead!

First, let's look at the items you'll want to have on hand before you begin:

- Computer
- Cable card
- Cable card software (this is typically available on a CD that comes with the card)
- Phillips-head screwdriver

It doesn't hurt to summon a little patience at this point, either. Not that this is a difficult process—it certainly isn't. But when you're working with the insides of your computer, you don't want to work quickly. There are lots of small pieces and connections. You don't want to accidentally disconnect one thing in your hurry to connect another.

NOTE *Before installing your cable card or opening your computer, check the back to be sure that you have an available PCI slot.*

TIP *When working inside a computer case, it's a good idea to "ground" your hands before placing them inside the box. This can be done by simply placing your hands on the case for a few seconds before touching any of the internal components. By doing this, you reduce the risk of creating a static charge and potentially damaging the intricate wiring.*

How to ... Install an Internal Cable Card

The following steps offer advice and instructions for installing your new cable card. Make sure to follow the directions carefully, and always read the directions that come with the hardware before starting.

To install a cable card:

1. It may seem obvious, but shut down your computer and unplug every cable or cord from the back. This gives you a power-free box that you can move to an open location for easier access.

2. Remove the PC cover (also known as the case). The steps here vary from computer to computer, but typically involve removing a few screws near the back of the case before the cover slips off.

3. Next, lay the computer on a flat surface with the exposed portion facing up.

4. Locate the unoccupied PCI slot. Typically, a PCI slot has two rectangular openings (one small and one large) that are white. When connected, a portion of the cable card will remain inside the computer and a small portion for connecting to the cable box will remain exposed on the back of the computer.

5. Remove the metal bracket that is covering the available PCI slot. You shouldn't need this small metal bracket again, as the opening will be filled by the new cable card once it's installed.

6. Now you're ready to insert the cable card. Slide the card into the PCI slot. You'll want to move slowly and deliberately. And, to get the card to snap into place, you'll need to apply some firm pressure.

7. Once the card is in place, screw it down so that the inputs and outputs are exposed on the back of the computer case. That's it!

8. Replace and screw the cover back into place. Hook your computer back up to all of the cables and cords you unplugged in the first step.

Installation

The first time you turn on your computer after installing a new cable card (or any hardware, for that matter), the Add New Hardware Wizard should run automatically. When prompted, insert the installation CD that came with the cable card.

Once you've completed the Add New Hardware Wizard, shut down your computer. After the computer has completely shut down, you can now (if you haven't done so already) plug your cable box into your cable card using the coaxial cable that likely came with the cable card and turn on your computer again.

If the Add New Hardware Wizard doesn't begin automatically, you can still move forward with manual installation and configuration. To install your new cable card manually, follow these steps:

1. Insert the installation CD.

2. On the Start menu, right-click Computer, and choose Properties from the shortcut menu.

3. In the Tasks pane, click Device Manager. The Device Manager window opens.

4. If prompted, click Continue.

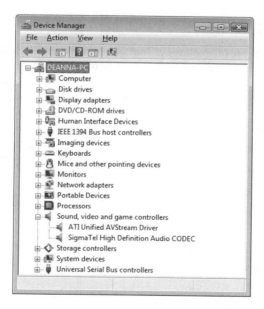

5. Click the plus sign (+) next to Sound, Video And Game Controllers.

6. Your cable card name or description should appear in the list. Double-click your cable card.

7. Click the Driver tab.

8. Click Update Driver. This launches the Add New Hardware Wizard. Once the wizard begins, you can follow the on-screen instructions to install your new hardware.

Configuration

As soon as you've installed your new cable card, you can configure Media Center to recognize it. Luckily, there's a wizard to walk you through the steps. To access the configuration wizard, follow these steps:

1. Open Windows Media Center.

2. From the Media Center main screen, under Tasks, click Settings. The Media Center Settings window opens.

3. Click TV.

4. Click Set Up TV Signal.

5. If prompted, click Yes to continue.

6. Click Next to begin configuring your TV signal.

7. Choose Yes to configure the signal for the United States. Click No to choose a different region.

8. To allow Media Center to configure your signal automatically, choose Configure My TV Signal Automatically, and then click Next. It may take several minutes as Media Center scans your computer for existing tuner cards.

The remaining steps in this process are based on your individual cable settings and cable card. Simply follow the on-screen instructions for the best results.

Chapter 22

Install, Configure, and Back Up
with an External Hard Drive

How to…

- Install an external hard drive
- Use Windows Backup And Restore Center
- Back up to the external hard drive
- Understand restore options

There are lots of backup strategies, from storing your data to an offsite, third-party, online server, to your own network drive, to an additional internal hard drive, to burning your own CDs and DVDs. Another way to back up your data is to use the Windows Backup And Restore Center in Windows Vista in conjunction with an external hard drive. Although you can use the Backup And Restore Center to back up to other types of media, an external drive provides lots of hard drive space, can be stored easily in a safe location, and can be taken with you if you need to get the data somewhere in a hurry (like to higher ground).

Although backing up data isn't technically a Media Center issue, the media you obtain and use in Media Center does need to be backed up in case of a computer failure or natural disaster (such as fire, flood, or earthquake). Since a basic backup and restore application is included with all versions of Windows Vista, we think it's a good choice. The first thing you need to do before you can use it the way we suggest is install an external hard drive.

> **NOTE** *Windows Backup And Restore is available in Vista Home Basic, Premium, and Ultimate editions. However, another version of the application, Windows Complete PC Backup And Restore, is only available in Vista Ultimate. If you have Vista Ultimate, you'll have more functionality than is provided with other versions.*

Install an External Hard Drive

External hard drives connect using a Universal Serial Bus (USB) or FireWire port. Some come with a driver disk, and some do not. For the most part, external hard drives are plug-and-play, meaning you connect them and they work automatically.

Once installed, you can view and access the external drive from the Computer window. Figure 22-1 shows an example. Here, PCBACKUP (E:) is the shared external drive for our PC and the networked PCs. (Notice the sharing icon beside the drive icon.) You can also see in Figure 22-1 that the external drive uses the file system FAT32, has a total size of 74.5 gigabytes (GB) with 43.2 GB free.

Windows Backup And Restore Center

The Windows Backup And Restore Center can help you create and configure automatic backups of your media. This is a good idea, since most people forget to make regular backups unless reminded by the operating system or other software. The Backup And Restore Center is located

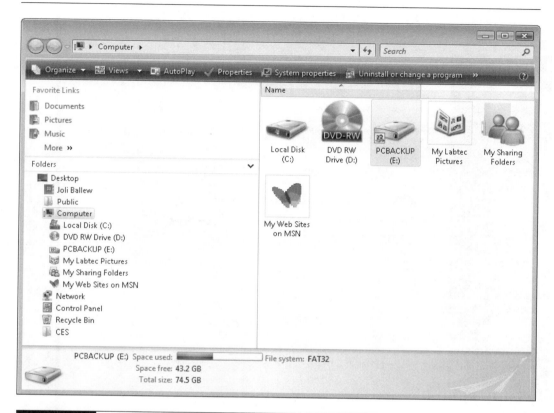

FIGURE 22-1   An external drive in the Computer windows

in Control Panel's System And Maintenance applet. Figure 22-2 shows the interface prior to the center's first use. There are really only two types of backups you need to be concerned with at this time. They include your personal data and the computer's system data.

Personal Data

Personal data includes but is not limited to the files and folders you create and modify, as well as data you obtain elsewhere—for example, music, pictures, and videos. You should back up your personal data regularly—at least once a week or whenever you make changes to your PC, like adding a new piece of hardware or software. You should also back up downloaded and purchased music each time you obtain it, as many online music subscription services won't let you restore purchased music if it's lost. You'll have to repurchase it, unless you have a backup. That being said, you should configure the Backup And Restore Center to back up your personal files on a regular schedule.

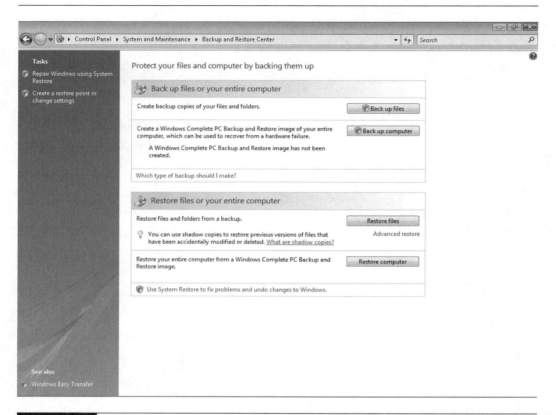

FIGURE 22-2 The Backup And Restore Center in Windows Vista

System Data and PC Images

A computer also has its own data. This includes but is not limited to system settings, the registry, drivers, all of your programs, and additional data the operating system needs to run. If something happens to your computer, you can restore it using this information. This type of backup is called a Complete PC Backup image, because it takes a complete "snapshot" of your system, including your personal data. If you need to, you can restore your PC to this image if you have a system-wide failure.

Note that you can't pick and choose what gets restored and what doesn't, which makes this an all-or-nothing recovery option based on your last complete backup. This option is not included with all versions of Windows Vista, either. You'll only have Windows Complete PC Backup And Restore if you have Windows Vista Ultimate. If you have Vista Ultimate, you should create a new Windows Complete PC backup image every six months.

NOTE

If your computer has more than one partition, the backup should include all files and programs on all partitions.

All About NTFS

A file system is the fundamental structure used to organize data on a hard disk. File structures exist on internal and external drives, network drives, and any other place data is stored. FAT32 is one option, as shown in Figure 22-1. New Technology File System (NTFS) is another. NTFS is preferred over any type of File Allocation Table (FAT) system, including FAT, FAT16, and FAT32. NTFS is preferred for many reasons, including the ability to recover automatically from disk errors, support for large disks, and better security using NTFS permissions and encryption.

TIP

If you want to create a Complete PC Backup image, your hard disk will need to be formatted using NTFS, as well as your external drive. If one or other is not NTFS, a complete backup cannot be created.

Without going into too much detail, which isn't really necessary at this time, note that an NTFS hard disk is better overall than a FAT disk. If you have a FAT disk, you should covert it to NTFS. There are a few things to consider first, however:

- Converting to NTFS does nothing noticeable to your data, your PC, or your operating system. You will not see any changes.

- Once you convert from FAT to NTFS, you can't convert back without wiping your hard drive clean by reformatting it and starting over.

- Earlier operating systems can't read NTFS partitions. Don't convert any disk you will need to access from a Windows 95 or 98 PC.

- You should always back up data prior to converting to NTFS.

To convert a hard disk or partition to NTFS:

1. Close any open files or programs running on the partition or disk you want to covert.
2. Click Start, and in the Start Search window, type **Command Prompt**.
3. Under Programs, right-click Command Prompt, and select Run As Administrator.
4. Click Continue.
5. In the Command Prompt window, type **convert**, insert a space with the SPACEBAR key, and type the drive letter for the disk you want to convert. Follow with a colon (:), another space, and then type **/fs:ntfs**. A sample command is: convert e: /fs:ntfs. Here, e: is the drive letter. Press ENTER. This is shown in Figure 22-3.
6. Type the name of the volume. You can find the name of the volume in the Computer window. As shown in Figure 22-1 earlier, the name of the external drive we're converting is PCBACKUP. Type the name of the drive when prompted. The name of the hard disk is technically called the volume label (see Figure 22-3).

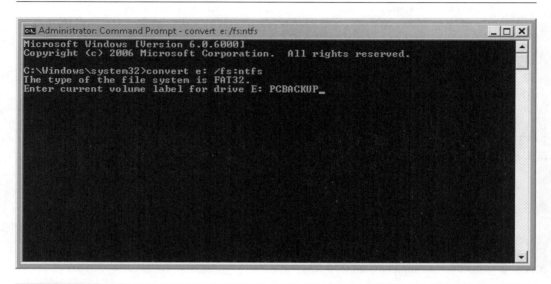

FIGURE 22-3 Use *<Drive Letter>*: /fs:ntfs to convert a FAT drive to NTFS.

If the partition you are converting is the partition or hard disk your operating system files are on, you will need to restart the computer to continue with the conversion. You will also be prompted to close any open files on the partition. If you aren't sure what to do, choose to convert the partition after the next restart. To close the Command Prompt window, type **exit**.

> **TIP** *NTFS is not required to back up and restore personal files. It is only required when creating a Complete PC Backup image.*

Back Up to the External Drive

To back up personal files on your computer, go to Start, click Control Panel, select System And Maintenance in the Control Panel Home view, and click Backup And Restore Center. Click Backup Files, shown in Figure 22-4. As with any system-wide application or change, click Continue to begin.

Continue through the pages of the wizard to complete the backup process:

1. On the Where Do You Want To Save Your Backup? page, use the drop-down list to locate your external drive. Note that you can also select a DVD or CD burner or a network drive. Click Next.

2. On the Which File Types Do You Want To Back Up? page, select each file type. While you can deselect file types, we do not recommend this. Figure 22-5 shows this page of the wizard. Click Next.

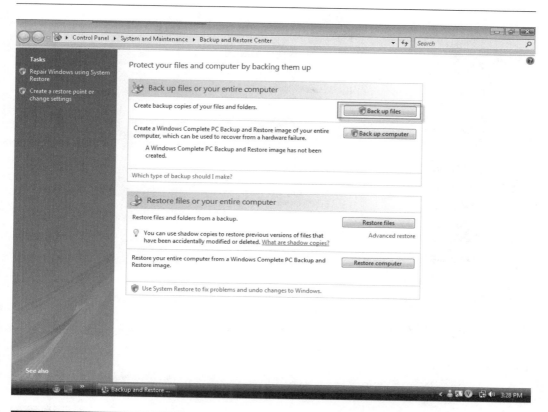

FIGURE 22-4   Select Back Up Files to begin backing up your personal data.

3. Select how often you want to create a backup. Choices include:

   ■ How often: Daily, weekly, or monthly

   ■ What day: Select from a weekday or day of the month. No choice is offered if Daily is selected.

   ■ Choose the time to perform the backup. Make sure the computer will be on during this time.

4. Select Save Settings And Start Backup.

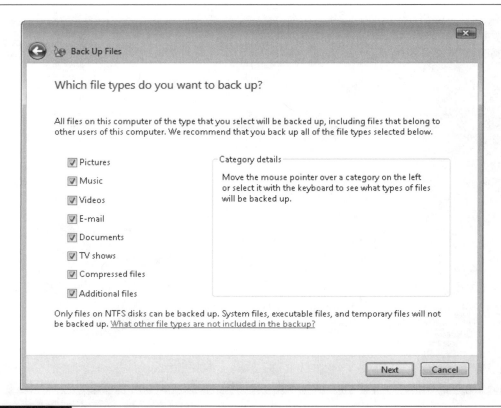

FIGURE 22-5   Select the file types you want to back up.

Restore Options

You don't always have to use the Backup And Restore Center when something goes wrong with your PC. Before restoring your computer using a backup you've created in Windows Backup And Restore Center, always try System Restore first. The System Restore feature comes with all editions of Windows Vista and is easy to use. System Restore is enabled by default and automatically creates its own restore points each day. You can find System Restore and configure restore settings by typing **System Restore** in the Start menu's Search window. Using System Restore won't affect your personal files, e-mail, or any related data.

If System Restore doesn't work, try a repair installation using your Windows Vista disk. Technically, it's the upgrade installation option. You won't lose any data upgrading with the disk, and generally, this restores files that are corrupt and gets the operating system working again. Try these two options before using a backup to restore your computer to an earlier time.

Restore Personal Data Using Windows Backup And Restore

To recover personal files using a backup, open the Backup And Restore Center, and click Restore. A wizard will walk you through the process. You'll need to make sure that the external drive is connected to the computer so that the restore process can obtain the data it needs from your backup.

Restore System Data Using a Complete PC Backup Image

If you've created a system image with Windows Vista Ultimate and aren't able to resolve your computer's problems with System Restore or an upgrade (repair) installation, you can use the system image you created with Vista Ultimate.

If you have a Windows installation disk:

1. Insert the disk and restart the PC.

2. When prompted during boot up to boot to the CD or DVD, press any key to enable the option.

3. Select your language settings, and click Next.

4. Click Repair Your Computer.

5. Select the operating system you want to repair, and click Next.

6. On the System Recover Options menu, click Windows Complete PC Restore, and follow the directions given.

If you don't have a Windows installation disk, reboot the computer, and press F8 repeatedly until you gain access to the Advanced Boot Options screen. (If you wait too long, Vista will boot and you'll need to try again.) Select Repair Your Computer when the choice becomes available. Select a keyboard layout, type a user name and password, and answer any other questions asked. On the System Recovery Options menu, click Windows Complete PC Restore, and follow the directions given.

Hopefully, you'll never need to restore from backup, but it never hurts to keep backups available. Almost anything, including a fire, flood, or spilled cup of coffee can ruin your most valuable data.

Index